The Global Mission of the Jim Crow South

Perspectives on Baptist Identities

The National Association of Baptist Professors of Religion is proud to join with Mercer University Press in the creation of a new academic series. *Perspectives on Baptist Identities* will explore the rapidly evolving questions of identity that press upon those who call themselves Baptist in the twenty-first century: What does it mean to be Baptist? What does the future hold for Baptists? How does the Baptist tradition relate to the global Church and other ecclesial traditions? How does Baptist identity impact Scripture reading and Christian practice? The series hopes to generate significant scholarly research and engender fruitful and lively conversation among various types of Baptists and non-Baptists.

SERIES EDITORS

Dr. Adam C. English
Professor of Theology and Philosophy
Department of Christian Studies, Campbell University

Dr. Alicia Myers
Associate Professor of New Testament and Greek
Divinity School, Campbell University

PUBLISHED TITLES

Ryan Andrew Newson, *Inhabiting the World: Identity, Politics, and Theology in Radical Baptist Perspective*

Mikeal C. Parsons, *Crawford Howell Toy: The Man, the Scholar, the Teacher*

Amy L. Chilton and Steven R. Harmon, ed., *Sources of Light: Resources for Baptist Churches Practicing Theology*

Anyone interested in Christian missions will be familiar with the enormous power of US-based ventures from the late nineteenth century onward. What we often forget is the distinctly Southern origins of so many of those missionaries, and their racial and segregationist assumptions. In *The Global Mission of the Jim Crow South*, João Chaves makes a really valuable contribution not just to the history of missions but to US religious history more generally, and to the history of Protestant churches in Latin America. This is impressively innovative work. I hope this thoughtful and wide-ranging study reaches the largest possible readership.

—Philip Jenkins, distinguished professor of History,
Baylor University, and author of *Fertility and Faith*

This exhaustively researched study of Southern Baptist missionary endeavors in Brazil illustrates both the long shadow cast by White supremacist Southern evangelicalism and the resistance to it by Brazilian converts. In presenting a complex story unfolding over more than a century of time, João Chaves illuminates in a way unlike any other book a story that is fundamental to the rise of Protestant evangelicalism in Brazil. I recommend it with enthusiasm.

—Paul Harvey, distinguished professor of History, University of Colorado, Colorado
Springs, and author of *Christianity and Race in the American South*

Meticulously researched and sharply argued, *The Global Mission of the Jim Crow South* reveals how US Baptists exported a faith intertwined with White supremacy and racial violence, one that took root in Brazil and gave rise to a theopolitical project with enduring consequences. An essential work for those seeking to understand Brazilian history, the history of global Christianity, and the racial imagination of American evangelicals.

—Kristin Kobes Du Mez, *New York Times* bestselling author of *Jesus and John Wayne:
How White Evangelicals Corrupted a Faith and Fractured a Nation*

This book is a significant and superbly documented investigation of American evangelicalism and its global impact theologically, politically, and ideologically. With Southern Baptist missionary impetus in Brazil as a case study, Chaves "recontextualizes" the ways in which evangelicals could rhetorically resist "worldliness" while linking their Gospel vision with the "Christian whiteness" of the world from which they came. It is a volume not to be overlooked.

—Bill J. Leonard, founding dean and professor of Divinity emeritus,
Wake Forest University School of Divinity

This meticulously researched and beautifully written book sheds much-needed light on how White supremacy was embedded in the transnational growth of evangelicalism in both Brazil and the United States. João Chaves has written a powerful and important work that is a must-read for anyone who wishes to understand the intersection of religion, race, and missionary movements in the modern era.

—Erika Helgen, associate professor of Latin American and Latinx Christianity, Yale
Divinity School, and author of *Religious Conflict in Brazil*

As a product of the Southern Baptist mission in Brazil, as an alumnus of Brazilian Baptist and Southern Baptist seminaries, and as someone who has researched and published on this topic for the past forty years, I am deeply impressed by the level of detailed evidence presented in this book. Before João Chaves, no one else in Brazil had had access to such revealing data, nor were we able to imagine the full extent of Southern Baptist captivity to the Lost Cause in the mission field. This book will mark a turning point in the study of Southern Baptist missions.

—H.B. Cavalcanti, emeritus professor of Sociology, James Madison University, and author of *Gloryland: Christian Suburbia, Christian Nation*

This compelling study examines the understudied world of Southern Baptist missionaries in Brazil from the nineteenth century to the present and how this group not only evangelized Brazilians but also sought to bring their US Southern culture forged in the mythology of the Lost Cause, commitment to White supremacy, male privilege, and zealousness for conversion to a country already saturated with centuries of racial animus. Chaves moves beyond the official story of the Southern Baptist Convention (SBC) and tells the story of missionaries who sought to wrest power away from the SBC and desired autonomy from their US-based overseers. This study marks a significant addition to the growing literature examining the role of missions, the global nature of the Religious Right, and the quest to decolonize the Brazilian Baptist experience.

—Arlene Sanchez-Walsh, professor of Religious Studies, Azusa Pacific University, and author of *Pentecostals in America*

Built on innovative research and unerring, critical questions about the historical dynamics of Southern Baptist missions in Brazil, this book represents an outstanding contribution. João Chaves has powerfully argued that the history of evangelism in Latin America cannot be viewed without considering detailed and personal stories from within institutions, as well as the contours of sending and receiving cultures—including racism and White supremacist ideology. The book's transnational perspective, drawing on marvelously thorough research in Brazil and the United States, makes for a nuanced, truly novel addition to our knowledge of Protestantism, denominational identity, imperialism, racism, Pentecostalism, and the roots of contemporary religious politics. Given its publication as Brazil solemnizes its first "terribly evangelical" supreme court justice (to use the descriptor coined by the President who nominated him), the book could not be timelier, nor more necessary.

—Benjamin Cowan, associate professor of History, University of California, San Diego, and author of *Moral Majorities Across the Americas*

The Global Mission of the Jim Crow South

Southern Baptist Missionaries and the Shaping of Latin American Evangelicalism

João B. Chaves

MERCER UNIVERSITY PRESS
Macon, Georgia
2022

MUP/P643

© 2022 by Mercer University Press
Published by Mercer University Press
1501 Mercer University Drive
Macon, Georgia 31207
All rights reserved

26 25 24 23 22   5 4 3 2 1

Books published by Mercer University Press are printed on acid-free paper
that meets the requirements of the American National Standard for
Information Sciences—Permanence of Paper for Printed Library Materials.

Printed and bound in the United States.

This book is set in Adobe Caslon Pro.

Cover/jacket design by Burt&Burt.

Cover Image: 1892 Missions Meeting with Bagbys, Entmingers, J.J. Taylors,
Ginsburgs, Sopers, and Downings.

Cover image courtesy of the International Mission Board,
Southern Baptist Convention.

ISBN   978-0-88146-836-6
Cataloging-in-Publication Data is available from the Library of Congress

To Clare Duffy.

Thank you for teaching me what I thought I knew!

MERCER UNIVERSITY

MERCER UNIVERSITY PRESS

Endowed by

TOM WATSON BROWN

and

THE WATSON-BROWN FOUNDATION, INC.

CONTENTS

ACKNOWLEDGMENTS

It is often stated that books are a communal effort. The community that helped put this work together is one that is multilingual, multiethnic, multinational, multireligious, and multidisciplinary. The idea of this book was birthed at Baylor University's Department of Religion, where I wrote my dissertation under Douglas Weaver's supervision. After my dissertation defense, Doug, Philip Jenkins, and Raimundo Barreto—who were part of the committee—encouraged me to extend the first half of that research into a book on race and missions. *The Global Mission of the Jim Crow South* is a result of their wonderful advice.

Douglas Weaver was indispensable in my training as a historian and his guidance has been central in many aspects of my journey. I would venture to guess, however, that he is most proud of the fact that he has taken me, a Brazilian immigrant, to a Yankees game, during which he taught me invaluable lessons about baseball rules and strategies. Under his influence, I have committed to simultaneously become a Yankees fan and to never watch a baseball game again in my entire life. Doug's commitment to his students, to scholarship, and to justice issues is inspiring. I cannot think of a better mentor and am delighted to consider him a friend.

People who read this work in its earlier versions, namely, Doug Weaver, William Pitts Jr., Philip Jenkins, Bill Leonard, Raimundo Barreto, David Whitford, and Beverly Gaventa, gave crucial feedback for its later development. I am thankful for their willingness to read and provide incisive and challenging comments. A number of Latin American scholars also contributed by providing questions and important information to versions of this manuscript. Amongst them were Ángel Gallardo, Flávio Conrado, Ivan Dias, Juçara Mello, Lyndon Santos, Marconi Monteiro, Marco Davi Oliveira, Maria Monteiro, Nora Lozano, Paul Barton, and Ronilso Pacheco. I am thankful for their insight.

The colleagues and friends in my cohort at the Hispanic Theological Initiative (HTI), many of whom are now important voices in the new generation of Latinx academics across the United States, provided great inspiration during our times together writing and discussing our respective projects at Princeton Theological Seminary. Andrés Albertsen, Antonio

Alonso, Elmer Guzman, Erica Ramirez, Leo Guardado, Maziel Barreto Dani, Rafael Reyes III, Tito Madrazo, and Yvette Garcia, among others, provided encouragement and insight even when they did not notice that was what they were doing. The Hispanic Theological Initiative is the most important institution for Latinx scholarship in a number of disciplines that relate to religious studies and theology. I am indebted to HTI for its financial, editorial, emotional, scholarly, spiritual, and logistic support. If I were to name every individual in the HTI network for whom I am thankful this section would become unmanageable. Suffice it to say that without HTI and Joanne Rodríguez—HTI's Executive Director—this book (and many, many others) would not exist.

Adam English and Alicia Myers, editors for the Perspectives on Baptist Identities series, welcomed this project warmly and provided helpful comments and observations. I am especially thankful for Adam's careful reading of the manuscript and suggestions for improvement. The Mercer University Press editorial team was helpful and encouraging. I am thankful for their help in general, and particularly for their genuine concern when family issues delayed the completion of the manuscript.

The archivists and staffs at the International Mission Board of the Southern Baptist Convention (particularly Jim Berwick), Moody Library at Baylor University, Texas Collection and University Archives also at Baylor, Wright Library at Princeton Theological Seminary, and James P. Boyce Centennial Library at Southern Baptist Theological Seminary were extremely helpful and central to the collection of primary sources. The wealth of resources and rare documents in Marconi Monteiro's private collection—compiled in a time when access to the archives of the North Brazil Baptist Theological Seminary (of which he is an alumni) and South Brazil Baptist Theological Seminary was possible—made this work much richer. I appreciate Marconi allowing me to analyze those sources freely for months.

The National Association of Baptist Professors of Religion (NABPR), Baptist History and Heritage Society (BH&H), and Society for Pentecostal Studies (SPS) communities allowed me to present parts of this research in regular sessions and plenary panels. I am thankful for the feedback I got from a number of historians, sociologists, and theologians who heard parts of this project. Earlier versions of chapter sections were published in the *Baptist History and Heritage Journal*, *Review and Expositor*, and *Perspectives in Religious Studies*. The feedback I got from the review process and the conversations I had after the articles came out helped me improve my language and sharpen my argument.

Finally, I want to thank my family for providing support, encouragement, and love as I invested much time in this project. Beijanete Bezerra da Silva, Jo Ann Duffy, Carla Chaves, Josias Bezerra, Julia da Silva, and Lucas da Silva provided great encouragement and support. My kids, Jonathan and Rebecca, asked, "are you still writing, dad?" at least one thousand times, and heard "I am almost done!" every single one of those times. They will be happy to see this in print and be able to finally believe me. The only one in my family who would actually read this book thoroughly would be my father-in-law, Michael Duffy. He will continue to be missed forever. My wife, Clare Duffy, to whom this work is dedicated, heard me read many sections of this project with my heavy Latin American accent. I benefited from her insight, wisdom, and language skills. I appreciate and love all of you. Muito obrigado.

LIST OF ABBREVIATIONS

BBC	*Brazilian Baptist Convention*
BETS	*Baptist Evangelical Theological Seminary*
FMB	*Foreign Mission Board*
IMB	*International Mission Board*
NBBTS	*North Brazil Baptist Theological Seminary*
NBC	*National Baptist Convention*
SBBTS	*South Brazil Baptist Theological Seminary*
SBC	*Southern Baptist Convention*
SEBTS	*Southeastern Baptist Theological Seminary*
WMB	*World Mission Board of the Brazilian Baptist Convention*

INTRODUCTION

A Contemporary Note on Hemispheric Evangelicalism

As I write these pages, the reality of global racial violence continues to show its destructive face. The latest iteration of the struggles of marginalized peoples is most evidently presented to White supremacist societies in the Américas today by two means: the wake of the brutal murder of George Floyd by a White police officer and the disproportional ways in which the COVID-19 pandemic affects racial and ethnic minorities. In Brazil, my country of origin, João Pedro, an unarmed Black teenager, was murdered by police officers during an operation in Rio de Janeiro just a few months ago. The favelas and ghettos of Latin America—overpopulated by Black and Brown bodies—are overburdened with the health, social, and economic effects of the COVID-19 pandemic. The term "twin pandemics" is being used to name the fact that the COVID-19 pandemic works together with the pandemic of racial violence upon which the Américas were invented. The truth of the undeniable and multifaceted brutalization of dark-skinned bodies is marching on in the United States and Latin America.

The racial violence demonstrated by the twin pandemics is not new or exceptional; the pandemics are examples of common ways in which the *modus operandi* of White supremacist societies manifests itself. At times, these White supremacist commitments show their global partnerships explicitly. For example, in this moment in history, the United States and Brazil—the largest country in Latin America—share a number of commonalities in this regard. Most importantly for the purposes of this book, former US president Donald Trump and Brazilian president Jair Bolsonaro have tremendous appeal in both evangelical and White supremacist groups. These two groups, which many times present overlapping affiliations, interests, methods, and assumptions, provide important foundations for the nationalist, populist, and authoritarian tendencies within the two countries. Steve Bannon, one of Donald Trump's most important campaign strategists, befriended and counseled Jair Bolsonaro's team and has been called a "guru" of Bolsonaro and his politician sons. Both Trump and Bolsonaro have been celebrated explicitly in evangelical pulpits in the

United States and Brazil as significant numbers of evangelicals praise them as their favored ones. Their constituencies share an overwhelming number of assumptions and a very similar worldview.

Although the research that resulted in this manuscript began much before Trump, Bolsonaro, or the twin pandemics became a reality, this book speaks directly to the current moment in the sense that it analyzes an underexplored aspect of the genealogy of the global influence of United States evangelicals—of which racial injustice is a major element. The crops Bolsonaro is harvesting as the first pan-Christian president of Brazil were planted by many hands, but the hands of Baptist Confederate exiles and Southern Baptist missionaries were most certainly among them. Beyond the way in which Southern Baptist missionaries and other United States evangelicals helped shape Brazilian political imagination, the national identity of the country itself was informed by an intellectual who became Baptist under missionary influence. Gilberto Freyre's presence in Baptist life was indispensable for the creation of a racial democracy ideology that was used by the Brazilian government in ways that shaped deep-seated aspects of Brazilian communal self-perception. The development of Brazilian national identity and Southern Baptist presence were surprising and unintended partners in the furthering of widespread forms of racial marginalization.

The Global Mission of the Jim Crow South, although focusing specifically on Baptists, speaks to concerns that go much beyond traditional denominational histories in the sense that it deals with issues at the intersection of global Baptist identities, missions, and ethnic studies in ways that speak to geopolitical realities significantly. The connections between Brazil and the United States' evangelicalisms are not exclusive to the Baptist fold in general or the Southern Baptist Convention (SBC) in particular. The influence of the gospel of the Southern Baptist, white-skinned Christ, however, goes much beyond Baptist circles and includes peoples of different places and languages as well as different ethnic, and even racial, backgrounds. Brazilian scholarship on the country's new conservatism, which is most visibly represented by Bolsonaro, has begun to uncover the importance of US-Brazil evangelical connections that were often facilitated by Baptist networks and led by Baptist individuals. The history of transnational evangelicalisms is at the center of the emergence of a global

Christian Right.[1]

Readers will notice that although I used the term "evangelicalism" in the title and sporadically throughout the book—I did not engage in debates about definitions of the term "evangelicalism," or distinguished between "evangelical" and "evangélico." Such distinctions often hinge on perceptions of Latin American evangelical "social Christianity" which, despite its rich history, has never had a sustained majority presence in Latin American evangelicalism.[2] I am keenly aware that such debates have captured the imagination of accomplished historians of US Christianity, whose work I respect. Two aspects of my approach make the details of this important debate less pressing for the purposes of this manuscript: (1) my focus on the Southern Baptist Convention, which would be considered an evangelical denomination whose evangelicalism fits within most definitions of the movement; and (2) the fact that I hope to demonstrate the strong ideological, political, theological, and racialized connections between the Southern Baptist Convention and the Brazilian Baptist Convention, which would not only place both comfortably within the evangelical camp but also render sharp distinctions between "evangelical" and "evangélico" unhelpful.

I hope to engage the debate about a proper conceptual framing of evangelicalism more directly in future contributions. For now, suffice it to say that when it comes to my own view of evangelicalism, I moved from

---

[1] For recent Brazilian scholarship on the topic, see Marina Bastos Lacerda, *O Novo Conservadorismo Brasileiro: De Regan a Bolsonaro* (Porto Alegre: Editoria Zouk, 2019); Andrea Dip, *Em Nome de Quem?: A Bancada Evangélica e Seu Projeto de Poder* (Rio de Janerio: Civilização Brasiliera, 2018); Juliano Spyer, *Povo de Deus: Quem São os Evangélicos e Por Que Eles Importam* (São Paulo: Geração Editorial, 2020); e Ricardo Alexandre, *E a Verdade os Libertará: Reflexões sobre Religião, Política e Bolsonarismo* (São Paulo: Mundo Cristão, 2020).

[2] David C. Kirkpatrick's history of what he called "the Latin American Evangelical Left," for example, is a welcome contribution to the history of Latin American evangelicalism which demonstrates not only the diversity of Latin American evangelicalism, but also the way in which evangelicals from the region influenced aspects of the movement globally. The rich diversity of the region's progressive evangelicalisms, however, must not distract from the fact that such expressions only rarely attained a sustained presence within majority representations of Latin American evangelicalism. For a history of Latin American progressive evangelicalism see David C. Kirkpatrick, *A Gospel for the Poor: Global Social Christianity and the Latin American Left* (Philadelphia, University of Pennsylvania Press, 2019).

an understanding that allowed theological self-perceptions and doctrinal articulations to overdetermine "evangelical identity" to an approach that pays attention to theological issues but also emphasizes political affiliations, social dispositions, gendered limitations, and racial imagination.[3] Other approaches consider these sociopolitical aspects to be consistent characteristics of evangelicalism. For example, Matthew Sutton recognized that historians of evangelicalism have tended to base their understanding of important aspects of the movement on the narratives of their subjects and thus have generally failed to offer a compelling account of the strong continuities between fundamentalism and evangelicalism in the US. For Sutton, when it came to political, economic, gender, racial, and cultural issues, "their ideology and agenda remained consistent."[4] Kristin Du Mez wrote that the affinities between fundamentalism and evangelicalism "ran deep, and it was not always possible to distinguish one from the other."[5] Similarly, Anthea Butler recognized that the evangelicalism of Baptist evangelist Billy Graham and his contemporaries differed from fundamentalism in some theological articulations while "their cultural and social racism held them together."[6] In line with the fundamentalist-evangelical disposition, Southern Baptist missionaries in Brazil offered significant continuity in their commitment to White supremacy, conversionism, male privilege, biblicism, homophobia, crucicentrism, conservative politics, and activism. Despite the fact that the term "evangélico" in Latin America is

---

[3] Almost ten years ago, I wrote about the complexities involved in defining "evangelicalism," especially as it related to Latin American Liberation Theology (LALT). Then, I concluded that "I am confident that LALT and Evangelicalism are not necessarily contradictory movements, and characterizing them as contradictory is not appropriate if their respective diversity and dynamism is taken into consideration." In retrospect, my confidence was based on an appropriation of a particular understanding of evangelicalism that focused almost exclusively on theological articulations and emphasized the importance of the diversity that exists within the movement without naming properly the dispositions of the majority of Latin American evangelicals. See João B. Chaves, *Evangelicals and Liberation Revisited: An Inquiry into the Possibility of an Evangelical-Liberationist Theology* (Eugene: Wipf & Stock, 2013), 130.

[4] Matthew Avery Sutton, *American Apocalypse: A History of Modern Evangelicalism* (Cambridge: Belknap Press, 2014), preface.

[5] Kristin Kobes Du Mez, *Jesus and John Wayne: How White Evangelicals Corrupted a Faith and Fractured a Nation* (New York: Liveright Publishing, 2020), 22.

[6] Anthea Butler, *White Evangelical Racism: The Politics of Morality in America* (Chapel Hill: University of North Carolina Press, 2021), 35.

largely used as a synonym of "Protestant," the Southern Baptist/Brazilian Baptist example shows that one could also speak of a "hemispheric evangelicalism" that revolves around the aforementioned octagon, which builds on the quadrilateral that David Bebbington helpfully suggested.[7] This book is in continuity with the growing literature that continues to point strongly in this direction.

The history of Southern Baptist missions is inseparable from the history of US evangelicalism and its traditional White supremacist connections and patterns that missionaries helped globalize. Although this book deals primarily with the history of Southern Baptist missionaries in Brazil, pointing out a few hemispheric and global implications that resulted from the SBC missionary enterprise in the country, this story is inevitably connected to the history of White evangelicalism in the United States. This study attempts to show in some detail how the SBC brand of US evangelicalism influenced Latin American Protestantism via missionary deployments of Christian Whiteness, especially in Baptist circles. The chronological limit of this study is 1982 partially because my focus on missionary correspondence precluded me from having access to more recent letters and papers according to the policies of the International Mission Board. In the last forty years, however, there is little indication that the SBC, the Brazilian evangelical establishment, or the leadership of the Brazilian Baptist Convention distanced themselves from the White supremacist spirit that characterized their general contours during the period on which this book focuses.

In addition, since I finished this manuscript's first drafts, important books on Southern Baptist connection to White supremacist convictions were published. Recent actions by SBC officials themselves also revealed the contemporaneity of dispositions similar to the ones uncovered by my research on Southern Baptist missionaries in Latin America. This book's particular denominational, geographic, and chronological focus may, in the mind of some readers, weaken its connection to the history of US evangelicalism broadly conceived. The story of Southern Baptist activity in Latin America, however, is an underexplored arm of the broader history of US evangelicalism in general—a history that has the SBC at its center.

---

[7] See David Bebbington, *Evangelicalism in Modern Britain: A History from the 1730s to the 1980s* (London: Routledge, 1989).

Southern, evangelical missionary activity in Latin America has often mediated the global dissemination of the US evangelical form of White supremacy even in spite of the good, religiously-legitimized intentions of missionary agencies. Emerging patterns of evangelical transnational engagement as well as the growing strength of social media technologies that encourage transnational communication provided avenues for the strengthening of US evangelical influence in Latin America even as physical missionary presence proportionally diminished.[8] It is important, therefore, to acknowledge that the history of US evangelicalism that was globalized via traditional missionary activity maintained its influence via diversified and adaptable means. In terms of Southern Baptist history and the history of White evangelicalism in general, developments that can be conceived as US-based quarrels continue to have global impact.

I agree with Melani McAlister's argument that the history of US evangelicalism must be recontextualized via international lenses in order to be properly understood, and I welcome her problematization of missionary self-perception regarding their role in colonial enterprises.[9] My assumption is that such studies must be multilingual and resist cross-regional characterizations of missionaries. In places like Brazil, where the broad social context encouraged strong forms of White supremacy and where appreciation for US culture became a post-WWII widespread reality, the connection between the US South and local dispositions were—and continue to be—stronger than in several other places. In other words, I am convinced that David Hollinger's thesis that the missionary project tried to make the world more like the US but instead "made the United States more like the world" could be problematized by demonstrating how successful US evangelical missionaries were in their attempts to shape the theopolitical imagination of Latin American evangelicals in general.[10]

---

[8] One of such emerging patterns of transnational evangelical partnerships is often referred to as the "sister church model" or the "congregation-to-congregation model." Such models, as Janel Bakker pointed out, remain characterized by Global North colonialism. See Janel Kragt Bakker, *Sister Churches: American Congregations and Their Partners Abroad* (Oxford: Oxford University Press, 2014), 207-8.

[9] Melani McAlister, *The Kingdom of God Has No Borders: A Global History of American Evangelicalism* (Oxford: Oxford University Press, 2018), 1-28.

[10] David A. Hollinger, *Protestants Abroad: How Missionaries Tried to Change the World but Changed America* (Princeton: Princeton University Press, 2017), 1. For the

When it comes to Latin America, it is indeed important to name instances of local influence on missionaries, for such relationships were not static. It is also important to recognize that Latin American evangelicalism is characterized most clearly by a North-South order of influence. The global influence of US evangelicalism has often been framed by specialists with regional research emphases that turned them away from Latin America in general and Latin American non-Pentecostal religious networks in particular. This tendency, that informed understandings of Latin American evangelicalism and its relationship to US evangelicalism, was largely constructed and imagined by US-based scholars. Regarding the continuing globalization of US evangelicalism, what happens in the US is often of crucial importance in Latin America.

In terms of the history of US evangelicalism, out of the many books published recently, two took center stage in public discussions about the connection between US evangelicalism and White supremacy, namely, Robert P. Jones' *White Too Long* and Kristin Kobes Du Mez's *Jesus and John Wayne*. Both books reveal ways in which US evangelicalism and White supremacist projects continued to partner in the maintenance of structural racism in the US. Jones demonstrates how White evangelical religious participation in the US, in its current form, continues to provide no adequate remedy to the social maladies of White supremacy.[11] Du Mez, pointed specifically to how this disposition affected Latin America directly. She wrote:

> Evangelicals in Brazil, drawing from their own culture of machismo and borrowing from the playbook of American evangelicals, helped install Jair Bolsonaro—a thrice-married strongman known for his misogynistic statements, his antigay agenda, and his defense of "traditional" family values—as the nation's president.[12]

---

purposes of this book, I will use the terms "theopolitical" and "theocultural" interchangeably to name the Southern Baptist tendency of conflating their quintessentially southern culture – and its ideal social arrangements – and their theological convictions. For a similar use of the term see Lilian Calles Barger, *The World Come of Age: An Intellectual History of Liberation Theology* (Oxford: Oxford University Press, 2018).

[11] Robert P. Jones, *White Too Long: The Legacy of White Supremacy in American Christianity* (New York: Simon & Schuster, 2020), 155-187.

[12] Kristin Kobes Du Mez, *Jesus and John Wayne: How White Evangelicals Corrupted a Faith and Fractured a Nation* (New York: Liveright Publishing, 2020), 301.

Afro-Brazilian, Baptist theologian and activist Ronilso Pacheco wrote recently, calling out the Brazilian Baptist Convention by name, that evangelical organizations in Brazil "contribute to the protection of a [Bolsonaro] administration whose primary language is violence, that prioritizes guns over vaccines, and that continues to attack social minorities [and democracy]."[13] Du Mez recorded interviews with Pacheco as well as with Rev. Caio Fabio—a Presbyterian minister who was the best-known evangelical leader in Brazil but left the evangelical movement. A few months before these interviews, the Djanira Institute of Research and Teaching, based in Rio de Janeiro, promoted a Brazil-US scholarly conversation that included several historians of evangelicalism. Scholars whose work appears primarily in English included well-respected voices in the scholarly conversation about US evangelicalism, namely, Molly Worthen, Bethany Moore, Amanda Porterfield, Axel Schaefer, and Darren Dochuk. Academics in Latin America and in the US have noticed the need for new historical narratives on the historical and contemporary influence of US evangelicalism in Latin America and are beginning to investigate this connection further.

The specific place of Brazilian Baptists in the historical trajectory of the Religious Right in the Américas is another important element connected to this book that should be mentioned. The Brazilian evangelicalism that undergirds such trajectory is poised to continue its growth in numbers and power; a phenomenon that will continue to be significant for the whole continent. Demographers project that by 2032 Brazil will be a majority-Protestant country with almost 100 million adepts – most of them belonging to churches that adopted theopolitical commitments similar to those of US evangelicalism.[14] Benjamin Cowan recently demonstrated that an appropriate understanding of the modern US Christian Right "must include Brazil as an essential platform – and Brazilians as essential proponents of – the development of cultural, moral, and political

---

[13] Ronilso Pacheco, "É impossível seguir Jesus e se calar sobre Bolsonaro: traíram o evangelho." Notícias UOL, February 21, 2021. https://noticias.uol.com.br/colunas/ronilso-pacheco/2021/02/21/e-impossivel-seguir-jesus-e-se-calar-sobre-bolsonaro-trairam-o-evangelho.htm Unless otherwise noted, all translations from Portuguese in this manuscript were made by the author.

[14] Mariana Zylberkan, "Evangélicos devem ultrapassar catolicos no Brasil a partir de 2032." VEJA, February 4, 2020. https://veja.abril.com.br/brasil/evangelicos-devem-ultrapassar-catolicos-no-brasil-a-partir-de-2032/.

agendas now taken for granted."[15] US-trained Brazilian Baptist leaders acting in the 1970s and 1980s were, according to Cowan, overseers of "evangelicals in the national legislature as a self-appointed vanguard against imminent moral calamity."[16] This transnational Christian Right project had already showed itself to be broadly influential in the hemisphere well before the Latin American religious context became characterized by Pentecostal numeric might. Brazilian Baptist leaders helped form a transnational Religious Right that became a continuous multi-denominational phenomenon with significant contemporary importance. Chronologically, my narrative stops roughly when Cowan's begins and focuses on narrating the Southern Baptist geneaology that connects to the geopolitical dynamics that scholars continue to trace.

The importance and contemporaneity of my focus on Southern Baptist racial imagination is further illustrated by the controversy surrounding the condemnation of critical race theory and intersectionality by the presidents of six Southern Baptist seminaries. This controversy represents a continuation of the White supremacist dispositions of Southern Baptists in the contemporary US. It is particularly interesting to notice that these are the presidents of the institutions that trained influential leaders of the Brazilian Baptist Convention and that, given recent partnerships, continue to form Brazilian Baptist leaders. For example, in 2016, Daniel Akin, the president of Southeastern Baptist Theological Seminary (SEBTS) and chairman of the Council of Seminary Presidents that signed the controversial statement on critical race theory and intersectionality, praised the partnership between SEBTS and the Brazilian Baptist Convention. The first graduating cohort of this partnership, who received a Masters of Theological Studies degree, consisted of executive and regional leadership in Brazilian Baptist entities, including the president of the Brazilian Baptist National Mission Board, Fernando Brandão. Akin said: "Southeastern loves its Great Commission partnerships around the world. None brings me more excitement and joy than the one we have with Brazilian Baptists. Our vision and passion for theological education, personal evangelism and world missions is one! We are true partners in building God's kingdom.

---

[15] Benjamin A. Cowan, *Moral Majorities Across the Americas: Brazil, the United States, and the Creation of the Religious Right* (Chapel Hill: University of North Carolina Press, 2021), 8.

[16] Cowan, 65.

What a blessing!"[17]

In 2020, Southwestern Baptist Theological Seminary (SWBTS) published a piece featuring Brandão, who by then was the president of the most important Baptist theological seminary in Brazil, the South Brazil Baptist Theological Seminary in Rio de Janeiro. The piece also quoted L. Roberto Silvado, a two-time graduate of SWBTS and a past president of the Brazilian Baptist Convention. Brandão, Silvado, and other SBC-trained Brazilian leaders were celebrating a new partnership between SWBTS and the seminary in Rio. They plan to continue a partnership whose focus is training the future leadership of the Brazilian Baptist Convention, which plans to plant five thousand new churches in the next five years.[18]

The statement signed by the presidents of the six SBC seminaries criticized critical race theory and intersectionality for being incompatible with the Southern Baptist faith. This document was put together in recognition of the twentieth anniversary of the adoption of a Southern Baptist statement of faith, the Baptist Faith and Message 2000. SBC seminary presidents made clear that they are committed to enforcing full compliance by seminary faculty. Talking about the statement, Daniel Akin said that SBC seminary professors must conduct their classes "in accordance with and not contrary to the Baptist Faith and Message," and that this commitment against critical race theory and intersectionality "is our sacred commitment and privilege, and every individual faculty member and trustee of our institutions shares this commitment."[19] It is, of course, no coincidence that this statement came when it did. The cultural pressures toward race and gender equality have clashed with Donald Trump's administration, favored of White evangelicals in general and Southern

---

[17] Amy Whitfield, "Southeastern Partnership with Brazilian Baptists Sees First Fruits," Southeastern Baptist Theological Seminary, March 21, 2016, https://www.sebts.edu/news-and-events/headlines/2016/03/SP16_Brazil.aspx.

[18] Adam Covington, "Dark Shadows & Bright Promises: The 'Missionary Vision and Passion' Planted in Brazil by the 'First Southwesterner' Continues to Grow," SWBTS, May 14, 2020, https://swbts.edu/news/dark-shadows-bright-promises-the-missionary-vision-and-passion-planted-in-brazil-by-the-first-southwesterner-continues-to-grow/.

[19] George Schroeder, "Seminary Presidents Reaffirm BFM, Declar CRT Incompatible," Baptist Press, November 30, 2020, https://www.baptistpress.com/resource-library/news/seminary-presidents-reaffirm-bfm-declare-crt-incompatible/.

Baptist Whites in particular. In September of 2020, Trump signed an executive order banning federal contractors, the military, federal agencies, and recipients of federal grants from citing critical race theory in government sponsored trainings.[20] The SBC statement is unsurprisingly in continuity with its historical ideological commitments and current political affiliations.

Reacting to the statement, African American pastors within the SBC and faith leaders across the nation accused the presidents of SBC seminaries of adding another shameful chapter to the SBC's long and transnational legacy of racism.[21] For example, Ralph D. West, a prominent African American pastor who left the SBC since the statement was released, said:

> I am uncertain as to why these men found it necessary even to associate their affirmation of the 2000 Baptist Faith and Message with a rejection of critical race theory. One would expect, with their sincere rejection of racism, they would speak to instances of it in our culture. They would stand against our president's attempts to maintain the names of Confederate generals on monuments and military bases.
>
> One would expect they would stand against the rise of anti-Semitism and racism seen in groups like the Proud Boys. They would stand against police violence against Black bodies and stand in solidarity with the Black community. They would call the names of George Floyd, Breonna Taylor and Ahmaud Arbery. But they have not done that. Their stand against racism rings hollow when in their next breath they reject theories that have been helpful in

---

[20] Yonat Shimron, "Southern Baptist Seminary Presidents Nix Critical Race Theory," Religion News Service, December 1, 2020, https://religionnews.com/2020/12/01/southern-baptist-seminary-presidents-nix-critical-race-theory/.

[21] Mark Markuly and Edward Donaldson III, "Southern Baptist Convention Makes Poor Decision on Racism," *The Tennessean*, January 21, 2021, https://www.tennessean.com/story/opinion/2021/01/21/southern-baptist-convention-makes-poor-decision-racism/4201688001/.

framing the problem of racism.[22]

Similarly, pastor Charlie Dates also criticized the SBC sharply. Recently, Dates led his Chicago congregation to join the SBC because he thought the SBC of the present was qualitatively different from what he called "the Old Southern Baptists." However, he left the denomination after being convinced that the change he thought he saw in the SBC was a mirage. Dates was optimistic about the SBC until 2020, but things changed after he could no longer overlook the White supremacist commitments of leaders in the Convention. He wrote:

> But as 2020 went on, I grew increasingly uneasy. When Albert Mohler, the president of the Southern Baptist Seminary, said the only politically moral option for Christians was the Republican Party, I asked other SBC leaders, good Christian men, to challenge him. They would not. I was shocked, but not surprised, when Mohler endorsed President Trump and watched the two men—on Reformation Day—celebrate each other on Twitter.
> And then, last week, a final straw.
> On Dec. 1, all six of the SBC seminary presidents—without one Black president or counter opinion among them—told the world that a high view of Scripture necessarily required a corresponding and total rejection of critical race theory and intersectionality.[23]

Dates confessed he was wrong to lead his church in joining the SBC, recognizing the continuity of the Southern Baptist racial imagination: "I had to tell my church I was wrong. There is no such thing as 'the Old Southern Baptists.'"[24]

---

[22] Ralph D. West, "Commentary: Where I Stand on the Statement by SBC Seminary Presidents," *Baptist Standard*, December 16, 2020, https://www.baptiststandard.com/opinion/other-opinions/commentary-where-i-stand-on-the-statement-by-sbc-seminary-presidents/.

[23] Charlie Dates, "'We out:' Charlie Dates on Why His Church Is Leaving the SBC over Rejection of Critical Race Theory," Religion News Service, December 18, 2020, https://religionnews.com/2020/12/18/we-out-charlie-dates-on-why-his-church-is-leaving-the-sbc-over-rejection-of-critical-race-theory/.

[24] Dates.

Dwight McKissic, an African American pastor who has been an internal critic of the SBC, went to his social media platforms to criticize the statement, saying that the SBC "is not a healthy place for African American professors. On the subject of race, they will not be given the freedom to speak their convictions, quote certain sources, or assign certain readings, without Anglo approval."[25] McKissic also put his affiliation to the SBC in check as the debates surrounding the statement against critical race theory and intersectionality develop, and broke ties with the Southern Baptists of Texas Convention (SBTC)—a state convention tied to the SBC. Because of his criticisms of the SBC, McKissic received a revealing racist letter from an SBC-affiliated individual. The letter, dated from January 25, 2021, reveals deep racial resentment and uses intentionally racist language. Signing under the name John V. Rutledge, the author concluded the letter saying:

> If Negroes had come to improve rather than to importune, they would have deployed the alleged-to-exist "collective wisdom of black Baptist pastors" to pick apart the Baptist Faith and Message, to challenge denominational denial of settled science, to extract the Convention from its unsophisticated doctrines and dogma of yesteryear. All desperately needed. But those are beyond the Negroes' intellectual capacities. Like two-year-olds, they know only how to whine and throw tantrums. The SBC should bid them goodbye and good riddance![26]

The SBC and the SBTC condemned the letter and denied that its author speaks for the Convention and its churches.[27] The language Rutledge use in the letter, however, is haughtily familiar; he sounds like

---

[25] Mark Wingfield, "SBC Seminary Presidents Meet with Black Pastors but Don't Change Position on Critical Race Theory," Baptist News Global, January 11, 2021, https://baptistnews.com/article/sbc-seminary-presidents-meet-with-black-pastors-but-dont-change-position-on-critical-race-theory/#.YDzmYWhKiCo.

[26] From John V. Rutledge to Dwight McKissic, January 25, 2021. This letter was shared publicly on social media platforms and is still broadly available on Twitter as I write this section of the manuscript.

[27] Brandi Addison, "Arlington Pastor Dwight McKissis Receives Racist Letter after Leaving Southern Baptists of Texas Convention," Dallas Morning News, February 3, 2021, https://www.dallasnews.com/news/faith/2021/02/03/arlington-pastor-dwight-mckissic-receives-racist-letter-after-leaving-southern-baptists-of-texas-convention/.

he would feel at ease among many of the missionaries quoted in the following pages and who are still celebrated as heroes in Latin America.

Located in the largest Black country outside of Africa, the Brazilian Baptist Convention has been pressured to address its own historical connections to White supremacist sensibilities—many times manifested through its relationship to the SBC. Many Black Brazilian Baptists consistently criticize the fact that the Brazilian Baptist Convention continues to fail to condemn the presence of structural racism within its initiatives and institutions. For example, in 2019, a panel entitled "Decolonizing the View: Does Racism Affect the Church?" was canceled by the leadership of the Brazilian Baptist Convention. The panel was planned to take place during an important biannual youth conference which, not unimportantly, was held at the Atitude Baptist Church, frequented by Brazil's first lady Michelle Bolsonaro.[28] Eventually the convention allowed the panel to take place, but without the presence of the two Black Baptist leaders who would originally lead the panel—pastor Marco Davi de Oliveira and activist and educator Fabíola Oliveira. The executive director of the Brazilian Baptist Convention, Sócrates de Oliveira Souza (none of these "Oliveira" are related)—who is a Black man—denied that the censoring of the speakers was racially motivated. According to Souza, the speakers' polemic social media profile was largely to blame for the retraction of their invitation.[29] Many, however, were convinced that the way in which the Brazilian Baptist leadership conducted the issue demonstrated their commitment to the ideological entanglements informed by their historical racial imagination, as well as by their commitment to the Jair Bolsonaro administration—once both speakers were known critics of the current president.[30]

Voicing their opposition to the way in which the Brazilian Baptist Convention acted during the event, the Alliance of Baptists of Brazil published an open letter condemning the move. The letter said that the deci-

---

[28] Marcelo Santos, "Congresso de jovens da Igreja Batista é acusado de racismo," Rede Brasil Atual, July 20, 2019, https://www.redebrasilatual.com.br/cidadania/2019/07/congresso-de-jovens-da-igreja-batista-e-acusado-de-racismo/.

[29] Ibid.

[30] Folha de S.Paulo, "Debate sobre racismo em igreja frequentado por Michelle Bolsonaro é cancelado," July 19, 2019, https://www1.folha.uol.com.br/poder/2019/07/debate-sobre-racismo-em-igreja-frequentada-por-michelle-bolsonaro-e-cancelado.shtml.

sion to retract the invitation to the speakers was done because the leadership succumbed to pressure from "ultraconservative, fundamentalist groups that, due to their alignment with the current [Bolsonaro] administration, find a point of contact with the [leadership of the Brazilian Baptist Convention]." The letter, expressing a sense of hemispheric solidarity with African American struggles in the US, also stated that

> Such a gesture, perpetrated by the Council of the Brazilian Baptist Convention, represents a historical, theological, and ethical setback to the anti-racist struggles led by Baptist pastor Dr. Martin Luther King, Jr., a militant against racism and for civil rights. Because of his struggle for justice in his country and in the world, MLK received the Nobel Peace Prize; such struggle was also carried out by other brothers and sisters of Baptist tradition in various parts of the world, and also in Brazil, among which Pr. Marco Davi must be counted as its main protagonist in the last decades.[31]

Examples like this illustrate that the temptation to connect the well-being of the Brazilian Baptist Convention to a denial of structural racism parallels similar moves made by the SBC, such as the statement against critical race theory and intersectionality.

These positions and decisions, in turn, are similarly entangled with racial imaginations, institutional structures, and political affiliations shared by the SBC and their Brazilian partners in the dissemination of the Southern gospel. In terms of a theological diagnostic of the Brazilian Baptist Convention, what White Baptist theologian Kristopher Norris said rings true even in a country predominantly populated by Afro-descendants: "Our diseased theological imagination has infected the world and re-created it in the image of the masked white supremacy that holds us captive. Put simply, white supremacy is an infection we gave to the world; it is our responsibility to do something about it."[32] Although some may perceive Norris' statement as being ambitious, a look at the shape of Brazilian evangelicalism will help confirm its general accuracy. Not only has the diseased

---

[31] Claudia Florentin, "Repúdio Da Aliança de Batistas Ao Desconvite de Marco Davi e Fabíola Oliveria," ALC Noticias – Portugues, July 23, 2019, https://alc-noticias.net/bp/2019/07/23/repudio-da-alianca-de-batistas-ao-desconvite-de-marco-davi-e-fabiola-oliveira/.

[32] Kristopher Norris, *Witnessing Whiteness: Confronting White Supremacy in the American Church* (Oxford: Oxford University Press, 2020), 59.

theological imagination of White evangelicalism infected the English-speaking world, but it also infected countries like Brazil, which continues to spread its own influence in the whole Latin America continent and beyond. Geopolitical dynamics and migration from Latin America to the United States, in turn, re-invigorate Christian-flavored conservatisms via new immigrants who often become religious entrepreneurs in their new country—a contemporary issue that I have tried to address in another volume.[33]

The book is organized into five major chapters that narrate the history of Southern Baptist influence in Brazilian Baptist life until 1982, when the Brazilian Baptist Convention celebrated its centenial. Chapter one gives a general overview of my argument and places the intended contributions of the book within the literatures of World Christianity and Baptist studies. More specifically, I argue for the centrality of the missionary White supremacy as a major theme in the history of American Protestantism in general and Brazilian Baptists in particular that remains understudied. Chapter two moves the narrative more intently to the history of the SBC missionaries to Brazil, where I remain for the rest of the manuscript. I begin by looking at how the decades that preceded a major clash between missionaries and local leaders over denominational control developed. From the beginning of Southern Baptist presence in Brazil until 1922, missionaries did not feel threated by the sporadic Brazilian resistance that manifested itself locally in denominational life. Rather, they established a successful denomination based on three main pillars: church planting/evangelism, education, and publication. Despite the missionary narrative that the power to control the denomination was going to be shifted to locals, until 1922 many Brazilian Baptists believed that no significant movement in that direction had been done. The trajectory of generally unchallenged missionary control, however, would begin to change in the early 1920s, when a group of dissenting Brazilians joined forces with one Southern Baptist missionary and started a movement that would split the denomination into two national bodies.

The creation, development, and resolution of the movement that split the denomination, which came to be known as the Radical Movement, is the topic of chapter three. The sporadic reactions that came before the

---

[33] João B. Chaves, *Migrational Religion: Context and Creativity in the Latinx Diaspora* (Waco: Baylor University Press, 2021).

16

Radical Movement did not materialize in an alternative movement within the Brazilian Baptist Convention. In the first decades of the twentieth century, however, a number of locals who saw missionaries as impediments to a full transition of power from Southern Baptist to Brazilian hands rebelled. The beginnings of the Radical Movement were regional—focusing mostly on the state of Pernambuco, where the North Brazil Baptist Theological Seminary was located. As the animosity between missionaries and dissenters strengthened, however, the movement grew in proportion and representation, eventually gaining national prominence. D.L. Hamilton, the one missionary who sided with locals, assisted the Brazilians in a number of ways during the administrative dissent that the Radical Movement represented. Hamilton did not see himself as a catalyst for the Radical Movement; rather, he sided with locals because he agreed with them that they were ready to transition into the leadership of the denomination.

Hamilton did not hold the alleged competence of a number of his fellow missionaries in high regard—which he made clear in his personal correspondence many years before the Radical Movement began. Missionaries in general, as Hamiltons' example will illustrate, did not tolerate fellow southerners who sided with Brazilians and against the missionary establishment in critical matters. Hamilton was seen as a threat to missionary power by some of his fellow missionaries for a long time, and when dissenters came knocking, he did feel he could mediate in their favor. Although Hamilton was indeed a part of the Radical Movement equation, structural factors such as the growth of Brazilian nationalism, the shape of missionary racial imagination in the 1920s and 1930s, and the ability to rule the denomination in Brazil were all central aspects of the disagreement. Eventually radicals won major aspects of the dispute, and by 1936, Southern Baptist missionaries, deeply affected by the economic recession affecting the United States, begrudgingly negotiated unprecedented leadership opportunities for Brazilians. When the Radical Movement dissolved, Brazilians began to lead seminaries, have stronger presence in national denominational boards, and feel like the Brazilian Baptist Convention had taken a major step towards the full nationalization of the denomination. The following decades, however, would prove them wrong, as missionaries adapted to the new reality by consolidating power sometimes by returning to leadership positions that had transitioned to local hands (such as the leadership of seminaries) and sometimes by being more careful in choosing Brazilian leaders and initiatives they would support.

Chapter four looks at the developments in Brazilian Baptist history that followed the resolution of the Radical Movement until 1982, the year when the Brazilian Baptist Convention celebrated their one hundred years of history. Missionaries lamented the victory of the Radical Movement and some came to resent the Foreign Mission Board officials who facilitated the transition that allowed Brazilians to have more institutional power. Field missionaries, however, soon began to plan the takeover of institutions of cultural output—especially the seminaries—from local hands. Foreign Mission Board officials who once were instrumental in allowing locals to have more power eventually partnered with field missionaries in their project to reestablish institutional domination. This time, however, missionaries who led important institutions within the denomination paid closer attention to the importance of creating a pipeline of missionary-friendly Brazilian leaders who would not represent resistance to Southern Baptist activity in Brazil.

As the denomination grew exponentially after the Second World War, the proportional number of missionaries gradually diminished and astute missionaries continued the implementation of strategies that ensured the continuation of the Brazilian Baptist ideological dependence on the Southern Baptist Convention. Brazilian Baptists also created their own agenda to "reach the world for Christ," and they began exporting Southern Baptist orthodoxy abroad. By 1982, the Brazilian Baptist Convention had missionaries in Chile, Portugal, Paraguay, Bolivia, Mozambique, Angola, Azores, Uruguay, Argentina, Rhodesia, Venezuela, France, Spain, Canada, South Africa, the United States, Peru, and Ecuador. The Convention also had a sense of strength and independence, but it continued to emulate Southern Baptists and sided with the most conservative elements in the struggles for control of the Southern Baptist Convention that eventually resulted in the split of the SBC. When they celebrated the one hundred years of presence in Brazil, Brazilian Baptists of the Brazilian Baptist Convention could be generally described as Southern Baptists abroad who happened to speak Portuguese.

The Brazilian Baptist Convention was not immune to the growth and influence of Global Pentecostalism. Although Brazilian Baptists grew rapidly after World War II, their growth was slower than that of Pentecostal churches. The influence of Pentecostalism entered the Brazilian Baptist Convention, however, through the ministry of Rosalee Mills Appleby, a

Southern Baptist missionary who worked in Brazil for thirty-six years. Appleby was influenced by the Keswick movement—with its emphasis on language of baptism with the Holy Spirit as an enduement of power for service. Appleby's mentees, however, went further than she would and became charismatic. They wanted to balance their Baptist and charismatic identities in a denomination that was aggressively anti-Pentecostal. The tensions engendered by differing interpretations regarding the role of the Holy Spirit in the believer's life led to a split within the denomination in 1965, and soon afterwards, a charismatic-friendly Baptist denomination was formed as an alternative to the Brazilian Baptist Convention. The National Baptist Convention, as the new denomination was called, represents the lack of ability of Brazilian Baptists to open a space for unity where there is no doctrinal uniformity. Chapter five tells the story of Appleby, her mentees and their opponents, and the controversy around the doctrine of the Holy Spirit that led to schism. This story illustrates that even when a sustainable doctrinal digression from Southern Baptist orthodoxy arose in Brazilian Baptist life, it was introduced and sanctioned by foreign figures of authority who had credibility within Southern Baptist circles. This chapter adds to the burgeoning study of Pentecostal/Baptist relations.[34]

Finally, the concluding chapter connects the threads of previous chapters and provides a brief overview of the ways in which the Brazilian Baptist Convention continued to nurture an imbalanced relationship with the Southern Baptist Convention. With the exception of sporadic and controversial initiatives that signaled a qualified acceptance of the ordination or women, no significant digression from SBC orthodoxy has been made by the Brazilian Baptist Convention. The sense of closeness and thankfulness that Brazilian Baptists feel towards the Southern Baptist Convention certainly is a testament to the commitment and work performed by field missionaries in Brazil. Works that celebrate missionary success, however, are myriad, and they tend to neglect the less celebratory aspects of Southern Baptist missionary work. The following pages represent an attempt to offer a counter-narrative that opens space for a more

---

[34] Douglas Weaver's *Baptists and the Holy Spirit* is the first major scholarly study that looks thoroughly at Pentecostal/Baptist interaction in the United States. Weaver mentions, for example, Rosalee Mills Appleby and her time in Brazil. See C. Douglas Weaver, *Baptists and the Holy Spirit: The Contested History with Holiness-Pentecostal-Charismatic Movements* (Waco: Baylor University Press, 2019), 262-65.

balanced view of SBC work in Latin America. Southern Baptist missionaries were convinced that they were doing the work of the Lord, and Brazilian Baptists agreed. The Southern tunes to which the missionary imagination danced, however, were not always heard by locals or even by missionaries themselves. Culture, after all, is too often our palace and our prison.

CHAPTER ONE

SOUTHERN BAPTIST MISSIONS AND WORLD CHRISTIANITY

In 2016, when doing a series of interviews for a study on immigrant communities in the United States, I was cautiously amused by a comment made by a Brazilian Baptist denominational leader. When I asked him about his opinion regarding the role of the Southern Baptist Convention in contemporary Brazilian Baptist life, he answered with a humorous metaphor: "when Southern Baptists sneeze, Brazilian Baptists catch a cold." The global influence of the largest Protestant denomination in the United States is not surprising. Southern Baptists have a unique set of qualities that have historically set them up for influence on a global scale. They are mission-minded, culture warriors, generally beholden to the Southern culture that sustained a cohesive set of values in the denomination's identity, and aggressive in their recruitment efforts. In the case of Brazil in particular and Latin America in general, however, the influence of the Southern Baptist Convention (SBC) is often uncritically praised with very little qualification. The more problematic aspects of the neo-colonialist, racially informed global "sneezes" of the SBC only rarely appear in the scholarly literature of the denomination's presence in the region. The role of SBC missions in this dynamic is central, and this study focuses on SBC missionary presence in Brazil throughout the first century of Brazilian Baptist history in order to reveal the role played by Southern culture in the extremely contagious presence of the SBC abroad.

Denominations that were disseminated globally through the agency of United States Protestant missions have a number of peculiar problems. For instance, the denominational identities appropriated by locals who embraced missionary proselytisms were often rife with colonial expectations.[1] The Protestantism that North American missionaries proclaimed

---

[1] I distinguish proselytism from evangelism and consider the tendency to recruit members from other Christian bodies, as was usually the case with evangelical mis-

globally generally bore the stamp of the religious nationalisms and religiously legitimized social imaginations of missionaries, and these missionaries themselves often struggled to distinguish between Christlikeness and cultural captivity. Making that distinction is certainly a herculean task that still permeates contemporary missiological debates. The ongoing attempts to differentiate between contextualization and syncretism, with their underlying desire to identify the ever-elusive transcultural core of the Gospel message, illustrate the complexities involved in this task. Translatability and hybridity are always elements in the transmission and appropriation of ideological messages across cultures and spaces, and the extent to which missionaries were capable to control their message is another complex element in studies of missionary activity. Resolving these theoretical dilemmas is not the concern of this project. Yet recognizing missionary cultural captivity is central for a proper understanding of both the missionaries themselves and also of the locals who chose to participate in expansionist transnational projects originally introduced to them through foreign missionary agency.

The language of modern missions itself, together with the White European attempts to subjugate the inhabitants of the New World that accompanied it, is a legacy from the colonial era.[2] Although Southern Baptist missionaries were not agents of traditional Western territorial expansion and subjugation, they shared a common disposition with the White missionaries that preceded them in that their mission was also concerned with reshaping their converts' social imagination. The subjugation they hoped to impose was cultural and it was guided by their self-perception as superior humans who were disseminators of a superior way of being. Southern Baptist missions to Latin America, as such, is in qualified continuity with the White European colonial projects that preceded them—even if their violence was more symbolic and epistemic than physical. Despite positive developments in missiological studies that recognize and try to transcend the uneasy tension between the violent, colonial roots of "missions" lan-

---

sionaries to Latin America, a clear example of the first. For a treatment in the distinction between proselytism and evangelism see Bryan Stone, *Evangelism after Pluralism: The Ethics of Christian Witness* (Grand Rapids: Baker Academic, 2018), 15–24.

[2] David Jacobus Bosch, *Transforming Mission: Paradigm Shifts in Theology of Mission* (Maryknoll: Orbis Books, 1991), 302–3.

guage and the goal of spreading the Gospel, missionary enterprises are often violent initiatives in either physical, symbolic, or epistemic terms.[3] The negotiation between the theological nature of the Church as the people of God on earth and the way in which such nature manifests itself in history has often been a difficult tension to navigate.

It is also important to note that the fact that missionary enterprises took place in a wide range of spaces and across long periods of time adds to the complexity involved in any appropriate understanding of missionary practice and belief. Different mission projects and contexts often meant different negotiations of missionary identity, and generalizations regarding "the missionary" often fall into the temptation to create a missionary *idealtypus* that is too general to withstand critical historical pressure. The fact that one can affirm unequivocally that the missionary enterprises of US Protestants bore the stamp of cultural captivity does not allow us to assume that such captivity manifested itself homogeneously across time and space. When it comes to the history of missions to Brazil, recognizing missionary cultural captivity challenges us not only to name the particular theocultural dispositions that missionaries brought to the country in their ideological luggage but also to recognize how the Brazilian context itself informed the manifestation of such dispositions on the ground. In the case of Southern Baptists, the mission to reach the Brazilians with the message of Christ was simultaneously the mission of the Jim Crow South, and a mission that developed in a national environment that was mostly receptive to the White supremacist dispositions of Southern Baptist missionaries.

The receptivity to missionary White supremacy implicit in Brazilian racial imagination helps us qualify the recent tendency, in the literature of World Christianity studies, to emphasize missionary adaptation and local agency in the context of foreign missionary work. This particular tendency gained strength partially because the examples of missionary contextual adaptation given by scholars who emphasize missionary flexibility tend to focus either on regions of the world where a phenotypical proximity between the dominant class and the general population could be imagined by Anglo-American missionaries (e.g. predominantly Black African countries and Asian countries such as China and Japan) or on independent

---

[3] For an overview of the use of "missions" language and an argument to transcend its use see Michael W. Stroope, *Transcending Mission: The Eclipse of a Modern Tradition* (Downers Grove: IVP Academic, 2017).

groups and denominations that were not under the auspices of foreign denominational structures. The work of four of the most influential scholars of World Christianity, Andrew Walls, Philip Jenkins, Dana Robert, and Lamin Sanneh, are illustrative of this general tendency. While all of them mention Latin America quite often, they tend to focus more prominently on African-Initiated Churches (AICs). Out of the four, Jenkins is the one whose work pays more attention to Latin America in general and Brazil in particular. Despite the fact that many of Jenkins' insightful observations are generally applicable to Brazilian Baptists, he focuses primarily on Latin American independent churches, such as the IURD, and other forms of nontraditional Christianities.[4] Furthermore, a look at edited volumes on World Christianity and Christianity in the Global South reveals the overwhelming presence of Africa and Asia in scholarly volumes. Non-Pentecostal Protestantisms in Latin America and Latinxs in the United States are comparatively underrepresented among major scholars of World Christianity.[5]

In terms of Southern Baptist missionary encounters in Asia and Africa, one must recognize that the widely different contexts between those

---

[4] See Philip Jenkins, *God's Continent: Christianity, Islam, and Europe's Religious Crisis* (Oxford: Oxford University Press, 2010); Jenkins, *The Next Christendom* (Oxford, Oxford University Press, 2007); Dana Robert, *Christian Mission* (Chichester, Wiley-Blackwell, 2009); and Lamin O. Sanneh, *Disciples of All Nations: Pillars of World Christianity* (Oxford: Oxford University Press, 2007).

[5] For examples see Hilde Nielssen, Inger Marie Okkenhaug, and Karina Hestad Skeie, eds., *Protestant Missions and Local Encounters in the Nineteenth and Twentieth Centuries: Unto the Ends of the World* (Leiden: Brill, 2011); Afeosemime U. Adogame and Shobana Shankar, eds., *Religion on the Move! New Dynamics of Religious Expansion in a Globalizing World*, International Studies in Religion and Society, vol. 15 (Leiden: Brill, 2013); Scott W. Sunquist and Mark A. Noll, *The Unexpected Christian Century: The Reversal and Transformation of Global Christianity, 1900-2000* (Grand Rapids: Baker Academic, 2015); Elaine Padilla and Peter C. Phan, eds., *Christianities in Migration: The Global Perspective*, Christianities of the World (New York: Palgrave Macmillan, 2016); and Miriam Adeney, *Kingdom without Borders: The Untold Story of Global Christianity* (Downers Grove: IVP Books, 2009).

regions and Brazil go beyond the dynamics of missionary racial imagination.[6] In contrast to Southern Baptist experiences in a number of the denomination's foreign missionary endeavors, however, the Brazilian context
allowed for (and at times encouraged) high levels of Southern Baptist racially informed ideological and structural domination. Regarding the Brazilian Baptist scenario, the racism imported from the Confederate, and
later the Jim Crow South by the majority of Southern Baptist missionaries,
despite contextual differences, found support in Brazil's own racial imagination, with a White dominant class and a marginalized Black and Brown
population. Although many Brazilians still reproduce the ideology of racial
democracy popularized by anthropologist Gilberto Freyre (a former Baptist himself), the history of Brazil is marked by strong racist tendencies.
Freyre became a Baptist as a youth and was positively impressed by the
missionaries under whom he studied in Brazil. Upon arriving at Baylor
University in 1918, however, Freyre was so appalled by the racism he witnessed that he not only left the denomination but also began a process of
developing a racial theory that eventually became a part of Brazilian national identity.[7] Freyre's racial democracy myth aimed at discrediting the
scientific racism of his time. Despite Freyre's intentions, the success of his
ideas in the country functioned as a mechanism that camouflaged forms of

---

[6] For examples see Calvin F. Parker, *The Southern Baptist Mission in Japan, 1889-
1989* (Lanham: University Press Of America, 1990); Travis Collins, *The Baptist Mis-
sion of Nigeria* (Ibadan: Associated Book-Makers Nigeria, 1993); Alan Scot Willis, *All
According to God's Plan: Southern Baptist Missions and Race, 1945-1970* (Lexington:
University Press of Kentucky, 2005); Li Li, "From Southern Baptist Identity to Chi-
nese Baptist Identity, 1850-1950," in *Baptist Identities: International Studies from the
Seventeenth to the Twentieth Centuries*, ed. Ian M. Randall, Toivo Pilli, and Anthony
Cross (Milton Keynes: Paternoster, 2006), 241–56; Kurt Bowen, *Evangelism and
Apostasy: The Evolution and Impact of Evangelicals in Modern Mexico* (Montreal:
McGill-Queen's University Press, 1996); James C. Enns, *Saving Germany: North
American Protestants and Christian Mission to West Germany, 1945 -1974* (Montreal:
McGill-Queen's University Press, 2017); and Melanie E. Trexler, *Evangelizing Leb-
anon: Baptists, Missions, and the Question of Cultures* (Waco: Baylor University Press,
2016).
   [7] Oral Memoirs of Gilberto de Mello Freyre, interview by Thomas Lee Chalton,
May 16, 1985, in Waco, Texas, transcript, Baylor University Institute for Oral History, Waco, TX, https://digitalcollections-baylor-quartexcollections.com/ Docu-
ments/Detail/oral-memoirs-of-gilberto-de-mello-freyre-tran-
script/1596408?item=1596409.

White supremacy in Brazil. Through Freyre's legacy, Southern Baptist racism informed much more than denominational issues and it had a role in the development of Brazilian national identity itself.[8]

During the period when the SBC sent the pioneering missionaries to Brazil, the racist ideology of "whitening" was at its peak. This ideology of whitening influenced Brazilian immigration policies that encouraged immigration from Europe and the United States based on the conviction that "the superior white race would prevail in the process of racial amalgamation."[9] Brazilian intellectual elites not only widely shared the ideal of whitening the country through immigration policies; they also valued eugenics-inspired ideas imported from White Europe and the United States. With the success of Freyre's understanding of race relations in Brazil, the persistence of the ideal of racial democracy was maintained by the country's legal maneuvers that discouraged people from identifying a number of racial issues in Brazil until recently, when the Brazilian government began to acknowledge openly the widespread racial discrimination in the country.[10] Although racial categories in Brazil are based mostly on phenotype rather than ancestry, as in the United States, the history of race relations in the country paralleled that of the United States in the sense that White Brazilians generally benefited from structural privileges and set the tone for the country's social organizations and institutions.[11] This environment was primed for the White supremacist ideology of SBC missionaries. The White supremacist structures already present in Brazil did not challenge the core of American racial ideology and thus White supremacy became

---

[8] João B. Chaves, *O Racismo Na História Batista Brasileira: Uma Memória Inconveniente Do Legado Missionário* (Brasília: Novos Diálogos, 2020), 84–86.

[9] Thomas E. Skidmore, *Black into White: Race and Nationality in Brazilian Thought* (Durham: Duke University Press, 1993): 44-46.

[10] Graziella Moraes Silva and Marcelo Paixão, "Mixed and Unequal: New Perspectives on Brazilian Ethnoracial Relations," in *Pigmentocracies: Ethnicity, Race, and Color in Latin America*, ed. Edward Telles (Chapel Hill: The University of North Carolina Press, 2014), 181-85.

[11] See Anthony W. Marx, *Making Race and Nation: A Comparison of South Africa, the United States, and Brazil* (Cambridge: Cambridge University Press, 1998); Micol Seigel, *Uneven Encounters: Making Race and Nation in Brazil and the United States* (Durham: Duke University Press Books, 2009); and Edward E. Telles, *Race in Another America: The Significance of Skin Color in Brazil* (Princeton: Princeton University Press, 2014).

institutionalized in the denominational structures. Southern Baptists intentionally dominated the Brazilian Baptist institutions of cultural production (e.g. seminaries, periodicals, and publishing houses) for almost a century with the clear goal of making Brazil an ideological extension of the Southern Baptist Convention—and they were very successful![12]

---

[12] In his work on the impact of American Christianity on World Christianity, Mark Noll argued that the primary reason for the similarities between Global South Christians and American evangelicals is not direct influence, but parallel development. For Noll, "social circumstances in many places of the world are being transformed in patterns that resemble in crucial ways what North American believers had earlier experienced in the history of the United States," and the bulk of the explanation for the similarities lies in these parallel experiences (Mark A. Noll, *The New Shape of World Christianity: How American Experience Reflects Global Faith* [Downers Grove: IVP Academic, 2009] 109). Noll himself singles out the SBC—the biggest Protestant denomination in terms of the numbers of foreign missionaries—as a notable exception to the growing independent missionary societies on which he focuses. The SBC example in Brazil does not fit Noll's view of the relationship between American Christianity and World Christianity. Direct influence—which Noll acknowledges but qualifies—is a much more prominent factor in the Brazilian Baptist case, as I hope to show. In terms of theology and its ramifications, Brazilian Baptists are by and large, to use Raimundo Barreto's words, "in conformity with the kind of evangelicalism that generated and nurtures" the denomination. See Raimundo Barreto Jr., "A Ética Social E Sua Relevância Para a Igreja Hoje," *Episteme* 3, no. 2 (2001): 73. In addition, new studies on the influence of North American, missionary schools in the transmission of United States religious and political dispositions also qualify Noll's thesis. The recent volume edited by Cesar Vieira and Ester Nascimento is particularly enlightening in this regard. See Cesar Romero Amaral Vieira and Ester Fraga Vilas-Bôas Carvalho do Nascimento, eds., *Contribuições do Protestantismo para a História da Educação no Brasil e em Portugal* (Piracicaba: UNIMEP, 2017). In terms of Southern Baptist influence, Maria Anjos and Carlos Carvalho traced the influence and strategy of missionaries who used schools in order to Americanize and evangelize locals. See Maria de Lourdes Amjos and Carlos Henrique Carvalho, "Ações Educacionais Dos Missionários Batistas Norte-Americanos No Início Do Século XX No Brasil," in *Contribuições Do Protestantismo Para a História Da Educação No Brasil E Em Portugal*, eds. Cesar Romero Amaral Vieira and Ester Fraga Vilas-Bôas Carvalho do Nascimento (Piracicaba: UNIMEP, 2017): 207-32. Finally, José Jardilino and Leandro Lopes gave a helpful introduction to a number of theses and dissertations that touch on aspects of the influence of imported Protestant educational goals and strategies. See José Rubens Lima Jardilino and Leandro de Proença Lopes, "Protestantismo E Educação, Construção de Um Campo de Pesquisa: Algumas Observações E Teses Inclusas" in *Contribuições Do Protestantismo Para a História Da Educação No Brasil E Em Portugal*, eds.

I readily accept the view that missionaries saw themselves as mechanisms of divine agency and that local converts often mystified their appropriation of missionary ideology accordingly. I also celebrate many initiatives of missionary humanitarianism from which locals benefited. Yet, the racially informed ideological and institutional missionary domination is not only part of the identity of Southern Baptist missionaries, but also a part of the very life of the Brazilian Baptist Convention. The shaping of Latin American evangelicalism, as I will show via a close look at the Brazilian Baptist example, cannot be understood apart from a proper demonstration of missionary domination that the literature largely neglects. The ideological ghost of the geographical area formerly known as the Confederacy, sometimes holding hands with the Holy Spirit, both haunted and blessed the Brazilian brethren of the SBC, and in the case of Brazil it is not always easy to distinguish when one acted apart from the other.

For the first decades of their history, despite sporadic local dissent, Brazilian Baptists—who were already generally socialized into a White supremacist society—readily internalized the doctrinal articulations of Southern Baptist missionaries, and during the first decades of Baptist work in Brazil, such sporadic dissent manifested itself as administrative disagreements rooted on nationalist sentiments rather than theological disagreements informed by the recognition of missionary theocultural racism. Generally speaking, if one wants to explore the history and development of Brazilian Baptist doctrine, all one needs to do is explore Southern Baptist theological development. Missionaries to Brazil were extremely driven and effective in the implementation of their ideological convictions, and such convictions often informed structural arrangements.

The missionary implementation of the Southern Baptist ethos in Brazil, therefore, was much more complex than the self-perception of Southern Baptist missionaries or that of their Brazilian proselytes allowed them to recognize. Despite the fact that pioneer missionaries saw themselves as immediate agents of the Gospel of Christ, their cultural anxieties of racial superiority pronouncedly affected their religious dispositions. Southern Baptist missionaries to Brazil perceived their beliefs and practices as being primarily theological, but they were also thoroughly racial.

Cesar Romero Amaral Vieira and Ester Fraga Vilas-Bôas Carvalho do Nascimento (Piracicaba: UNIMEP, 2017): 291-322.

They were concerned with theological orthodoxy, but their racial ortho-doxy was also a central aspect of their *modus operandi*. The racial imagina-tion of these missionaries marked the structural and ideological develop-ment of Brazilian Baptists, and this reality demands that we consider the theocultural arrangements that Southern Baptist missionaries attempted to impose on Brazilian Baptist life since its earliest days. Such a consider-ation is still understudied in either English or Portuguese as the great ma-jority of historians who have tackled this topic at all have written as if the White supremacist components of Southern Baptist missions should have been forgotten or are easily explained away. This book explores the ways in which pioneering Southern Baptist missionaries to Brazil implemented racialized strategies of denominational control in the first century of Southern Baptist missionary work in Brazil.

In terms of the history of Global South Protestantism, the im-portance of the history of Southern Baptist missions to Brazil transcends the number of Brazilian Baptists in the Brazilian Baptist Convention (BBC)—which today is estimated at around 1.7 million people distributed throughout over nine thousand churches and congregations. The BBC forms the tenth largest Baptist Convention in the world and the largest Baptist body outside the United States and Africa. The National Baptist Convention—also SBC-inspired, as I will show—has over four hundred thousand members distributed throughout almost three thousand churches. Put together, all Baptists in Brazil are the second largest Protestant denominational identification in the country, second only to the Assemblies of God. They account for almost fifty percent of traditional denominations and are more numerous than some of the most significant denominations and religious bodies in the United States, such as the Pres-byterian Church (USA), the Presbyterian Church in America, The Lu-theran Church (Missouri Synod), the American Baptist Churches USA, the Baptist General Convention of Texas (Texas Baptists), the United Church of Christ, and the Christian Church (Disciples of Christ).[13]

Brazilian Baptist numbers are only disappointing if measured against the explosive recent growth of Brazilian Pentecostal churches. Despite the fact that Baptists are only a fraction of the Brazilian population, the success of the missionary enterprise can be seen by the fact that Baptist numbers

---

[13] Juliano Spyer, *Povo de Deus: Quem são os evangélicos e por que eles importam*, (Rio de Janeio: Geração Editorial, 2020), 76.

grew at a much faster rate than those of the general population. This is evident in the periods of Baptists in Brazil that I will analyze. From 1890 to 1938, Brazilian Baptists went from 312 people to over fifty thousand members distributed in next to six hundred churches around the country.[14] In the same year, there were ninety-three Southern Baptist missionaries in Brazil—only China received greater attention from the denomination.[15] By the end of the celebration of the one hundred years of the Brazilian Baptist Convention in 1982, there were over six hundred thousand Baptists in the BBC—almost half of those joined Baptist ranks after 1970.[16] The SBC investment in Brazil remained considerable, with 321 missionaries in the country in 1982, but the missionary/local ratio diminished drastically.[17] Yet, the Brazilian population was over 120 million people in 1982, which makes the number of Brazilian Baptists seem irrelevant vis-à-vis the overwhelming strength of Roman Catholicism in 1980s Brazil. But sheer numbers are only part of the story.

Brazilian Baptists not only have been sending missionaries to both Latin American countries since 1908 and European countries since 1911, but today they also have missionary presence in over eighty countries, including the United States.[18] Also, it was in a Baptist church founded by a Southern Baptist missionary that the Swedish immigrants who founded the Assemblies of God in Brazil—which has an estimated twenty million

---

[14] See Israel Belo de Azevedo, *A Celebração Do Indivíduo: A Formação Do Pensamento Batista Brasileiro* (Piracicaba: Editora Unimpep, 1996), 196; and Anônio Neves de Mesquita, *História Dos Baptistas Do Brasil* (Rio de Janeiro: Casa Publicadora Baptista, 1940), 349–50.

[15] Annals of the Southern Baptist Convention, May 12, 1938. A number of denominational reports, such as this one, can be accessed through the online archives of the International Mission Board (IMB) and will not indicate page numbers. The IMB electronic archives can be accessed at www.imb.org/research/archives/. Unless otherwise noted, all denominational documents in English that do not provide page numbers were accessed via the IMB online archives.

[16] Azevedo, *A Celebração Do Indivíduo: A Formação Do Pensamento Batista Brasileiro*, 196.

[17] Annals of the Southern Baptist Convention, 1982, 102.

[18] Few scholarly works in English address the history of Brazilian Baptist global missions. For a recent example of the global impact of Brazilian Baptists, see Edward L. Smither, *Brazilian Evangelical Missions in the Arab World: History, Culture, Practice, and Theology* (Eugene: Wipf & Stock, 2012).

members today—began their Brazilian ministry.[19] As a matter of fact, scholars have suggested that the founders of the Assemblies of God in Brazil only formed the Pentecostal denomination because they first failed to convert Baptist churches to Pentecostalism.[20] In addition, churches that were once a part of the Brazilian Baptist Convention, such as the charismatic-leaning *Igreja Batista da Lagoinha*, became global powerhouses of the Brazilian gospel industry and its influence permeates Brazilian Protestantism irrespective of denominational affiliation or lack thereof. A Southern Baptist missionary who had connections to United States revivalists directly influenced the pastor who led the *Igreja Batista da Lagoinha* toward its charismatic stance that, in turn, opened space for its widespread success in the gospel industry.

In 1982, the seminaries connected to the Brazilian Baptist Convention served 3,608 students—including students of other denominations and countries. Then, Baptists also had seventeen K-12 schools, two universities, twelve orphanages, one hospital, three clinics, and two assisted living facilities that served beyond Baptist ranks.[21] In 1982, the Brazilian Baptist publishing house published twenty-three periodicals, fifty-nine new books, twenty-eight tracts, and a total of nine million pieces of literature that were consumed by Baptists and non-Baptists alike.[22] The presence of Baptist religious products in the Brazilian religious market today is even more significant than in the 1980s, once the recent explosion of Brazilian Protestantism—despite its primarily Pentecostal forms—means a larger receptive audience for Baptist religious goods. In short, the Southern Baptist influence in the religious history of the country with the second

---

[19] Mark Noll aptly put the significance of the Brazilian Assemblies of God in comparative perspective when he wrote that "this past Sunday there were more members of Brazil's Pentecostal Assemblies of God at church than the combined total in the two largest U.S. Pentecostal denominations, the Assemblies of God and the Church of God in Christ in the United States." See Noll, *The New Shape of World Christianity*, 20. He could, however, have added the membership of mainline denominations such as the Presbyterian Church (USA) and the American Baptist Churches (USA) to the two largest Pentecostal denominations in the United States and the number still would have been smaller than that of the Brazilian Assemblies of God.

[20] John M. Landers, "Eric Alfred Nelson, the First Baptist Missionary on the Amazon, 1891-1939" (PhD diss., Texas Christian University, 1982), 90.

[21] J. Reis Pereira, *História Dos Batistas No Brasil (1882-1982)* (Rio de Janeiro: JUERP, 1982), 314–15.

[22] Annals of the Southern Baptist Convention, 1982, 99.

largest Christian community in the world is felt much beyond the walls of Brazilian Baptist churches and it highlights the importance of the group's presence both in the country and globally.[23]

Brazilian Baptists were also part of the history of the SBC in the United States since the beginning of the twentieth century. For example, C.D. Daniel, who helped form the *Convención Bautista Mexicana de Texas* and served as its first president in 1910, came to the United States from Brazil, where he had been raised among the Confederate Exiles who went to Brazil after the Southern loss in the Civil War. Daniel's fluency in Portuguese helped him work successfully among the Spanish-speaking population in Texas. David Cameron demonstrated that, in typical Southern Baptist fashion, KKK-friendly Daniel was a warrior for Christ and Southern culture—if he could differentiate those at all.[24] According to Cameron, "C.D. Daniel sought to control the leadership and development of Mexican American Baptist evangelism as a means of reinforcing the doctrine of segregation and employing Americanization and evangelization programs."[25] Similarly, J.F. Plainfield, who became a prominent leader in Southern Baptist home missions, was an Italian-born former Roman Catholic priest who became a Baptist in Brazil. Plainfield worked among immigrants in the United States and wrote influential pieces, including a widely popular book among Southern Baptists.[26] Although not a Southerner himself, Plainfield was an avid defender of the project for Americanizing foreigners and saw non-Americanized immigrants as a potential threat to "the moral and religious life of the South."[27] Since very early on,

---

[23] Jenkins, *The Next Christendom*, 107.

[24] David J. Cameron, "Race and Religion in the Bayou City: Latino/a, African-American, and Anglo Baptists in Houston's Long Civil Rights Movement" (PhD diss., Texas A&M University, 2017), 84–91.

[25] Cameron, 84.

[26] J.F. Plainfield, *The Stranger Within Our Gates* (Atlanta: Home Mission Board of the Southern Baptist Convention, 1938).

[27] Joseph Frank Piani Plainfield, "The Missionary Challenge of the Foreigner," *Home and Foreign Fields* 13, no. 2 (1929): 15. See also Joseph Frank Plainfield, "Building a Christian America in Italian Tampa," *Home and Foreign Fields* 16, no. 2 (1932): 10; Joseph Frank Plainfield, "Among the Italians: Ring Bells, Ring!," *Home and Foreign Fields* 16, no. 3 (1932): 7; Joseph Frank Piani Plainfield, "The Challenge of the Foreigner," *The Teacher* 52, no. 4 (April 1938): 1–3, 64; J.F. Plainfield, "A Chasm: The Religious and Political Contrast Between Italy and America," *The Commission* 5, no. 3 (1942): 142–43.

Baptists in Brazil were a part of the history of Southern Baptist denominational life in the United States, but mostly by giving the SBC resources for furthering the xenophobic agenda so prominent in Southern culture.[28] In other words, the history of Baptists in Brazil has interesting connections to the history of religiously-legitimized xenophobia in America.[29]

Southern Baptist missionaries to Brazil were responsible for a number of initiatives that benefited Brazilians, such as the creation of schools and the implementation of initiatives of poverty alleviation. In addition to Southern Baptist evangelistic strategies, these initiatives—which were often themselves motivated by evangelistic goals—helped the qualified success attained by missionaries in Brazil. A number of texts produced by pastors and scholars connected to the denomination celebrate the positive aspects of Southern Baptist missionary presence in Brazil.[30] This celebration, however, led to a lack of attention to the less explored but equally present dominating tendencies so common among White, Southern missionaries to Brazil. This project focuses on the tendencies of Southern Baptist missionaries to subjugate locals and privilege White, male, and Southern individuals, mentalities, and practices. To be sure, disregarding the bravery, commitment, and convictions of missionaries in general—and the missionary self-perception as primarily religiously motivated individuals in particular—is not the primary aim here. The dominating, controlling, and racist dispositions of Southern Baptist missionaries to Brazil,

---

[28] Nick Pruitt wrote on this issue. J.F. Plainfield also appears prominently in his work. See Nicholas T. Pruitt, "Open Hearts, Closed Doors: Native Protestants, Pluralism, and the 'Foreigner' in America, 1924-1965" (PhD diss., Baylor University, 2017).

[29] For an excellent analysis of the ways in which foreigners were perceived as threats to American culture and life see Erica Lee, *America For Americans: A History of Xenophobia in the United States* (New York: Basic Books, 2019).

[30] The vast majority of the histories of Brazilian Baptists celebrate missionary accomplishments and presence and pay little attention to the ambiguities in missionary action and ideology. For examples, see A.R. Crabtree, *História Dos Baptistas Do Brasil*, vol. 1 (Rio de Janeiro: Casa Publicadora Baptista, 1937); Anônio Neves de Mesquita, *História Dos Baptistas Do Brasil* (Rio de Janeiro: Casa Publicadora Baptista, 1940); Zaqueu Moreira de Oliveira, *Ousadia E Desafios Da Educação Teológica: 100 Anos Do STBN* (Recife: STBN Edições, 2002); Edgar Francis Hallock and Ebenezer Soares Ferreira, *Historia Do Seminario Teologico Batista Do Sul Do Brasil: 1908 a 1998* (Rio de Janeiro: JUERP, 1998); J. Reis Pereira, *História Dos Batistas No Brasil (1882-1982)* (Rio de Janeiro: JUERP, 1982).

however, will be emphasized because they not only played a key role in the initiatives that shaped Brazilian Baptist imagination, they also still inform the theopolitical anxieties of the Brazilian Baptist Convention.[31]

Among histories of Brazilian Baptists, a published work that traces the racial and cultural components among Southern Baptist missionaries critically is lacking.[32] The monolingual tendencies often manifested in a number of English-speaking histories of the denomination's presence in England and/or the United States is also apparent, and works that look at Baptist identity as it developed across national borders are also rare in the English language. The few histories written by and about United States missionaries to Brazil focus overwhelmingly on the contribution of these individuals in the numeric growth of Brazilian Baptists and thus do not

---

[31] Brazilian Baptist scholars have noted the continuous dependence of Brazilian Baptist imagination on SBC anxieties and positions. Yet a thorough historical assessment of how such dependency developed remains absent from the literature. For examples, see Paulo D. Siepierski, "Localização Histórica Do Racismo No Protestantismo Brasileiro," *Episteme* 2, no. 1 (2000): 61–72 and João Ferreira Santos, "A Teologia Protestante No Brasil Nesse Ultimos Trinta Anos," *Episteme* 3, no. 1 (2001): 29–40. That said, it is important to note that anxieties that paralleled those of the original SBC missionaries to Brazil (e.g. Landmarkist successionism) are still debated on public discussions in Baptist publications that carry a scholarly veneer. See Othon Ávila Amaral, "A Origem Dos Batistas: Três Teorias," *Visão Missionária* 82, no. 1 (2004): 24–25 and Zaqueu Moreira de Oliveira "Os Batistas: A Versão Histórica de Sua Origem," *Refexão E Fé* 4, no. 4 (December 2002): 9–20.

[32] A look at the major works on Baptist history in Brazil will reveal either a lack of the effect of Southern culture on the relationship between locals and missionaries, a hagiographical tendency that obscures any critical assessment, or both. For examples, see Betty Antunes de Oliveira, *Antonio Teixeira De Albuquerque: O Primeiro Pastor Batista Brasileiro* (Rio de Janeiro: Edição de Autora, 1982); Joel Fortunato Oliveira, "Missões Mundiais: Uma Obra Incontestável," *Jornal Batista* (March 1981); Zaqueu Moreira de Oliveira, *Perseguidos, Mas Não Desamparados: 90 Anos De Perseguição Religiosa Contra Os Batistas Brasileiros (1880-1970)* (Rio de Janeiro: JUERP, 1999); Zaqueu Moreira de Oliveira, *Panorama Batista Em Pernambuco* (Recife: Departamento de Educação Religiosa de Junta Evangelizadora de Pernambuco, 1964); J. Reis Pereira, *História Dos Batistas No Brasil (1882-1982)* (Rio de Janeiro: JUERP, 1982); Marcelo Santos, *O Marco Inicial Batista*, Coleção Sem Fronteiras (São Paulo: Autor, 2003); Elizete da Silva, *William Buck Bagby: Um Pioneiro Batista Nas Terras Do Cruzeiro Do Sul* (Editora Novos Diálogos, 2011); and Enéas Tognini, *História Dos Batistas Nacionais: Documentário* (Brasília: Convanção Batista Nacional, 1993).

pay attention to the process of the brazilianization of the Baptist denomination in Brazil as it is related to Southern Baptist presence.[33]

---

[33] In terms of published academic manuscripts, there are only a few exceptions to the encyclopedic and/or pro-missionary tendency in analyses of Southern Baptist presence in Brazil, and most of them are recent publications. In the 1950s, in his book on Brazilian Protestantism, French scholar Emile Leonard provided an exceptional non-confessionally driven account of Southern Baptist presence in Brazil, looking at some of the tensions between locals and missionaries. But once Leonard's concern was providing a general account of all major denominations, he did not pay exclusive attention to Baptists. See Emile G. Leonard, *O Protestantismo Brasileiro: Estudos de Eclesiologia E Historia Social* (São Paulo: ASTE, 1963). Jorge Pinheiro e Marcelo Santos edited a volume with short essays that signaled toward a critical analysis of several themes in Brazilian Baptist history that remain understudied, such as the presence of nationalism in grassroots Baptist movements, controversies surrounding women's ordination, and the issue of the correct date of the official beginnings of Brazilian Baptist history. See Jorge Pinheiro and Marcelo Santos, eds., *Os Batistas: Controvérsias E Vocação Para a Intolerância* (São Paulo: Fonte Editorial, 2012). On the issue of Brazilian Baptist beginnings, Marcelo Santos and Alberto Yamabuchi uncovered problematic aspects of the Brazilian Baptist attempt to establish the date of the beginning of Brazilian Baptist work. See Marcelo Santos, *O Marco Inicial Batista* (São Paulo: Convicção, 2003) and Alberto Kenji Yamabuchi, *O Debate Sobre a História Das Origens Do Trabalho Batista No Brasil: Uma Análise Das Relações E Dos Conflitos de Gênero E Poder Na Convenção Batista Brasileira Nos Anos 1960-1980* (São Paulo: Novas Edições Acadêmicas, 2015). João Araújo authored two volumes that were published in 2015 and touch on the domination of Southern Baptist missionaries over Brazilian Baptists in general. In *História, Tradições, e Pensamentos Batistas*, Araújo argued that contextualizations of Southern Protestantism by Brazilian locals were very limited and generally done against missionary desire. See João Pedro Gonçalves Araújo, *Historias, Tradições E Pensamentos Batistas* (São Paulo: Fonte Editorial, 2015). It is in *Batistas: Dominação e Dependência*, however, that Araújo laid out his argument that Brazilian Baptists were by and large dominated by Southern Baptist missionaries institutionally and still are dominated ideologically. Although Araújo focused mostly on the two-volume work by A.R. Crabtree and Antônio Mesquita as primary sources and only consulted sources in Portuguese, he was correct in his observation that a compelling narrative of Southern Baptist missionary domination is lacking from the literature. Araújo was convinced that his book represented the first scholarly counterpoint to the americophile literature available. For Araújo, "After the writings of A.R. Crabtree and Antônio Mesquita, all the books that were written about Baptists in Brazil had the same tendency of praising missionaries, their mission, and the churches of the United States. Therefore, over 130 years after the first Baptist churches were planted in Brazil, there has been little literary production and, all of the few works that exist deal with

A leading methodological limitation of historians of Baptists in Brazil is their lack of attention to—or selective positive use of—the correspondence of missionaries. By focusing primarily on denominational documents and official publications, historians have neglected the fact that the private dispositions often voiced explicitly only in intra-missionary exchanges informed public articulations of supposed administrative and theological tendencies. This book uncovers the private articulations present in missionary correspondence and shows how and to what extent they echoed or differed from the public expressions of denominational publications. This approach uncovers particular ways in which the pronounced tendency toward domination present in the missionary imagination was operationalized. In addition, this study welcomes a transnational tendency in historical narratives and thus opens the possibility of looking at the influence on those narratives of structural developments across nation-state borders. This is key for an appropriate understanding of the impact of United States Southern culture in Brazilian Baptist life, since missionaries imported their theocultural anxieties from a foreign land and attempted to impose them abroad.

The steady establishment of the Southern spirit in the denominational structure in the country characterized Southern Baptist missionary work in Brazil. Only six years after the end of the Civil War, former Confederates who migrated to the country after the Southern loss founded Brazil's first Baptist church. The sustainable phase of Southern Baptist missionary work, however, began with the arrival of the Bagbys in 1881. Since the arrival of the Bagbys, a number of Southern Baptist missionaries arrived in Brazil, deeply committed to their Southern culture, and implemented a system of institutions of cultural output that disseminated and maintained Southern Baptist theology, culture, and social anxieties. The next pages will tell the story of how that happened in more detail.

---

the issues in the same way. There are no counterpoints, criticisms, re-readings, or disagreements. Such attitudes are rejected and silenced" (13). Araújo is correct in pointing out a lack of criticism in the literature on Brazilian Baptist history. Araújo's welcomed contributions to the conversation about missionary domination, however, are informed by a limited source selection both in terms of primary sources and language. In many parts of Araújo's research, his conclusions are more stated than demonstrated. See João Pedro Gonçalves Araújo, *Batistas: Dominação E Dependencia* (São Paulo: Fonte Editorial, 2015).

CHAPTER TWO

SHAPING LOCAL SUBJECTS: CONFEDERATE EXILES, SOUTHERN MISSIONARIES,AND EARLY INSTITUTIONAL DEVELOPMENT

Baptist history in Brazil is complex, diffuse, and multifaceted. It started with a failed attempt by the SBC to establish foreign missionary work in the country, then it turned into a story of migration as Confederate Exiles came to Brazil after the Southern loss in the Civil War, later it developed into a story of sustainable foreign missionary presence, it increasingly included aspects of local administrative autonomy, and moved to Brazilian-led institutions with a strong global presence through their own missionary agencies. Most of these elements coexisted throughout the history of Baptists in Brazil, which adds to the complexity of analyzing the rich history of the group. A consistent element of Baptist history in Brazil, however, is the presence of the controlling shadow of the Southern Baptist Convention, which manifested itself in more or less explicit ways depending on historical circumstances. This Southern Baptist presence was most explicitly embodied in missionaries, who were overwhelmingly committed to the Southern culture in which most of them were nurtured much before they knew of the existence of missions, Baptists, or Brazil.

In the first decades of Southern Baptist missions in Brazil, missionaries were very successful in establishing the foundational structure of the Brazilian Baptist Convention. With the help of local converts, missionaries planted churches, began schools, established seminaries, developed regional conventions, started a national convention, began foreign missionary initiatives from Brazil, purchased a number of properties, and built many buildings. Southern Baptist success in the country was celebrated by both Brazilians and missionaries, and the more success missionaries attained, the more they became convinced that their success was to be partially credited to the Southern aspects of their *modus operandi*.

Despite the fact that local converts did not always notice how the Gospel preached by missionaries was flavored by the cultural norms of the

South, Southern commitment to American and White superiority flooded the imagination of Southern Baptist missionaries. In this chapter, I will tell the story of Brazilian Baptists until 1922, focusing on the aspects of missionary practice that reveal the White supremacist dispositions of Southern Baptists in Brazil. The implementation of such dispositions became so strong that they eventually energized the national conflict that divided the denomination in the country for more than a decade, which I narrate in the next chapter.

Immigrant Beginnings

There was a time in Brazil when being a Protestant usually meant one was an immigrant. A great number of Protestant denominations trace their initial presence in Brazil to European and United States immigrants who came to Brazil looking for a better life.[1] In this sense, the beginning of Baptist work in Brazil was also a story of migration. Not only does this story find its genesis in British and United States migration, but migration stories also inform denominational life for decades. The Foreign Mission Board of the Southern Baptist Convention (hereafter FMB) supported denominational workers in Brazil who were born in many places, such as England, Poland, Latvia, Russia, Italy, Brazil, Sweden, Spain, and Portugal. The FMB was, in other words, a transnational enterprise with some ethnic diversity in its ranks. The control of denominational institutions in Brazil, however, was placed mostly in the hands of United States-born individuals or in the hands of those who identified with the strategies chosen by Southern Baptist missionaries. The presence of a qualified ethnic diversity must not distract from the strong ideological drive of missionary work in Brazil. Baptist work in Brazil was, in the first decades of its existence, the work of the missionary South abroad.

The Foreign Mission Board Turns to Brazil

Historian Israel Belo de Azevedo argued that "Brazilian Baptist thought is North American Baptist thought reproduced in its general outlines."[2]

---

[1] Emile G. Leonard, *O Protestantismo Brasileiro: Estudos De Eclesiologia E Historia Social* (São Paulo: ASTE, 1963), 27-46.

[2] Israel Belo de Azevedo, *A Celebração Do Indivíduo: A Formação Do Pensamento Batista Brasileiro* (Piracicaba: Editora Unimpep, 1996), 225.

The literature on Brazilian Baptist history bears the mark of this North American influence as well as the mark of the robust appreciation that Brazilian Baptists have for their American "founding fathers." The controversy regarding the date of the beginnings of Baptist work in Brazil illustrates how this appreciation manifests itself in the historical memory of Brazilian Baptists. Until 2009, the Brazilian Baptist Convention (BBC), despite abundant historical proof to the contrary, considered 1882 to be the starting point of Baptist work in Brazil, thus attenuating the complexities of the role played by Confederate Exiles (or immigrants from the Southern United States) in the history of the group.[3] The later recognition of an earlier starting date for Baptist beginnings in Brazil may have been the result not of any desire for historical accuracy, but of the fact that the church founded by William Buck Bagby in 1882 became Pentecostal and was no longer under the BBC's umbrella by 2009.[4]

To consider the place in Brazil of immigrants from the Southern United States is important because it pushes us to identify the general characteristics that such immigrants brought to Brazil and compare them to the Brazilian culture with which such immigrants dialogued.[5] Using the year 1871 as a starting point, as some historians have suggested, certainly does offer a better alternative for Brazilian Baptist history than 1882 because it marks the founding of the first Baptist church in the country. But doing so would neglect two important aspects of Brazilian Baptist history:

---

[3] Alberto Kenji Yamabuchi, "O Debate Sobre a História Das Origens Do Trabalho Batista No Brasil: Uma Análise Das Relações E Dos Conflitos De Gênero E Poder Na Conveção Batista Brasileira Do Anos 1960-1980" (PhD diss., Universidade Metodista de São Paulo, 2009); Betty Antunes de Oliveira, *Centelha Em Restolho Seco* (São Paulo: Vida Nova, 2005); and J. Reis Pereira, *História Dos Batistas No Brasil (1882-1982)* (Rio de Janeiro: JUERP, 1982).

[4] Alverson de Souza, *Thomas Bowen: O Primeiro Missionário Batista No Brasil* (Rio de Janeiro: Novos Dialogos, 2012), 48.

[5] Zaqueu Moreira de Oliveira, "The Persecution of Brazilian Baptists and Its Influence on Their Development" (PhD diss., Southwestern Baptist Theological Seminary, 1971).The doctoral dissertation of Brazil's most prolific historian of Baptists illustrates the general lack of attention to the dynamics of Southern religion in the beliefs and behaviors of the United States missionaries who go to Brazil. Talking about the beginnings of Baptist work in Brazil, Oliveira does not provide any overview of Southern Christianity in the United States and, as such, overlooks its potential cultural force on Brazilian Baptist life. This tendency shown by Oliveira has attained normative status in Brazilian Baptist historiography.

1) that it was thirteen years earlier in 1858 that the Foreign Mission Board of the Southern Baptist Convention (SBC) began to seriously consider sending missionaries to Brazil; and 2) that the dynamics of Southern religion in the United States, both before and after the Civil War, were key to the self-understanding of the immigrants from the Southern United States to Brazil among whom Baptist work in Brazil began.

On September 6th, 1858 the FMB, attentive to the emigration of "young men from Virginia and other Southern States,"[6] considered sending missionaries to Brazil to pastor American-only ethnic communities as well as to reach the Brazilians. Although the economic and personnel limitations worked against the initiative of sending missionaries to Brazil at the time, the FMB listed a number of advantages of sending missionaries to Brazil. Among these reasons, the fact that Brazil was a slaveholding country, like the United States, was prominent.[7] The report read:

> [Brazil] is, like our own, a slaveholding country. No missionary can go thither, from any portion of the Christian world but this—who would not probably feel himself called on, either by his own feelings, or by the demands of the public at home who sent him, to broach this vexed question—and to war, either openly or covertly, with the domestic institutions of the land. A missionary from the southern states of America would be free, at least, from this liability to embarrassment. He would have nothing to preach to them but the gospel of Jesus Christ—and need not commence by laying a foundation either of practical or theoretical abolitionism.[8]

For the FMB, Brazil's slaveholding status was important enough to be included in the list of things that should compel the Board to consider its stance on new foreign fields despite its financial and personnel struggles. Instead of voicing opposition to slaveholding, the FMB brazenly suggested that Brazil's slaveholding status would free missionaries from the emotional burden and from the public embarrassment potentially present

---

[6] Foreign Mission Board report, September, 6, 1858.

[7] Foreign Mission Board report, May 6, 1859. A.R. Crabtree had already pointed out that this report includes the celebration of Brazil's slaveholding status, but he minimizes its importance and mistranslates the English text in his Portuguese account. See A.R. Crabtree, *História Dos Baptistas Do Brasil* vol. 1 (Rio de Janeiro: Casa Publicadora Baptista, 1937), 37.

[8] Foreign Mission Board report, May 6, 1859.

in mission fields where the Black population was not treated as property.

In the second half of the nineteenth century, Brazil was the country with the highest number of slaves in the world, and it was partially for this reason that the first Southern Baptist missionary to Brazil, Thomas Bowen, went to the country in 1860.[9] Bowen had been a missionary in Nigeria, but he had to leave Africa for health reasons.[10] His interest in Brazil was not accidental: many of the Black people who had been kidnapped in Nigeria became slaves in Brazil. Whereas the FMB report that mentioned Bowen's appointment ended with a note that millions of the Brazilian Catholic Christians would find Christ through the agency of the Board's appointment of Bowen, in fact, Bowen's actions in Brazil indicate that he was primarily concerned with preaching to Yoruba-speaking slaves in the hopes that they could return to their country as missionaries.[11] One could say that the FMB took Bowen from Africa, but not Africa from Bowen. Bowen's time in Brazil was short, and the mission was abandoned by the beginning of 1861, allegedly once again for reasons of Bowen's health.[12] Ten years after Bowen's return to the United States, the FMB was once again in a position to consider a Brazilian mission.

Why the ten-year hiatus? The United States Civil War had had a considerable impact on the financial situation of the SBC.[13] Between 1861 and 1871, neither the FMB nor the SBC mentioned Brazil prominently in their reports. Defeat in the Civil War, however, provided additional impetus for United States Southerners to immigrate to places like Brazil, which continued to be a slaveholding country until 1888. It was among

---

[9] Foreign Mission Board report, August 6, 1860. The FMB reported his transfer to Brazil as taking place on April 2, 1860.

[10] Souza, *Thomas Bowen: O Primeiro Missionário Batista No Brasil*, 27. This is contested. Souza argues that Bowen's presence in Africa was jeopardized because of his disagreement with the policies of the FMB.

[11] Souza, 27.

[12] Foreign Mission Board report, May 10, 1861. Bowen still had a productive professional life after his return to the United States, which led his Brazilian biographer, Alverson Souza, to speculate that claims of his ill health were how the FMB covered up the fact that he was too progressive for the FMB's taste.

[13] Many Baptist publications attest to the way in which the Civil War impovished Southern Baptist churches. For an example see "Review," *Home and Foreign Journal* 1 (May 1862): 2.

these immigrants from the Southern United States, also known as Confederate Exiles, that the first Baptist church in Brazil, the First Baptist Church of Santa Barbara, was founded in September 1871.[14]

The First Baptist Church of Santa Barbara had for several years asked the FMB for approval as a self-supporting mission, but by the time that happened, Brazil already had a second church in the city of Station. The FMB approved both churches in 1879 and in 1880. The annual report of the SBC read: "last year the convention authorized the Board 'to enter Brazil.' Two stations have been opened in that country—one at Santa Barbara, known as 'the First Baptist Church of Brazil,' and the other at a place called 'Station.'"[15] This same report referred to Rev. E.H. Quillen's favorable impression of Brazil.[16] The FMB approved Quillen, who was the pastor of the Santa Barbara church, as a missionary and he became the second Southern Baptist missionary in Brazilian Baptist history. He wrote about the financial advantages of immigrating to Brazil as well as of his confidence that missionaries in the country would be able to be self-supporting within their first year of work. Quillen also had a disposition that was characteristic of much of Southern Baptist missionary demeanor toward Brazil and Brazilians: a paternalistic optimism for the country's and countrymen's potential—as long as its resources and their decisions conformed to Southern Baptist expectations.[17]

Despite all the proselytizing rhetoric of the FMB's reports, the two first Baptist churches in Brazil did not engage in significant efforts to reach the locals. In this sense, they were not very different from the immigrant churches of other immigrant groups who went to Brazil, whose primary function was to preserve their ethnic customs rather than to proselytize the Brazilians.[18]

---

[14] Crabtree, *História Dos Baptistas Do Brasil* 1, 39.

[15] Southern Baptist Convention report, May 6, 1880.

[16] E.H. Quillen's name also appears as "Quillin" in some sources. I will use "Quillen" throughout this manuscript for consistency.

[17] Southern Baptist Convention report, May 6, 1880.

[18] Gedeon Alencar, *Protestantismo Tupiniquim* (São Paulo: Aret Editorial 2007), 26; Betty Antunes de Oliveira, *Antonio Teixeira De Albuquerque: O Primeiro Pastor Batista Brasileiro* (Rio de Janeiro: Edição de Autora, 1982). Betty Antunes de Oliveira argued that the fact that the American churches consecrated the first local pastor, former Catholic priest Antonio Teixeira de Albuquerque, shows their missionary zeal. There is no indication, however, that the churches planned to create mixed Brazilian-

The Immigrant and Missionary South in Perspective

The first wave of United States Baptist work in Brazil was quintessentially Southern. Between the end of the nineteenth century and the second half of the twentieth century, being a United States White Southern Christian had clearly identifiable contours. A key characteristic of this general disposition was its religious legitimation of slavery as a divinely-ordained institution. The abolition of slavery in the United States and the loss of the Confederate states in the American Civil War did not eliminate this conviction immediately, but it did prompt its progressive reshaping into the myth of a Southern Lost Cause that had a strong element of racial superiority.[19] In the words of Douglas Weaver, "it is practically impossible to read Southern religion in the decades after the Civil War through any lens but race."[20] In turn, the identification of the Southern Baptist Convention with Southern culture is so strong that Bill Leonard highlighted the harmony between SBC values and Southern values and Andrew Smith said that "to study Southern Baptists during the period between the Civil War and the Civil Rights Movement is to study the nerve center of distinctively white Protestantism."[21] Racial and ethnic tension, even if often implicit

---

American congregations. In addition, the first missionaries who left the US with the specific purpose of reaching the Brazilians did not stay in Santa Barbara, partially because of the lack of interest of that church in such an endeavour. Teixeira, then the only national member of the church, left with them. This lack of interest in traditional evangelism, however, may have occurred because of the perceived failure of other Protestant denominations. Quillen wrote to the Board in 1881 that the best way to resist Brazilian "Romanism" was through the creation of schools rather than traditional evangelism. It was this very issue that would later partially account for the conflicts between local leaders and American missionaries.

[19] Charles Reagan Wilson, *Baptized in Blood: The Religion of the Lost Cause, 1865-1920* (Athens: University of Gerogia Press, 2009), 4; John Lee Eighmy and Samuel S. Hill, *Churches in Cultural Captivity: A History of the Social Attitudes of Southern Baptists* (Knoxville: University of Tennessee Press, 1987); C. Douglas Weaver, *In Search of the New Testament Church: The Baptist Story* (Macon: Mercer University Press, 2008), 146-50; Paul Harvey, *Redeeming the South: Religious Cultures and Racial Identities in the South, 1865-1925* (Chapel Hill: University of North Carolina Press, 1997), 8-10.

[20] Weaver, *In Search of the New Testament Church*, 146.

[21] Bill Leonard, *God's Last and Only Hope: The Fragmentation of the Southern Baptist Convention* (Grand Rapids: Eerdmans, 1990), 15; Andrew Christopher Smith,

and unspoken, was central to the way in which a number of Brazilian Baptist leaders eventually reacted against American missionary leadership. The literature on Brazilian Baptist history, however, has yet to consider properly the importance of Southern religion in their account of Baptist work in Brazil. But the presence of Southern migration to Brazil is an important, often-forgotten marker of this history. Just like the new immigrants who come to the United States, United States immigrants to Brazil also brought their gods with their luggage, and thus the White supremacist God of the South arrived in the land of the Southern Cross together with its White American creators. Not all United States immigrants to Brazil were Southerners, but the ethnic enclaves of the *Confederados*—as the groups of United States immigrants who wanted to preserve their appreciation for the Confederacy became known—were of particular importance for the history of immigration to Brazil in general and Brazilian religious history in particular.

Brazil abolished slavery twenty-three years after the end of the Civil War in the United States. Although Brazilian imperial policy eventually encouraged immigration from the Southern United States, it did so partially as a response to the numerous inquiries made by Southerners after the Civil War.[22] Among the eight-to-ten thousand Southern families who went to Latin America as a whole following the Civil War, about four thosand migrated to Brazil.[23] Despite the fact that, as mentioned earlier, a strong motivation for this trip was the fact that Brazil was still a slaveholding country,[24] the complexity of Brazil's multiracial context, in which there

---

Fundamentalism, Fundraising, and the Transformation of the Southern Baptist Convention, 1919-1925 (Knoxville: The University of Tennessee Press 2016), 4.

[22] Célio Silva's study on Yankee and Confederate immigration to Brazil deals with the letters sent by Americans who wanted to go to Brazil after the Civil War. See Célio Antonio Alcantara Silva, "Confederate and Yankees under the Southern Cross," *Bulletin of Latin American Research* 34, no. 3 (2015).

[23] Silva, "Confederate and Yankees under the Southern Cross"; Judith Mac Jones, *Soldado Descansa! Uma Epopéia Norte-Americana Sob Os Céus Do Brasil* (São Paulo: Fraternidade Descendência Americana, 1998); Laura Jarnagin, *A Confluence of Transatlantic Networks: Elites, Capitalism and Confederate Immigration to Brazil* (Tuscaloosa: University of Alabama Press, 2008), 25-27; Cyrus Dawsey and James M. Dawsey, eds., *The Confederados: Old South Immigrants in Brazil* (Tuscaloosa: University of Alabama Press, 1998), 18-19.

[24] There is some debate about the status of slavery as a motive for Southern migration to Brazil. Eugene Harter, Judith Jones, Frank Goldman, and Ana de Oliveira

was much more racial mixing among the free population than the United States-born people were accustomed to, presented a challenge to the social imagination of these Southern United States immigrants, who at times adapted to their new country by segregating themselves and forming ethnic enclaves with clearer racial-ethnic boundaries.[25] Commitment to Confederate ideals, of course, was not an exclusively Baptist trait. Southern Presbyterians and Methodists also migrated to Brazil and just like their Baptist counterparts, they were amazed by the comparative freedom the Brazilian dominant groups granted to free Blacks as well as by the perceived leniency Brazilian slaveholders showed their slaves.[26] In terms of White supremacist Christianity, the immigrant South was ecumenical in Brazil and the history of Presbyterian and Methodist missions in the country also contains elements of racially driven tensions between missionaries and locals.[27]

---

downplay the purchase of slaves by Southern immigrants, saying it was due either to lack of interest or lack of purchasing power. See Eugene Harter, *The Lost Colony of the Confederacy* (College Station: Texas A&M University Press, 2006); Jones, *Soldado Descansa! Uma Epopéia Norte-Americana Sob Os Céus Do Brasil*; Frank Goldman, *Os Pioneiros Americanos No Brasil: Educadores, Sacerdotes, Covos E Reis.* (São Paulo: Pioneira, 1972); Ana Maria Costa de Oliveira, *O Destino (Não) Manifesto: Os Imigrantes Norte-Americanos No Brasil* (São Paulo: União Cultural Brasil-Estados Unidos, 1995). More recent research, however, indicates that a major factor in the Southern migration to Brazil was the possibility of perpetuating the Southern lifestyle through slavery or, in the case of poor White southerners, the possibility of acquiring slaves in Brazil. Gerald Horne, *The Deepest South: The United States, Brazil, and the African Slave Trade* (New York: NYU Press, 2007); Célio Antonio Alcantara Silva, "Capitalismo E Escravidão: A Imigração Confederada Para O Brasil" (PhD diss., Universidade Estadual de Campinas, 2011).

[25] Silva, "Confederate and Yankees under the Southern Cross," 379; Charles Willis Simmons, "Racist Americans in a Multi-Racial Society: Confederate Exiles in Brazil," *The Journal of Negro History* 67, no. 1 (1982): 35-37.

[26] José Carlos Barbosa, *Slavery and Protestant Missions in Imperial Brazil: "The Black Does Not Enter the Church, He Peeks in From Outside,"* trans. Fraser G. MacHaffie and Richard K. Danford (Lanham: University Press of America, 2008), 4–6.

[27] Similarly to the case of Brazilian Baptists, the study of White supremacy among United States missionaries in Brazil of other Protestant denominations is not sufficiently developed. A few examples of Protestant White supremacy in other denominations, however, can be found in a number of manuscripts. For examples of racially-driven tensions among locals and Anglo-American missionaries of other

The Santa Barbara do Oeste region, where the First Baptist Church started in 1871, was where these United States immigrants settled most successfully in terms of their ability to preserve culture and language, and part of this success was precisely due to the self-imposed separation of the community from Brazilian metropolitan centers.[28] The cohesion of this community was so effective that its inhabitants preserved their culture, customs, and language generally unburdened by Brazilian multiculturalism up to the first decades of the twentieth century.[29] We can trace the Baptist connection with Santa Barbara do Oeste back to the parents of the founder of the settlement in the region, Confederate Colonel William H. Norris. William Norris, father of William H. Norris, was a longtime member of a Baptist church in Harris County, Georgia.[30] According to William Norris' obituary, published in the *Christian Index* in 1844, he had been a member of a Baptist church for at least forty-two years, and his son, William Hutchison Norris, attended Baptist churches since he was at least two years old.[31] It is unclear how Norris maintained his Baptist affiliation throughout his life, but he was certainly familiar with the ways of Baptists in the Southern United States.

Protestant denominations, see Frank Goldman, *Os Pioneiros Americanos No Brasil: Educadores, Sacerdotes, Covos E Reis.* (São Paulo: Pioneira, 1972); Emile G. Leonard, *O Protestantismo Brasileiro: Estudos de Eclesiologia E Historia Social* (São Paulo: ASTE, 1963); Mário R. Martins, *Missionários Americanos E Algumas Figuras Do Brasil Evangélico* (Goiânia: Kelps, 2007); Peri Mesquida, *Hegemonia norte-americana e educacão Protestante no Brasil: um estudo de caso* (Juiz de Fora; São Bernardo do Campo: Editora da Facultade de Teologia da Igreja Metodista, 1994); Mendonça and Filho, *Introdução Ao Protestantismo Brasileiro*; and Barbosa, *Slavery and Protestant Missions in Imperial Brazil.*

[28] Karina Esposito, "Confederate Immigration to Brazil: A Cross-Cultural Approach to Reconstruction and Public History," *Public History Review* 22 (2015); John Lowe, "Reconstruction Revisited: Plantation School Writers, Postcolonial Theory, and Confederates in Brazil," *The Mississippi Quarterly* (Winter 2003); and Silva, "Confederate and Yankees under the Southern Cross," 379.

[29] Lawrence F. Hill, "Confederate Exiles to Brazil," *The Hispanic American Historical Review* 7, no. 2 (1927); Simmons, "Racist Americans in a Multi-Racial Society: Confederate Exiles in Brazil"; and Harter, *The Lost Colony of the Confederacy,* 77.

[30] "Obituary of William Norris," *Christian Index*, April 26, 1844.

[31] Personal communication with descendant.

In 1871, the First Baptist Church of Brazil was founded within a cohesive community of former Confederates who wanted to recreate the old South. Before the Civil War, the great majority of Baptist state conventions in the South had passed resolutions siding with the Confederate cause after hostilities began.[32] There is no indication that the United States-born Southern Baptist immigrants who made their way to the Santa Barbara region were much different in their commitment to Southern identity in their new home than they were before the Civil War ended. Célio Silva's study of the United States and Brazilian census and slave registration documents, for instance, suggests that the family of Rev. Richard Ratcliff, founder of the First Baptist Church in Brazil, had no slaves in the United States, but acquired two slaves in Santa Barbara.[33] Rev. E.H. Quillen, who succeeded Ratcliff when the latter went back to the United States, resented the Southern loss and migrated with his whole family to Brazil immediately after the war. Quillen, the second Baptist missionary in Brazil, was an active participant in recruiting other heartbroken Southerners to sail to Brazil.[34] A.T. Hawthorne, son of Baptist minister Kedor Hawthorne, was also a key figure in Brazilian Baptist History.[35] Hawthorne had been a brigadier general in the Confederate Army. He went to Brazil but decided to return to the United States, from where he used his influence to advocate for the FMB to adopt a more intentional stance on sending missionaries to Brazil.[36] Hawthorne was also a direct influence on the Bagbys and the Taylors, whose work made a lasting mark on Brazilian

---

[32] Robert A. Baker, *The Southern Baptist Convention and Its People, 1607-1972* (Nashville: Broadman Press, 1974), 226-27.

[33] Silva, "Confederate and Yankees under the Southern Cross," 381; "Capitalismo E Escravidão: A Imigração Confederada Para O Brasil."

[34] William Clark Griggs, *The Elusive Eden: Frank Mcmullan's Confederate Colony in Brazil* (Austin: University of Texas Press, 1987), 37.

[35] William Cathcart, *The Baptist Encyclopedia* (Paris: The Baptist Standard Bearer, 1881), 512.

[36] Donald C. Simmons Jr., *Confederate Settlements in British Honduras* (Jefferson: McFarland & Company, 2001), 117; Crabtree, *História Dos Baptistas Do Brasil* 1, 43; Daniel Lancaster, *The Bagbys of Brazil: The Life and Work of William Buck and Ann Luther Bagby* (Austin: Eakin Press, 1999), viii; Donald C. Simmons Jr., "Confederate Exiles in Latin America," in *Encyclopedia of U.S. - Latin American Relations* (Thousand Oaks: Sage Publications, 2012), 915.

Baptist history.[37] Pioneer missionary Z.C. Taylor's own exposure to the idea of moving to Brazil came when his father, a former soldier of the Sixth Mississippi Regiment, wanted to leave the United States because of the Southern loss.[38]

The impact of Southern religion in Brazil is not limited to the disposition of the individuals who migrated there, but in the case of Southern Baptists it was sustained by institutional tendencies.[39] Henry Allen Tupper, corresponding secretary of the FMB from 1871 to 1893, had been a chaplain of the Ninth Georgia Infantry[40] and was an avid defender of both the Confederate cause and Anglo-Saxon superiority.[41] Under Tupper's tenure a number of the most influential Southern Baptist missionaries were sent to Brazil. A number of family members of William Bagby, who was the third Baptist missionary to be endorsed by the FMB, had served in the Confederate Army. In a letter written to his then future wife, Anne, Bagby mentioned that one of the reasons they should go to Brazil was

---

[37] Lancaster, *The Bagbys of Brazil: The Life and Work of William Buck and Anne Luther Bagby*, viii; Helen Bagby Harrison, *The Bagbys of Brazil* (Nashville: Broadman Press, 1954), 19. General Hawthorne's direct involvement in Brazilian missions is evident in many FMB reports. See FMB reports from October 11, 1880; January 03 1882; and November 06, 1882.

[38] Z. C. Taylor, *The Rise and Progress of Baptist Missions in Brazil: An Autobiography.* (Unpublished Manuscript), 1-2, accessed at the International Mission Board Archives in Richmond, VA.

[39] Robert Norman Nash Jr., "The Influence of American Myth on Southern Baptist Foreign Missions, 1845-1945" (PhD diss., The Southern Baptist Theological Seminary, 1989); Adrian Lamkin Jr., "The Gospel Mission Movement within the Southern Baptist Convention" (PhD diss., The Southern Baptist Theological Seminary, 1979); Bill Leonard, *Baptist Ways: A History* (Valley Forge: Judson Press, 2003), 204. Robert Nash and Adrian Lamkin wrote compelling studies that show how deeply commited to the Southern Cause the SBC was during the Civil War and to the Lost Cause after the South was defeated. According to Bill Leonard, "in the search for ways to cope with defeat, Southern Baptists and other Southern Protestants looked to the 'religion of the Lost Cause' — the idealization of the South's culture and religion. Defeated politically, the South turned to the cultural superiority of its mythic past."

[40] John Wesley Brinsfield Jr., *The Spirit Divided: Memoirs of Civil War Chaplains* (Macon: Mercer University Press, 2006), 12.

[41] H. Allen Tupper, *Armenia: Its Present Crisis and Past History* (New York: John Murphy & Company, 1896); Nash Jr., Robert, "The Influence of American Myth on Southern Baptist Foreign Missions, 1845-1945," 95.

because the race of the dominant class in Brazil was Caucasian.[42] Many of the most influential American missionaries sent to Brazil by the FMB who attempted to reach the Brazilians (e.g. William Bagby, Z.C. Taylor, W.E. Entzminger, and J.J. Taylor) were born before the American Civil War and raised in the South during and after the hostilities that so shaped Southern memory and identity.

Most pioneering missionaries to Brazil worked in the country for a long time and were able to institutionalize in Brazil certain dispositions born in the Old South. Z.C. Taylor, for instance, stayed for twenty-seven years in the country, William Bagby stayed in Brazil for fifty-eight years, and W.E. Entzminger edited the denomination's official periodical, the *Jornal Batista*, for twenty years.[43] Although they left the South while they were still young men, the South, both in its theological as well as in its racial manifestations, had a deep and continuous effect on their imaginations. Baptist work in Brazil thus began in a particular kind of immigrant and continued through the agency of a missionary South, whose message was informed by a hyper-racialized Southern cultural captivity.[44]

---

[42] William to Anne, August, 20, 1880. Unless otherwise noted, missionary correspondence and papers were made available to me electronically by archivists of the International Mission Board and originals are housed in the Archives of the International Mission Board in Richmond, VA. The imagination of early Southern Baptist missionaries such as Bagby about Brazil was informed by their exposure to A.T. Hawthorne and to works written by United States immigrants who had been or were in Brazil. Some of the most influential writings about Brazil intended for an English-speaking audience included Daniel Kidder's two-volume "Sketches of Residence and Travel in Brazil" (1845), Daniel Kidders' and James Fletcher's "Brazil and the Brazilians" (1857), Ballard Dunn's "Brazil, Home for Southerners" (1866), and General W.W. Wood's "Ho! for Brazil!" For a list of other publications that intend to showcase Brazil to an American audience, see Blanche Henry Clark Weaver, "Confederate Emigration to Brazil," *The Journal of Southern History* 27, no. 1 (February 1961): 33-53.

[43] Pereira, *História Dos Batistas No Brasil (1882-1982)*, 49.

[44] Eighmy and Hill, *Churches in Cultural Captivity: A History of the Social Attitudes of Southern Baptists*; Harvey, *Redeeming the South: Religious Cultures and Racial Identities in the South, 1865-1925*, 4; 257-58; Alan Scott Willis, *All According to God's Plan: Southern Baptist Missions and Race, 1945-1970* (Lexington: The University Press of Kentucky, 2004). In *Churches in Cultural Captivity*, John Eighmy shows "how the prevailing secular values gained confirmation from a denomination that lacked institutional leadership capable of independent judgment and action." Using Eighmy's thesis for the study of the Brazilian-American Baptist experience would mean

The Training of the Missionaries
and Southern Mythology

The training of Southern Baptist missionaries was an element in the the-ocultural apparatus that informed and legitimized their feelings of superi-ority. The pioneer missionaries who went to Brazil received their theolog-ical training in what would later enter into denominational memory as flagship institutions of the Baptist denomination. These institutions op-erated in dialogue with the Southern culture that surrounded them and, as such, gave a Southern flavor to the Gospel recipe. Most of the missionaries who played influential roles in the construction and development of Bra-zilian Baptist identity graduated from Waco University, Baylor University, or Southern Baptist Theological Seminary.[45] Some of the missionaries had connections to more than one of these schools. Z.C. Taylor and H.H. Muirhead went to both Baylor University and the Southern Baptist The-ological Seminary. A.L. Dunstan spent one year studying at Southern Seminary before sailing to Brazil,[46] and O.P. Maddox as well as W.E.

---

presupposing that Anglo-American Baptists broadly appropriated the social values of wider culture of the late nineteenth and early twentieth centuries. Paul Harvey complicates Eighmy's thesis by providing a dynamic account of African American agency in the post-bellum South, but he does acknowledge that "the cultural captivity thesis highlights the moral failings of white southern religion, as it was originally designed to do." Harvey succeeds in demonstrating that in the post-bellum South there was a measure of interracial cooperation in ecclesiastical settings that was paired with a White commitment to racial "subjugation and humiliation." Alan Willis's work on Southern Baptist missions and race in the mid-twentieth century shows the persistence of Anglo-American racial prejudice in the denomination. For an introductory study of racial tensions among Southern Baptist in Texas see Joao B. Chaves, "Where Should We Go Next?: A Call for the Critical Investigation of Possible Racial Encounters between Anglo-American and Mexican-American Baptists in Texas During the Pioneer Period," *Baptist History and Heritage* 49, no. 3 (Fall 2014).

[45] Waco University and Baylor University merged soon after William Bagby graduated from Waco.

[46] Foreign Mission Board report May 1, 1901. In 1902, the *Jornal Batista* states that Dunstan graduated from William Jewell college before going to Southern Semi-nary.

Entzminger, the latter a longtime editor of the major denominational publication in Brazil, also went to Southern Seminary.[47] Helen Bagby Harrison, writing about her father, William Buck Bagby, said that "father attended Waco University and became Dr. B.H. Carroll's first pupil in the department of theology, which developed into the Southwestern Baptist Theological Seminary."[48] William Bagby planned on attending Southern Seminary for three years, but decided against it partially due to Anne Baby's missionary drive.[49]

Many of the early missionaries to Brazil, therefore, were exposed to leading thinkers in the denomination. B.H. Carroll was a direct influence on William Bagby and Z.C. Taylor. Taylor mentioned his appreciation for the "masters of theology" at Southern Seminary, and he named James Petigru Boyce, John Broadus, Basil Manly, William Whitsitt, and John Sampey as people who influenced him during his time there.[50] Some of the Southern Baptist intellectual luminaries, after all, had also been willing to give their lives for the Southern Confederate cause. During the war, B.H. Carroll served in McCullough's Texas Rangers and entered into Confederate service. He eventually enlisted in the regular army and served in the Seventeenth Regiment of the Texas Infantry.[51] James Petigru Boyce served in the Sixteenth Regiment of the South Carolina Volunteers, John Broadus did chaplaincy work for General Robert E. Lee's army,[52] and Basil Manly was an avid advocate of slavery and the Confederate cause.[53] It is therefore not surprising that as late as 1926, John Sampey, one of Taylor's theological heroes, wrote about his uneasiness about non-segregation in

---

[47] To R.J. Willingham on July 8, 1901. Gregory Willis demonstrated that one of the pressing issues regarding the perceived need of a Baptist seminary in the South was the growing overlap between theology and Southern culture on the part of Southern Baptists. See Gregory A. Willis, *Southern Baptist Theological Seminary, 1859-2009* (Oxford: Oxford University Press, 2009), 6-8.

[48] Harrison, *The Bagbys of Brazil*, 3.

[49] Harrison, 14-17.

[50] Taylor, *The Rise and Progress of Baptist Missions in Brazil: An Autobiography*, 14.

[51] Robert A. Baker, *A History of Southwestern Baptist Theological Seminary, 1908-1983* (Nashville: Broadman Press, 1983), 58-59.

[52] John R. Sampey, *Southern Baptist Theological Seminary* (Baltimore: Wharton, Barron & Company, 1890), 30-32.

[53] Although Taylor did not specify, he was probably referring to Basil Manly Jr., son of Confederacy advocate Basil Manly Sr. See A. James Fuller, *Chaplain to the Confederacy: Basil Manly and Baptist Life in the Old South* (Baton Rouge: LSU Press, 2000), 212–20.

Brazil.[54] As expected, and like many other Southern Baptist intellectuals of his time, Sampey was against racial equality and despised racial mixing.[55]

The grip of Southern commitment to Confederate ideals in post-bellum Southern Baptist life was so significant that important denominational figures such as Baptist minister, prolific writer, and Southern Baptist Theological Seminary employee J. William Jones saw no conflict between the Lost Cause and Southern Baptist identity. In addition to producing influential books and articles, Jones lectured several times on the virtues of the Confederacy in official events of Southern Seminary during his time as a seminary employee.[56] John Broadus showed his support for Jones' project of equating the Confederate cause with Baptist ideals by encouraging Jones to write more Confederate hagiographies.[57] Another of Taylor's theological giants, William Whitsitt, also praised Jones' work and provided his own Baptist contributions to the mythology of the Lost Cause.[58] John Sampey had a deep affection for Robert E. Lee and even kept a picture of Lee in his office.[59] In short, many of those who would later become missionaries to Brazil had gone to Southern and Southwestern institutions and had been taught by Baptist intellectuals committed to their Southern culture. Racism was in the DNA of Southern Baptist educational institutions.[60]

The course of studies at Southern Seminary during its first decades taught biblical context, Old Testament, New Testament, hermeneutics, systematic theology, homiletics, apologetics, church history, and Baptist polity.[61] But no specific courses on missions seem to have been offered at

---

[54] John R. Sampey, "The People of Brazil: Potentialities, Problems, and Needs of This Great Growing Nation," *Home and Foreign Fields* 10 (January 1926): 12-13.

[55] G.S. Dobbins, "The Race Problem's One Solution," *Home and Foreign Fields* 8 (August 1924).

[56] Christopher C. Moore, *Apostle of the Lost Cause: J. William Jones, Baptists, and the Development of Confederate Memory* (Knoxville: University of Tennessee Press, 2019), 85-86.

[57] Moore, 85-86.

[58] Moore, 85-86.

[59] Mikeal C. Parsons, *Crawford Howell Toy: The Man, the Scholar, the Teacher* (Macon: Mercer University Press, 2019), 38.

[60] Parsons, 37.

[61] William A. Muller, *A History of Southern Baptist Theological Seminary* (Nashville: Broadman Press, 1959), 113-15.

Southern Seminary until William Owen Carver's hiring in 1898. Carver espoused the triumphalist spirit that characterized turn-of-the-century American Protestantism, including the need for missions to civilize the proselytized.[62] Generally speaking, therefore, the education of the most important missionaries who went to Brazil not only solidified a general Baptist theological consensus but also helped legitimize their religious, cultural, and racial biases. The key academic architects of the SBC grounded elements of their theology in a racial superiority fostered by the South's slave-based culture. The Gospel of the SBC missionaries, in turn, was seasoned with racist sensibilities that were already present in the plausibility structure of Southern culture but received a special anointing through theological training.

Southern Baptist missionaries globalized the Lost Cause mythology that was legitimized by the context and content of their theological education through aggressive methods of ideological dissemination. At times, missionary commitment to Southern ideals led to an explicit rewriting of history. For example, in 1901, the major denominational publication printed an article about the famous story involving composer and singer Ira Sankey that reversed Sankey's role in the American Civil War and placed him in the Confederate Army—even though Sankey fought in the Union Army. In this story as popularized in the United States, Sankey escaped death because the Confederate soldier who ambushed him decided to spare Sankey's life after Sankey sang one of his hymns. In the missionary version of the story, however, Sankey fought in the Confederate Army and was an instrument in the conversion of the Union soldier. In the same year, the *Jornal Batista* celebrated triumphantly:

> The countries of greatest progress today are the United States, England, Germany, the Netherlands, Switzerland, Denmark, Sweden, Norway and France, to an extent: these are Protestant nations. Their colonial power is enormous, and the Anglo-Saxon and Germanic Protestants are called to conquer the world. And you still ask me if I am Protestant? Yes sir, I am! And I am so with great pride because I find myself in great universal company among men whose

---

[62] William O. Carver, *Syllabus of Lectures on Missions* (Louisville: Southern Baptist Theological Seminary, 1905), 6-7.

calling is restoring this world in a state of mental and physical slavery to a state of liberty, prosperity, and happiness.[63]

The ability of printing stories in Portuguese gave Southern editors
freedom to reimagine stories in order to highlight the Confederacy's moral
superiority and an ideology that claimed the right of White men to dominate the world. Brazilian readers were likely to accept the translated narrative, even when such narrative was inspired by Lost Cause revisionism
and rabid American White nationalism. Southern Baptist missionaries,
therefore, brought with them aggressive forms of their Southern
worldview and deployed the mythologies of the South—together with the
structural manifestations of their racist sensibilities—in several ways and
through a number of means that will be further explored in the following
pages. The theocultural imaginations of missionaries ran deep and their
manifestations were not always obvious, but lack of education was not
what caused the missionaries' sense of White supremacy; rather, Southern
Baptist theological education sustained and even strengthened their commitment to their peculiar self-perception.

The New Testament Church Arrives in Brazil

On March 2nd, 1881, with the arrival of the Bagbys in Rio de Janeiro, the
sustained phase of the Baptist work among the Brazilians began. There
were other Baptists from the United States and Britain in Brazil, but they
did not have sustainable missionary initiatives in the country. Soon after
William and Anne Bagby arrived in Brazil, for instance, one Mrs. M.M.
Ellis, a Baptist, sent two horses and a slave to bring over their baggage
when they visited her.[64] Bagby also knew of three Baptist preachers who
were already in the region, but "one of them (became) a Spiritualist" and
the others did not preach often and were thus considered unfit in his eyes.[65]
The Bagbys were the first of a number of missionaries to be credited for

---

[63] "O Que São os Protestantes," *Jornal Batista* 1, no. 9 (1901): 3.

[64] Letter sent to the FMB in March 12, 1881. In Anne Bagby's diary, the entry
for March 7, 1881 makes no mention of slaves, despite the fact that slavery was still
legal in Brazil. William Bagby, however, mentions the presence of slaves in a letter
sent to his mother. I could not find the letter in the Bagby Papers at Baylor University.
Daniel Lancaster, however, quotes from the letter in Lancaster, *The Bagbys of Brazil:
The Life and Work of William Buck and Anne Luther Bagby* (Austin: Eakin Press, 1999).

[65] Lancaster.

the conversion of locals and the growth and organization of the Baptist denomination in Brazil.

Early Missionaries and their Beliefs

Early Southern Baptist missionaries in Brazil held a set of theological beliefs common in the Southern Baptist denomination. Z.C. Taylor, for instance, felt its clear articulation of Baptist convictions warranted his translation into Portuguese of the New Hampshire Confession, which was adopted as the official confession for Brazilian Baptists in 1916 under the name "Declaration of Faith of Brazilian Baptist Churches" (*Declaração de Fé das Igrejas Batistas do Brasil*).[66] The sufficiency of the Bible, the ability of the individual to interpret the Bible properly, the traditional Christian narrative of fall and salvation, the Baptist focus on liberty of conscience, separation of church and state, the foundational insistence on the "Believers' Church," and the ordinances of Baptism (believer's baptism by immersion) and Lord's Supper were all part of the core theological apparatus of the missionaries. These elements formed the cornerstone of the Southern Baptist theological orthodoxy disseminated by SBC missionaries in Brazil. Beyond such consensus documents and beliefs, early missionaries also held a number of convictions that showed a clearly identifiable influence of the missionaries' social location.

Despite some diversity among the early missionaries that the FMB sent to Brazil, a significant proportion was from Texas or had studied at Texan institutions. Their educational formation and denominational upbringing were heavily informed by the Landmarkist tendencies that characterized nineteenth-century Baptists in Southern and Southwestern United States. The Landmark Movement appeared in Southern Baptist circles around the middle of the nineteenth century and defended, among other things, the idea that Baptists were the only true New Testament church. Landmarkists were generally against denominational centralization and focused on the independence of local congregations.[67] During the

---

[66] Pereira, *História Dos Batistas No Brasil (1882-1982)*, 87. This translation of the New Hampshire Confession was the only official confession of faith of the Brazilian Baptist Convention until the 1986 Doctrinal Declaration.

[67] For a fuller picture of Landmarkism in Southern Baptist life, see James E. Tull, *High-Church Baptists in the South: The Origin, Nature, and Influence of Landmarkism* (Macon: Mercer University Press, 2000).

period when early Southern Baptist missionaries were receiving their theological education, the identity of Southern Baptists—especially those with Southwestern regional connections—was becoming increasingly affected by Landmarkist convictions. According to Rosalie Beck, in the second half of the nineteenth century, "the Baptist consciousness, for many, rested on the assertion of uniqueness found in Landmark teaching."[68] In Brazil, the particular Landmarkist characteristic that was prominent was the idea that Baptists were direct descendants of the church started by Jesus and, as such, its only true manifestation on earth. This Landmarkist disposition appeared in and was disseminated through the publications translated by missionaries. The first director of the Baptist publishing house in Brazil, Z.C. Taylor, chose S.H. Ford's "Origin and History of the Baptists," which had an introduction written by Landmarkist icon J.R. Graves, as the foundational text for teaching Baptist history in Brazil.[69] W.E. Entzminger, who succeeded Taylor in the publishing house, was an avid advocate for the translation of James Pendleton's theology and its dissemination through the Baptist publication house in the country.[70] In a letter to the FMB's corresponding secretary, Dr. R.J. Willingham, Entzminger showed a sense of urgency in introducing Pendleton, one of the most influential Landmarkist thinkers, to a Brazilian audience.[71] Yet there is no indication that the FMB ever showed signs of concern with the Landmarkist-leaning literature that the missionaries were introducing in Brazil.[72]

It must be kept in mind, however, that in the Brazilian case, missionary Landmarkist dispositions were not a significant issue for denominational centralization. Whereas Landmarkism may be connected to a commitment to the local congregation and a suspicion of denominational

---

[68] Rosalie Beck, "The Whitsitt Contorversy: A Denomination in Crisis" (PhD diss., Baylor University, 1984), 60.

[69] Solomon L. Ginsburg, *A Wandering Jew in Brazil: An Autobiography of Solomon L. Ginsburg* (Nashville: Sunday School Board of the SBC, 1922), 73.

[70] It is unclear from the sources which of Pendleton's works Entzminger wanted to introduce in Brazil. His admiration for Pendleton, however, is clearly and explicitly stated.

[71] From W.E. Entzminger to R.J. Willingham Sep. 27, 1901.

[72] Azevedo, *A Celebração Do Indivíduo: A Formação Do Pensamento Batista Brasileiro*, 213-14. Israel Azevedo argues that the Landmarkist ideal was not controversial in Brazil, and was inserted into denominational identity.

centralization, the practical, financial, and organizational benefits of denominational centralization in Brazil limited the Landmarkist tendencies of Southern Baptist missionaries. Azevedo correctly observed that the permanence of the "Landmarkist ideal" as made popular by J.R. Graves was not fully appropriated in Brazil. If, in Brazilian Baptist historiography, Landmarkism—which was popularized through translations of Landmarkists such as Graves—made its mark, Landmarkist anti-denominationalism "did not become hegemonic among Brazilian Baptists."[73] Southern Baptist Landmarkism in Brazil was, most clearly, historiographical successionism, that is, the idea that the Baptist church had an unbroken historical lineage that connected them directly to the first disciples of Christ. Another central characteristic of classical Landmarkism, namely, a suspicious stance toward denomination centralization, however, did not find success in Brazil. The historical sources fail to show missionaries complaining about their salaries being paid by the centralizing missionary agency that employed them or the ability to shape their centralizing denomination in Brazil. As a matter of fact, the opposite is true: they seemed to want more of both.

Most White Southern Baptist missionaries in Brazil reflected—even if only implicitly—the prejudices and biases of their countrymen who remained in Dixie. Pioneer missionary William Buck Bagby demonstrated his White supremacist dispositions in his early observations about Brazil. Writing to his United States audience, Bagby described the inhabitants of Brazil as follows:

> Besides these [White Portuguese], there are many Indians in the far interior, untaught, uncivilized, and living in a manner even more rude and animal-like, perhaps than our North American Indians. The negroes form a large portion of the inhabitants of the country, of whom some are slaves and some are freemen. The races are very much mixed, and all shades of color are daily seen in any of these cities, from coal black, up through brown and olive, mulatto, and yellow, and white. Of course, where such unnatural unions exist, all kinds of deformities appear and many hereditary diseases are known.[74]

---

[73] Azevedo, 213.

[74] W.B. Bagby, "Brother Bagby on Brazil and Its People," Foreign Mission Journal, 12 (1882):3.

Oftentimes, pioneering missionaries' displays of such superiority were abundantly clear. For example, in contrasting Brazilian people with Americans, Z.C. Taylor—who during his tenure as missionary refused to marry couples of different races—said that

> [Brazil] has been a dumping ground of Portugal, to which were exiled the worst criminals. These mixed with Indians. Later Africans were imported and the mixture went on. The mixed population far exceeds the Portuguese or white population. Those who colonized the United States were mostly God-fearing men and women, fleeing from tyrants and despotism in Europe.[75]

Taylor was convinced of American superiority on the grounds of his distorted view of the different histories of colonization of the United States and Brazil, but also because of his White supremacist commitments. Brazilian Whites and those of pure European stock, whom Taylor called "Portuguese," he accorded a level of respect not granted to Afro-Brazilians or Brazilians of mixed blood. He said: "the Portuguese, though degenerated through long centuries of pagan and Catholic idolatry, are descendants of that grand old Roman race which began before the Christian era, and which includes some of the greatest names in history."[76] Taylor recognized the differences in racial relations between the Brazilian and United States context. For him, Brazil adjusted better to the post-slavery era because "the African is more docile here [in Brazil], more humble, more polite to the whites."[77] But despite Taylor's limited contextualization of racial relations, he still had deep-rooted commitments to his feelings of racial superiority. For him, "the Negro in Brazil, as everywhere, lives for the present as the Chinese live in the past and the Caucasian for the future."[78] In Taylor's social imagination, evangelizing was inseparable not only from civilizing but also from Anglicizing. For him, the FMB should flood Latin America with Anglo-Saxon missionaries because only if people from other racial groups "were joined with the Anglo-Saxon race" could the denomination "take the world for Christ."[79]

---

[75] Taylor, *The Rise and Progress of Baptist Missions in Brazil: An Autobiography*, 19-20.

[76] Taylor, 20.

[77] Taylor, 48.

[78] Taylor, 48.

[79] Taylor, 205.

In a letter to the FMB corresponding secretary T.B. Ray, W.E. Entzminger showed a disposition similar to Taylor's. Writing to ask for support for the preparation of young men for preaching and young women for teaching, Entzminger mentioned a diligent ministerial student who had made some progress in his studies, but whose future Entzminger deemed not to be promising due to his mixed-race status. He wrote that the young man's "future usefulness as a preacher seems to be a doubtful quantity. He is a dark Mulatto, which is against him."[80]

The racial imagination of US-born missionaries affected their relationships with those born elsewhere. The tensions between Entzminger and Polish-born, Jewish missionary Solomon Ginsburg, who became an FMB missionary through Z.C. Taylor's initiative, illustrates this reality.[81] Entzminger wrote regularly to different FMB corresponding secretaries not only complaining that Ginsburg was bad at what he thought a Jew should do well—handling money[82]—but also that Ginsburg, deep inside, could "never overcome being a Jew."[83] Entzminger stated that many of the Anglo missionaries did not like Ginsburg and he wanted the board to send a replacement to help him at the publishing house. Not just any replacement, not an Englishman or a Jewish person "but a genuine American"[84]— by which he also presumably meant a *Southern* American.

A guiding anxiety for Southern Baptist missionaries in Brazil was their deep entrenchment in a gospel-culture-race identity that preached a gospel whose effectiveness was measured, to a great extent, by its power to shape social interactions in their image and according to the prescription of a God partially fashioned in the American South. A letter sent from Jephthah Hamilton to H.H. Muirhead exemplifies this widespread characteristic among Southern Baptist missionaries in Brazil. Both of these missionaries were avid defenders of education and both played leading roles in the denominational schools in Brazil. Hamilton wrote: "Good evangelical schools are not only needed for the children of the native

---

[80] From W.E. Entzminger to T.B. Ray, May 21, 1917.

[81] Tensions between H.H. Muirhead and Latvian-born Dr. Inke as well as between H.H. Muirhead and J.W. Shepard and Italian-born Dr. Piani can also be pointed out.

[82] For the clearest example, see W.E. Entzminger's letters to corresponding secretary R.J. Willingham in July 1908.

[83] From W.E. Entzminger to R.J. Willingham, June 2, 1903.

[84] From W.E. Entzminger to T.B. Ray, February, 28, 1917.

Christians, but also for the young native Christians, to give them a more general preparation for their social, civil, and Christian lives."[85] Other pioneering Southern Baptist missionaries to Brazil such as William Bagby, Z.C. Taylor, W.E. Entzminger, A.L. Dunstan, and O.P. Maddox shared this concern for a comprehensive education that involved a strong doctrinal element, but also aimed to indoctrinate local leaders socially, ideologically, and culturally. Their social imagination was informed by their connection with the developments in their home country, which was informed by an ideological reconstruction of their past into the racial and geographical exceptionalism of Lost Cause mythology. The value given by Southern Baptist missionaries to the projection of their anxieties about the effective dissemination of their cultural dispositions through formal education would, somewhat paradoxically, eventually be a major stumbling block to their ability to control Brazilian Baptist activity undisturbed—a topic dealt with in the next chapter.

Missionary-Local Interactions in the Field

In light of their racialized worldview, Southern Baptist missionaries were reticent about including local leaders in the structural control of the denomination. In theory, missionaries seemed eager to establish greater Brazilian participation; several reports sent to the FMB from the Brazilian mission emphasized what appeared to be a sincere concern on the part of Southern Baptist missionaries about developing a strong local leadership structure. In practice, however, Southern Baptist missionary work in Brazil was characterized by Southern Baptist ideological and structural control of the denomination. Feelings of racial and denominational superiority were so pervasive among Southern Baptist missionaries that "Anglo-Saxon supremacy became an integral part of Southern Baptist foreign mission strategy" not only in Brazil but also in other countries.[86] In the first five decades

---

[85] From Jephthah Hamilton to H.H. Muirhead, August 11, 1902. The distinction Hamilton made between "children of native Christians" and "young native Christians" is unclear in the sources. It is possible, however, that here he is dintinguishing between students who lived in Baptist households (children of native Christians) and those who did not (young native Christians).

[86] Robert Norman Nash Jr., "The Influence of American Myth on Southern Baptist Foreign Missions, 1845-1945" (PhD diss., Southern Baptist Theological Seminary, 1989), 167–73.

of missionary work in Brazil, wherever there was local leadership, it was exercised under the supervision of SBC missionaries and expected to operate according to the theocultural forms of the American South. An example of this disposition is provided by the most celebrated Brazilian-born pastor and denominational leader, F.F. Soren. Soren was educated at William Jewell College and Southern Baptist Theological Seminary and was initially against the inclusion of Brazilians into the formation of a national convention.

Initially, Soren thought that only missionaries should lead the denomination nationally, and when it was decided that locals would also participate in the Brazilian Baptist Convention, he became a prominent denominational leader. Soren stands as a classic example that the local leaders who were able to have influence in the denomination were protective of missionary power and ideology. Missionary appreciation for Soren was so pronounced that Southern Baptist Missionary L.M. Bratcher wrote Soren's biography.[87] Daniel Lancaster argued that F.F. Soren played an important role in the implementation of Southern Baptist strategies. Soren, whose academic career at William Jewell College and Southern Baptist Theological Seminary was facilitated by his missionary connections, was selected by the Foreign Mission Board to pastor the First Baptist Church in Rio de Janeiro, was appointed the first president of the Brazilian Baptist Convention, and became the first president of the Baptist Education Society of Brazil. Z.C. Taylor's unpublished autobiography also praises Soren as an ideal national leader. There is no strong indication from the sources that Soren, a White man with a clear European lineage, ever digressed strongly from his support of Southern Baptist ideological dispositions.[88] To use Araújo's words, Soren "thought just like [SBC missionary] Entzminger" and just like many other Brazilians, "had his practices and thoughts dictated" by Southern Baptist missionaries.[89]

Yet missionaries were keenly aware of the importance of Brazilian involvement and, at times, they showed themselves to be optimistic regarding their strategy for using local help. In 1896, the annals of the SBC

---

[87] See L.M. Bratcher, "Francisco Fulgencio Soren: Christ's Interpreter to Many Lands (Nashville: Broadman Press, 1938).

[88] See Daniel Lancaster, "The Bagbys of Brazil," 72-73; and Z.C. Taylor, *The Rise and Progress of Baptist Missions in Brazil: An Autobiography*, 147.

[89] Araújo, *Batistas: Dominação e Dependencia*, 199.

show that Southern Baptist missionaries asked the convention not to send them American help, convinced that their local helpers (and alleged colleagues!) would be enough.[90] Other FMB reports show that missionaries understood that the future of their work in Brazil depended on locals, not foreigners.[91] This conviction on the part of missionaries came from their own expectation regarding the growth of the denomination in Brazil, which would affect the missionary/local ratio progressively. Such realization, however, did not translate into real action or a smooth leadership transition. The theocultural commitments of the missionaries, together with their controlling disposition, meant they would not relinquish structural power without a fight.

During the first five decades of Southern Baptist work in Brazil, mechanisms that were generative of what Steven Lukes called "three-dimensional power" helped missionaries to avoid widespread conflict. Lukes explained that three-dimensional power has "the capacity to secure compliance to domination through the shaping of beliefs and desires, by imposing internal constraints under historically changing circumstances."[92] Missionaries, primarily through their proselytizing, evangelizing, teaching, and publishing practices, actualized such power. This does not mean that all conflict was eliminated or that Southern Baptist missionaries to Brazil always acted in a unified way. The missionaries that were not aggressively protective of their structural power, however, were the exception, not the rule.

The controversy regarding the expulsion of Antônio Campos from the denomination shows this sometimes-multifaceted dynamic of power in the Brazilian Baptist mission. Most Baptists in Brazil became acquainted with Campos' story through the official denominational account, that is, the account printed in the *Jornal Batista*—the main denominational publication. It would be hard to overstate the importance of the *Jornal Batista*, and certainly by 1903, when the Campos story took place, it was already the denomination's key publication.[93] On April 30, 1903, under

---

[90] Annals of the Southern Baptist Convention, May 8, 1896.

[91] See Foreign Mission Board report May 7, 1897 and Foreign Mission Board Report May 12, 1899.

[92] Steven Lukes, *Power: A Radical View*, 2nd ed. (New York: Palgrave Macmillan, 2005), 143-44.

[93] In May 8, 1903, missionaries in Brazil reported to the SBC that the *Jornal Batista* was distributed almost universally among churches. The report read: "during

the editorial authority of W.E. Entzminger, the *Jornal Batista* notified its audience that Antonio Campos "is no longer an employee of the mission and no longer a part of this denomination."[94]

Campos was the pastor of a church in the Rio de Janeiro Mission. At the beginning of 1903, in light of altercations between him and SBC missionary A.L. Dunstan, his church excluded Dunstan and the members who sided with the missionary.[95] Campos lost the financial support of the FMB and his dissent was short-lived. The missionaries in the south of Brazil united in repudiating Campos and taking back the group that initially had followed the local minister. The public condemnation of Campos in the *Jornal Batista* claimed that Campos and his group had no denomination and were schismatics; they had usurped the church building, and Campos had been disloyal and incited people against Dunstan. The periodical noted that no compromise that allowed Campos to return to the denomination "in any part of Brazil or the world" would be accepted.[96]

In a letter to corresponding secretary R.J. Willingham, W.E. Entzminger chided Antonio Campos and his friend, Polish-born missionary Solomon Ginsburg. He wrote:

> It would be, I think, difficult to exaggerate the utter unworthiness of Antonio Campos to even belong to a Christian church, not to speak of being a minister of the holy Gospel. For seven years he has been in the employ of Mr. Ginsburg against the wishes and counsels of the Baptist missionaries and to the astonishment of the missionaries of the other denominations.[97]

For Entzminger, Ginsburg's protection of Antonio Campos represented an affront to the missionaries of Southern Brazil, who were united against

---

the year we published a weekly edition of 1,700 copies of the *Jornal Batista*, which circulates wherever there is a Baptist work in progress, even among the German colonies in the States of Santa Catarina and Rio Grande do Sul." See Annals of the Southern Baptist Convention, May 8, 1903.

[94] W.E. Entzminger et al., "Declaração E Protesto," *Jornal Batista* (April 30, 1903).

[95] Crabtree, *História Dos Baptistas Do Brasil* 1, 290. Crabtree's account of this event takes the perspective of the missionaries and, thus, is clearly against Antonio Campos and his supporters.

[96] Entzminger et al., "Declaração E Protesto."

[97] From W.E. Entzminger to R.J. Willingham, May 1, 1903.

the local worker. The matter was so serious that Entzminger wrote that Ginsburg's attitude "has severed the last tie that may have identified him with us in a common cause" and wanted him to resign.[98]

William Cannada, however, had a different perspective about the Campos story. In 1903, Cannada worked closely with Ginsburg, and he wrote to R.J. Willingham warning him that if Campos and Ginsburg were asked to resign, as the missionaries in the South of Brazil were demanding, "half of the churches will go with them."[99] Cannada also criticized his fellow Southern Baptists in the South of Brazil for circulating damaging stories about Campos in the denominational periodicals.[100] Jephtah Hamilton, who also worked closely with Ginsburg, criticized the missionaries in Southern Brazil, pointing out not only what he thought was an unfair rendering of the situation in the *Jornal Batista* but also the potentially ethnic dynamics of the affair. He wrote to Willingham saying: "I think the language of the document was too strong and bitter, and that its publication in our paper was unfortunate. If they are not careful down there, they will make it appear that it is in part a question of American against Brazilian and will arouse against us all a 'race prejudice'."[101]

Addressing the animosity missionaries in Southern Brazil had directed at Solomon Ginsburg, Hamilton said (perhaps presciently) that "if those brethren should speak evil of Bro. Ginsburg because of this matter, many would say that we were wanting to Americanize everything."[102] What instigated the tension between Campos and Dunstan is unclear from the sources and, in his autobiography, Ginsburg did not mention the controversy. Rather, in a conciliatory tone, Ginsburg praised A.L. Dunstan, who was at the center of the dispute, and other missionaries as deserving credit for the success of Baptist missions in that region.[103] The outcome of this controversy was that Campos was banished from the Baptist church, as the missionaries in the South of Brazil had wanted, and Ginsburg was not forced to resign his position.

The controversy involving Antonio Campos and A.L. Dunstan is but

[98] From W.E. Entzminger to R.J. Willingham, May 1, 1903.
[99] From William Cannada to Willingham, May 12, 1903.
[100] From William Cannada to Willingham, May 12, 1903.
[101] From Jephtah Hamilton to Willingham, May 27, 1903.
[102] From Jephtah Hamilton to Willingham, May 27, 1903.
[103] Ginsburg, *A Wandering Jew in Brazil: An Autobiography of Solomon L. Ginsburg*, 93.

one of several instances in which there was friction between Southern Baptist missionaries and Brazilian workers.[104] In general terms this controversy is particularly illuminating not only because of its potential to split the denomination, but also because it shows clearly that Southern Baptist missionaries at times disagreed on how to treat dissenting local workers. The resolution of this particular controversy, however, was typical of how challenges to Southern Baptist control were resolved. The dissenting leadership lost funding and was excluded, a significant part of the membership was reincorporated under new management, American structural power remained virtually unchallenged, and no alternative denominational body with significant competitive appeal was established.[105]

The Routinization of Brazilian Baptists

As in other mission fields, pioneering Southern Baptist missionaries in Brazil had little local logistical support, institutional structure, or available personnel in bringing about the sustainable phase of the Baptist missionary enterprise. The United States immigrants that preceded William and Anne Bagby's trip and gave birth to the first two Baptist churches in Brazil provided a number of missionaries with significant stability for their initial introduction to the country. At times, American and British immigrants who were not a part of close-knit ethnic communities, such as the colony of Santa Barbara, provided pockets of financial and emotional relief to missionaries who had a more robust cultural identification with them than with the people in whom they invested a significant portion of their lives trying to convert-educate-civilize. When William Bagby, Anne Bagby,

---

[104] Leonard, *O Protestantismo Brasileiro: Estudos De Eclesiologia E Historia Social.* In addition to A.R. Crabtree and Antonio Mesquita, Emile Leonard also presented a number of minor conflicts between Brazilians and United States workers. None of these conflicts, however, was widespread or lasted long.

[105] Crabtree, *História Dos Baptistas Do Brasil* 1; Anônio Neves de Mesquita, *História Dos Baptistas Do Brasil* (Rio de Janeiro: Casa Publicadora Baptista, 1940); Pereira, *História Dos Batistas No Brasil (1882-1982)*; Azevedo, *A Celebração Do Indivíduo: A Formação Do Pensamento Batista Brasileiro*; Taylor, *The Rise and Progress of Baptist Missions in Brazil: An Autobiography*; Ginsburg, *A Wandering Jew in Brazil: An Autobiography of Solomon L. Ginsburg.* The great majority of controversies recorded by historians of Brazilian Baptists follow this general description. It is only the Radical Movement that, as I will argue in the next chapter, has deeper structural effects on the denomination in Brazil.

Antonio Teixeira de Albuquerque, Z.C. Taylor, and Kate Taylor left Santa Barbara and established their base of operations in the state of Bahia in 1882, however, they were venturing into a bold project—a project for which they could not always comfortably count on the financial support of the FMB.

Within a few decades of the founding of the Baptist church in Bahia in 1882, the Baptist denomination in Brazil had become a considerable institutional machine. Despite all the obstacles faced by United States and Brazilian Baptist workers, by 1936 the denomination had 539 churches, 250 pastors and missionaries, 78 evangelists, 10 schools, and 2 major seminaries.[106] The reasons for this growth include but transcend the commitment and methods of Southern Baptist missionaries and their Brazilian help. The aggressive evangelistic and church-planting efforts of the missionaries included a number of factors such as rabid anti-Catholicism, the Baptist practice of direct recruiting of leadership that was aided by a congregational free-church structure, and the rigorous ethical demands that facilitated the development of a cohesive communal identity. These were major elements that informed the conversion of Brazilians. Structural factors, however, also help account for Baptist growth in Brazil. The geographical proximity between Brazil and the United States, the technological innovations that came to Brazil from Protestant countries and helped create an admiration for "Protestant progress," and the widespread dissatisfaction among significant sectors of Brazilian society with the Roman Catholic Church that was reinforced by the unprecedented institutional weakness of the Roman Catholic Church, also factor into the reasons for Baptist success in the country.[107] An assessment of the church planting

---

[106] Annals of the Brazilian Baptist Convention in 1936, accessed at the Archives of the North Brazil Baptist Theological Seminary.

[107] Walter Wedeman, "A History of Protestant Missions to Brazil, 1850-1914" (PhD diss., Southern Baptist Theological Seminary, 1977); Antônio G. Mendonça, "Evolução Histórica E Configuração Atual Do Protestantismo Brasileiro," in *Introdução Ao Protestantismo No Brasil*, eds. Antônio G. Mendonça and Prócoro Velasques Filho (São Paulo: Edições Loyola, 1990); Antônio Gouvêa Mendonça and Prócoro Velasques Filho, eds., *Introdução Ao Protestantismo Brasileiro* (São Paulo: Loyola, 1990); H.B. Cavalcanti, "Southern Baptist Abroad: Sharing the Faith in Nineteenth-Century Brazil," *Baptist History and Heritage* (Spring 2003); and Roberto Motta, "Social Scientists and Disenchanters: Some Basic Themes of Brazilian

efforts of Southern Baptists missionaries, therefore, must acknowledge that there were a number of structural factors that help explain their success.

Baptist Denominational
Organization in Brazil

Daniel Lancaster noted that Baptist missionary work in Brazil progressed in a similar way to that of the Baptists on the United States frontier, as "missionaries organized churches, associations, schools, colleges, seminaries, and a convention in Brazil."[108] First, several missions were created, such as Bahia (1882), Rio de Janeiro (1884), Pernambuco (1896), Amazonas (1897), Alagoas (1901), and Piauí (1903). As soon as the number of churches in a particular geographical area started to grow, associations that organized local churches into a cooperative relationship came into being— a common occurrence in Baptist development worldwide. The association in Rio de Janeiro began in 1894, in the northeast in 1900, in São Paulo in 1904, and in the Amazon in 1906. The Brazilian Baptist Convention was created in 1907 after brief discussion about whether Brazilian workers would be included in the national organization or only missionaries.[109] In 1908, the FMB divided the Brazilian field into a Southern mission and a northern mission. In the same year the Brazilian Baptist Convention already began to spread its transnational influence. The World Mission Board of the Brazilian Baptist convention established missionary presence in Chile in 1908 and Portugal in 1911—reverse mission came early in Brazilian Baptist life.[110] In terms of macro-organizational dynamics, therefore, Brazil followed the pattern established by Southern Baptists, and had implemented the general contours of denominational organization by the end of the first decade of the twentieth century.

The establishment and organization of church communities into cooperative arrangements, however, was only a part of the denominational dynamic. Unlike Christians operating in the Southern United States, the

---

Sociology of Religion," in *Sociologies of Religion: National Traditions*, eds. Giuseppe Giordan and Anthony J. Blasi (Leiden: Brill 2015).

[108] Lancaster, *The Bagbys of Brazil: The Life and Work of William Buck and Anne Luther Bagby*, xv.

[109] Mesquita, *História Dos Baptistas Do Brasil*, 20–24.

[110] Mesquita, 116–17.

missionaries in Brazil did not count on a wider culture with which they shared a variety of biases and presuppositions. The context of the missionaries in Brazil made the establishment of mechanisms of ideological dissemination and control even more important than in places where major concerns were guided primarily by the competitive spirit of a religious market characterized by voluntarism. In addition to preaching to and pastoring communities, missionaries had to develop aggressive forms of denominational indoctrination, which they did through publishing and teaching. For these reasons, Baptist work in Brazil was strongly characterized not only by direct evangelization and church planting, but also by the implementation of publishing and educational institutions (particularly seminaries).[111] To be clear, missionaries may not have been aware of all the aspects involved in the indoctrinating practices in which they engaged. My purpose here, however, is primarily highlighting function rather than motivation. That is, denominational indoctrination was a widespread outcome of Southern Baptist practice, even if Southern Baptist missionaries did not perceive their *modus operandi* as anything other than divinely-ordained work.

Baptist Publishing in Brazil

Before 1900, Baptist publishing advanced primarily through a number of publications that were managed by strong editors but had little national impact.[112] In 1900, however, the Baptist Publishing House was established after a meeting between W.B. Bagby, Z.C. Taylor, S.L. Ginsburg, and J.J. Taylor. The group decided that W.E. Entzminger would be the editor of the main periodical. He was also the second manager of the publishing house. In April 25, 1901, the first issue of the *Jornal Batista* came out, and the periodical remains the official publication of the Brazilian Baptist

---

[111] The correspondence of missionaries and their reports to the FMB and SBC corroborate this assessment. Perhaps the clearer articulation of this tripartite arrangement is found in F.M. Edwards' report to the SBC in May 17, 1922. He wrote: "I might say that there are three distinct phases of the work in its present stage of development in the evangelistic, educational and publication."

[112] See Crabtree, *História Dos Baptistas Do Brasil*, 1, 79, 107, 13, and 221. A.R. Crabtree notes that the periodcials *A Nova Vida* and *As Boas Novas* were considered successful by the missionaries, but had only regional influence.

Convention. During the five years before the national convention was organized, the *Jornal Batista* already developed a deeper sense of denominational ideological and cooperative unity among Baptists in Brazil. Other periodicals existed alongside the *Jornal Batista* and some were even created with the objective of resisting it under particular circumstances, but no publication became so important so quickly. The importance of the *Jornal Batista* in developing a denominational identity is so central that the first academic work devoted exclusively to the publication argues that after the Bible, the *Jornal Batista* is the most important writing in the development of the denomination.[113]

The *Jornal Batista* is also a good source for measuring the level of cultural and political engagement of Brazilian Baptists. Israel Azevedo provided an in-depth analysis on the themes of the Jornal Batista articles from 1901 until 1964. The overwhelming percentage of articles was directed toward themes of piety, doctrine, and denominational organization. In the period analyzed by Azevedo, only 3.8% of articles dealt with politics, 1.1% with culture, and 4.9% with secular news.[114] Of course Baptists had political preferences, but they were explicitly mentioned in the *Jornal Batista* only rarely and they by and large reflected Southern Baptist anxieties. As Azevedo pointed out,

> The Jornal Batista was uncritical of the economic, political, and cultural penetration of the United States in Brazil, seeing such entrance in Latin America as holding exclusively religious interests, even though it presented the other America as a bigger sister who served as a political and religious model for the "archaic" country of Brazil.[115]

Brazilian Baptists were individual-focused conversionists and countercultural in their social thinking, and they engaged social movements and ideologies mostly in order to combat what they saw as threats. The lack of

---

[113] Israel Belo de Azevedo, "A Palavra Marcada: Teologia Política Dos Batistas Segundo Jornal Batista" (master's thesis, Recife, Seminário Teológico Batista do Norte do Brasil, 1983). This work is a master's thesis written in Portuguese and recently made available only in Kindle edition, therefore, there will be no page numbers whenever this source is cited.

[114] Azevedo.

[115] Azevedo.

involvement with socio-political causes that characterized Brazilian Baptists was interpreted by sociologist Gedeon de Alencar as the separation of church and society, not only of church and state as Baptists claimed.[116] This Baptist general self-understanding, up to their centennial in 1982, is clear in the words of José dos Reis Pereira, the former editor of the *Jornal Batista* who wrote the history of the denomination's first hundred years:

> Officially, the Brazilian Baptists do not take political positions. They are part of no political party. Respecting the New Testament principles in Romans 13:1-7, 1 Timothy 2:1-2, Titus 3:1, and 1 Peter 2:13, the Brazilian Baptists pray for the constituted authorities and respect them. ... For the Brazilian Baptists what really matters is the evangelization of the country. The hymn that can be considered the official Brazilian Baptist hymn begins with these words: "My nation for Christ, this is my prayer."[117]

Official Baptist interaction with broader social, cultural, and political issues is limited and should be interpreted in light of this countercultural, individualistic, and Southern Baptist-informed background.

In addition to the *Jornal Batista*, the books translated by the missionaries, the Sunday School material they made available to their Brazilian audience, and the hymns they translated, compiled, and composed also helped form the theocultural imagination of Brazilian Baptists in general. As Israel Azevedo noted, "the thought of Brazilian Protestants is less contained in the books of their theologians than in the hymns they sing and periodicals they read."[118] Publication work was so important in Brazil that missionaries involved with publishing made little distinction between the value of publishing and of preaching. W.E. Entzminger, writing to R.J. Willingham, made this disposition clear. Facing the possibility of losing funding for denominational publications, Entzminger wrote:

> At this juncture it appears that the question is not whether to have or not to have a printing plant, but whether or not it is worthwhile to have publications. And it would be easy to decide this question

---

[116] Gedeon Alencar, *Protestantismo Tupiniquim* (São Paulo: Aret Editorial, 2007), 62–64.

[117] Pereira, *História Dos Batistas No Brasil (1882-1982)*, 317–18.

[118] Azevedo, *A Celebração Do Indivíduo: A Formação Do Pensamento Batista Brasileiro*, 154.

by deciding whether or not it is important, whether or not it is worthwhile, to continue the work of evangelizing in Brazil. If we should close up the enterprise, the publication enterprise, it would be because we should abandon the whole evangelization enterprise.[119]

For Entzminger, the success of the whole Brazilian mission hinged on its ability to publish, and the *Jornal Batista* was "the only means of cultivating any denominational spirit [and of] stimulating cooperation [and] indoctrination."[120]

The administrative and editorial leadership of the Baptist Publication house in Brazil was reserved for non-locals until 1934, when the Brazilian Constitution mandated that only Brazilians could lead publishing houses. Article 133 of the Constitution of 1934 stated that "the primary responsibility of intellectual or administrative orientation of political or news presses can only be exercised by Brazilians."[121] The Southern Baptist missionaries in control of the publishing house, however, were resourceful and creative, and they named a Brazilian as chief editor who would be the legal face of Baptist publications while creating an executive editor position that would be filled by the person who would make final editorial decisions.[122] Given the new law, S.L. Watson left the management of the publishing house, and Teodoro Teixeira, a native of Spain and longtime mentee of W.E. Entzminger, stepped down from the senior editor position. Moisés Silveira became the first Brazilian manager of the house and Manoel Avelino the first senior editor, but it was Teixeira, who then became the new executive editor, who made the decisions.[123]

When it came to the denominational boards and committees that dealt with publications and Sunday school administration and process, missionaries also led the way during the first three decades after the creation of the BBC. In 1922, when the beginnings of the first notable phase

---

[119] From W.E. Entzminger to Willingham, November 2, 1909.

[120] From W.E. Entzminger to Willingham, November 2, 1909.

[121] Article 133 of the *Constituição da República dos Estados Unidos do Brasil* (July 16, 1934), the constitution of 1934 can be accessed online at http://planalto.gov.br/ccivil_03/constituicao/constituicao34.htm.

[122] Pereira, *História Dos Batistas No Brasil (1882-1982)*, 131-32.

[123] Mesquita, *História Dos Baptistas Do Brasil*, 271-72. Teodoro Teixeira had been W.E. Entzminger's assistant editor for many years and had the trust of the FMB to lead the publishing house in accordance with missionary expectations.

of the Radical Movement[124] that would temporarily split the denomination took place, Southern Baptist missionaries led the great majority of the influential denominational departments: the Publishing House (S.L. Watson), the Department of Sunday Schools and Youth (T.B. Stover), the Department of Books (W.E. Entzminger), the Department of Baptist Popular Schools (W.W. Enete), and the Department of Periodical Literature (T.R. Teixeira—Spanish-born).[125] In his annual report to the SBC, S.L. Watson's list of the regular contributors to the denominational publishing work in Brazil is comprised mostly of United States missionaries.[126] In short, Southern Baptist missionaries, sometimes contradicting the intention of Brazilian law, controlled not only the operational organization, but also the ideological production of the denomination in Brazil during the first decades of the twentieth century. The rhetoric of transfer of power to the locals, which was prominent in missionary communication, was not intentionally implemented by the missionaries.

Education: The Major Seminaries

Baptist missionaries started a number of educational initiatives in Brazil. Some of them, such as the *Collegio Industrial*, founded with the help of Z.C. Taylor in 1894, lasted just a few years.[127] Other initiatives, such as the Brazilian Baptist School for children and youth in São Paulo, founded by the Bagbys in 1902, remain in operation to this day. Most of these initiatives, however, were aimed at the education of Brazilian youth. When it came to the training of future local ministers and denominational leaders, with the exception of the few Brazilians they chose to send to the United States for education, missionaries initially turned to on-the-job training; that is, they would train locals while pastoring churches, rather than setting aside formal schools for ministerial training. Though this arrangement was taxing on the missionaries, they often insisted on closely

---

[124] For the purposes of this project, the term "Radical Movement" refers to the nationalist-inspired Baptist movement in Brazil that advocated the need to implement local autonomy in Brazilian Baptist denominational life.

[125] Mesquita, *História Dos Baptistas Do Brasil*, 269.

[126] Annals of the Southern Baptist Convention, May 12, 1921.

[127] Crabtree, *História Dos Baptistas Do Brasil* 1, 93.

monitoring the training of Brazilians.[128] Writing to the FMB in 1900, Z.C. Taylor stated that he was "studying a plan that will allow nine churches without a pastor to have their own ministers. First, the mission cannot employ any national pastor; second, that the churches send every year, one or more members to study the Bible with me, so that they can prepare for pastoral work."[129]

In 1899, both Z.C. Taylor and T.C. Joyce asked the board for money to build seminaries.[130] Missionaries such as Taylor and Joyce had been offering forms of intentional ministerial education since at least 1895,[131] but it was only in 1902 that the North Brazil Baptist Theological Seminary (henceforth NBBTS) was founded in the city of Recife, the capital of the state of Pernambuco. In 1908, the South Brazil Baptist Theological Seminary (henceforth SBBTS) would be founded in the city of Rio de Janeiro.[132] Similar to the developments in denominational organization and publication, the imported Southern Baptist tendency to dominate Brazilian institutions ruled in the major centers of theological training in Brazil.

The North Brazil Baptist Theological Seminary. The NBBTS is the oldest Baptist seminary in Latin America and was the first in the region to offer graduate theological education. The solemn inaugural ceremony of the NBBTS was at Solomon Ginsburg's residence on April 1, 1902, and missionary Jephtah Hamilton was the first president of the institution.[133] In the same year, missionary William Cannada arrived in Brazil to lead

---

[128] The taxing nature of the initial stages of theological training in Brazil is evident in many places, but nowhere more clearly than in the correspondence of Jephtah Hamilton, who constantly complained about having to split his time between his evangelistic work and his responsibilities training the locals.

[129] Quoted by A.R. Crabtree in Crabtree, *História Dos Baptistas Do Brasil* 1, 124.

[130] Annals of the Southern Baptist Convention, May 12, 1899.

[131] Z.C. Taylor, "Gracious Blessings" *The Foreign Mission Journal* 26, no. 10 (1895).

[132] For the most comprehensive histories of both seminaries, see Zaqueu Moreira de Oliveira, *Ousadia E Desafios Da Educação Teológica: 100 Anos Do Stbn* (Recife: STBN Edições, 2002); Edgar Francis Hallock and Ebenezer Soares Ferreira, *Historia Do Seminario Teologico Batista Do Sul Do Brasil: 1908 a 1998* (Rio de Janeiro: JUERP, 1998).

[133] Emiliano Kerr, "Acta Da Instalação Do Seminário Baptista Em Pernambuco " *Jornal Batista*, no. 16 (April 25, 1902).

the seminary. This would mark a tendency of Southern Baptist missionaries to lead the seminary, a tendency that would only end in the 1980s, with the exception of two local presidents who, as a result of the Radical Movement, led the institution from 1938 to 1940. When it came to the faculty, out of the seventeen professors who taught in the seminary from its inception until the controversy of the Radical Movement in the early 1920s, only four were Brazilian born. Of these four Brazilian-born professors, only two taught for more than four years, whereas of the thirteen of United States heritage only four taught less than four years.[134]

In the first years of the seminary, the school had no permanent place and the FMB sent very little financial support for the institution.[135] William Cannada came to preside over the seminary in 1902, after Jephtah Hamilton chose to invest more time to his evangelistic work,[136] and only Cannada and the Ginsburgs taught classes until 1906. When J.W. Shepard arrived to help the seminary, he only stayed for one year, and in 1907 both Shepard and Cannada left the seminary to work on establishing what would become the official denominational seminary.[137] After the establishment of the Brazilian Baptist Convention in 1907, the denomination in Brazil decided to have one official theological seminary and that it would be in the South of the country. According to missionary W.C. Taylor, with the founding of SBBTS in Rio de Janeiro in 1908, the NBBTS operated for several years as if it was a clandestine work.[138]

The two missionaries that were largely responsible for the survival of the NBBTS were D.L. Hamilton and H.H. Muirhead, who not only took care of the teaching and administrative duties by themselves until 1915,[139]

---

[134] Oliveira, *Ousadia E Desafios Da Educação Teológica: 100 Anos Do Stbn*, 193-95. Oliveira's book, which is the only major published work on the seminary, includes a list of all presidents, professors, and graduates of NBBTS until the year 2001.

[135] Jerry S. Key, "The Rise and Development of Baptist Theological Education in Brazil, 1881-1963: A Historical and Interpretive Survey" (PhD diss., Southwestern Baptist Theological Seminary, 1965), 34-35.

[136] Hamilton had to travel significant distances to teach at the seminary, and he complained about the difficulties of traveling often in his correspondence with FMB corresponding secretary R.J. Willingham.

[137] Zaqueu Moreira de Oliveira, *Perfil Histórico Da Educação Teológica Batista No Brasil* (Fortaleza: ABIBET, 2000), 16.

[138] W.C. Taylor, "O Seminário Do Norte," *Revista Teológica*, (January 1951), 33.

[139] Oliveira, *Ousadia E Desafios Da Educação Teológica: 100 Anos Do Stbn*, 193; *Perfil Histórico Da Educação Teológica Batista No Brasil*, 16. Oliveira, citing Antônio

but also helped facilitate mechanisms of local financial support for the seminary and invested their personal money in the institution.[140] When H.H. Muirhead was able to garner some financial support from the FMB in 1915, L.L. Johnson and W.C. Taylor came to the seminary, and in 1917, with the help of the Building Committee of the BBC, the seminary got its first building. In 1918, the NBBTS was officially accepted as the second seminary of the denomination in the country, even though it was established years before the national convention.

Regional scars and ill-feeling developed because of the eleven years that it took the national convention to support the seminary officially as a denominational institution. There was no significant theological chasm between north and South, and so Baptists in the Brazilian north widely perceived that the actions of the BBC were a form of neglect and even disrespect. Antônio Mesquita, who began teaching in the NBBTS in 1919, said that the acceptance of the seminary into the BBC did not come without "a few obstacles from both Richmond and some brothers in the South."[141] Mesquita likewise wrote that

> The [NBBTS] remained outside the Brazilian Baptist Convention until 1918, meanwhile the institutions in Rio de Janeiro enjoyed all the privileges of the direction of a board elected by the convention. Without wishing to accuse the missionaries in the south, and fearing not interpreting all the facts properly, I venture to say that there really was an opposition to the approval of the institutions in Recife on the part of the national convention.[142]

Mesquita's account went further. He claimed that by the time the national convention in 1918 approved the seminary as an official denominational school, people in Northern Brazil had already developed distrust

---

Dorta's unpublished work "O Jubileu teologico Batista do Norte do Brasil" in his shorter assessment of the seminary's history, says that in 1909 Ginsburg tried to lead the seminary but that due to lack of time he appointed a congregationalist missionary, F.A. Gallimore, as president for the institution. In his longer, official history of the seminary, however, Oliveira does not list Gallimore as a former president, although he leaves the account of the year 1909 without mentioning the name of a president.

[140] Oliveira, *Perfil Histórico Da Educação Teológica Batista No Brasil*, 16-18.

[141] Mesquita, *História Dos Baptistas Do Brasil*, 100.

[142] Antônio Mesquita, *Historia Dos Baptistas Em Pernambuco* (Recife: Typographia do C.A.B., 1930), 125.

and suspicion of the denominational workers in the South. Mesquita observed that "a form of dangerous regionalism was slowly taking over the spirit of our national leaders and it would soon break the good relationship between the South and the north."[143] When the controversy did indeed break out in 1922, missionary D.L. Hamilton, who had sacrificed much to save the NBBTS, was the only Southern Baptist missionary to stay on the locals' side. The controversy, to which I devote the next chapter, was not primarily theological, but was fundamentally about the power to steer the administrative arm of the denomination away from the historic pattern of missionary domination.

The South Brazil Baptist Theological Seminary. In similar fashion to the NBBTS, the SBBTS had a significant history of missionary rule. Only in 1936, after twenty-eight years of operation and after the terms that set the stage for the end of the Radical Movement controversy were mostly settled, did the seminary appoint its first Brazilian president (Djalma Cunha) and chairman of the administrative board (José Marques).[144] This faculty likewise was made up mainly of Southern Baptist missionaries. Until 1930 the seminary had thirteen professors, of whom only three were locals.[145]

The SBBTS was founded as a result of the decision made in 1907—with the establishment of the Brazilian Baptist Convention—that despite the existence of a theological seminary in the north of the country, the only official denominational training school for ministers would operate in Rio de Janeiro. J.W. Shepard, who was elected president, together with W.H. Cannada left the NBBTS and started working at SBBTS when it started offering classes in 1908. Cannada's stay at SBBTS, however, was not long due to conflicts between him and Shepard. In his letter of resignation, signed on April of 1909, Cannada mentioned that Shepard was not only an authoritarian leader, but also that "brother Shepard is trying to transport an American College and Seminary and fit them down upon the Brazilian customs and temperaments, but it doesn't work. What we want

---

[143] Mesquita, 184.

[144] Hallock and Ferreira, *Historia Do Seminario Teologico Batista Do Sul Do Brasil: 1908 a 1998*, 122.

[145] Hallock and Ferreira, 28

is tactful adaptation to Brazilian customs and temperaments."[146] Shepard would not put up with insubordinations, and his tenure was marked by a number of conflicts with fellow missionaries who challenged his initiatives or disagreed with him.[147] In 1911, Shepard led a reorganization of the school "in accord with our schools in the South in North America."[148] He remained president of the seminary until 1930, and before H.H. Muirhead accepted his appointment as president, he demanded that Shepard be released from the school.[149] The sharpest edges of missionary attachment to Brazilian Baptist seminaries, however, would become more explicit only when they could no longer take their positions of leadership for granted. After 1922, when missionary authority over the schools and seminaries began to be challenged, missionaries, in general, became viciously aggressive against local leadership that was not unquestionably subordinate.

Conclusion

Until 1922, the authority of Southern Baptist missionaries in Brazil remained virtually unchallenged by Brazilians, and missionaries did not move toward a denominational transition of power to the locals, as they often proposed. Rather than implementing strategies of power transitions, SBC missionaries infused the spirit of the Jim Crow South into the denominational institutions they helped create. More specifically, the institutions of cultural production were dominated by missionaries well into the 1930s, when Brazilian legislation called for the nationalization of institutions such as publication houses and periodical boards. Even then, missionaries found creative ways to circumvent the intent of the law and maintain tight editorial control of published content. When it came to seminaries, both the NBBTS, despite its turbulent history, and the SBBTS were missionary-dominated and implemented in their classrooms the content and form of schools in the American South. The Jim Crow-

---

[146] William H. Cannada, *Letter of Resignation to the Board of Trustees of Rio Baptist College and Seminary.* April, 26, 1909.

[147] Hallock and Ferreira, *Historia Do Seminario Teologico Batista Do Sul Do Brasil: 1908 a 1998,* 13.

[148] From J.W. Shepard to R.J. Willingham, May 29, 1911.

[149] Hallock and Ferreira, *Historia Do Seminario Teologico Batista Do Sul Do Brasil: 1908 a 1998,* 33.

inspired structural manifestations of SBC institutions in Brazil were responsible for the local appropriation of ideologies and biases inspired in Dixie, and the history of racism in Brazil itself informed the freedom with which SBC missionaries exercised their White supremacist anxieties.

When the Radical Movement broke out in the 1920s, it did so in an environment in which Southern Baptist missionaries had controlled the institutions of denominational theocultural output for decades, and, as will become clearer in the following chapter, such control was part and parcel of the anxieties that energized the Radical Movement itself. The three-legged foundation of denominational work in the country, consisting of church organization/planting, publishing, and education, were thoroughly controlled by Southern Baptist missionaries and ordered according to their theocultural preferences. Yet in Brazilian Baptist historiography, this missionary domination is only rarely stated, nowhere thoroughly demonstrated or investigated, and almost never criticized.

When it came to theological articulations of foundational denominational commitments, the missionary legitimation of their cultural gospel, despite sporadic challenges, remained mostly legitimized among locals. The focus of the Radical Movement, however, was the most explicit manifestation of denominational power, which was manifested in administrative representation. One must remember, however, that although the Radical Movement represented the first major local resistance against missionary White supremacy in Brazilian Baptist life, it took place in mostly non-theological terms. Religious groups often change ideologically as a result of shifts in power structures, rather than changing power structures as a result of burgeoning ideologies. In Brazilian Baptist life, the threatening possibility represented by the Radical Movement was, to a great extent, precisely the freedom that the denomination, under the "wrong" hands, would have to steer off the path of the White, Southern Gospel. According to SBC missionaries, local administrative freedom represented the danger to disrupt the path of the one true Gospel of their Lord and Savior Jesus Christ, who had appointed them with normative leadership authority.

CHAPTER THREE

NATIONALISM AND THE RADICAL
REACTION AGAINST
MISSIONARY DOMINATION

In the 1920s and 1930s, a group of Brazilian Baptists would shake the foundations of denominational life in Brazil through a movement that wanted more autonomy from foreign missionary control. This series of events was so significant that Erika Helgen, in her study of Brazilian religious conflict, argued that it "transformed the face of Protestantism" in the Northeast region of Brazil.[1] The movement began in the northern region of the country, and the northern state of Pernambuco was the epicenter of the resistance that came to be known in Brazilian Baptist history as the Radical Movement. The name given to the movement itself and a number of terms that came to be associated with this group that resisted missionary domination—such as "anti-missionary" and "nationalist"—were informed by historiographical and polemical articulations that tended to favor missionary perspectives. The Radical Movement was indeed influenced by nationalist sentiments, but these sentiments were heightened by the way in which the nationalism and the racialized imagination of missionaries themselves informed the operationalization of their denominational control. The control of denominational structures by foreign missionaries was, to varying extents, expected by Brazilians and even appreciated at times. As the national and local conventions, as well as their auxiliary institutions matured, however, cries for additional local autonomy became more common while, at the same time, US and Brazilian social-cultural contexts encouraged more explicit confrontations.

The history of the Radical Movement, therefore, must acknowledge the context of Brazilian nationalism in general and the regionalism in the state of Pernambuco—the geographical and intellectual center of the movement—in particular. In terms of countrywide nationalism, World

---

[1] Erika Helgen, *Religious Conflict in Brazil: Protestants, Catholics, and the Rise of Religious Pluralism in the Early Twentieth Century* (New Haven: Yale University Press, 2020), 64.

War I contributed to the growth of nationalist sentiments in the country, which came accompanied by a suspicion of foreign influences.[2] The history of the state of Pernambuco itself, where the Pernambuco Baptist College and the North Brazil Baptist Theological Seminary (NBBTS) were located,[3] is rife with wars and revolutions that are widely interpreted as generators of the regionalist spirit that still characterizes the region.[4] The United States, in addition to its widespread nativist sentiments, was also going through its own peculiar phase in the first decades of the twentieth century. Some of the features of this historical period in United States religious history included the expansion of Ku Klux Klan activity in the South, the Fundamentalist controversies, and the crisis of the Protestant establishment.[5] More specific to the SBC, the convention was growing and was moving toward greater centralization and effectiveness,[6] and the "seventy-five million campaign," launched in 1919, despite its eventual failure, reflected an optimistic spirit within the denomination.[7] The

---

[2] Steven Topik, "Middle-Class Brazilian Nationalism, 1889-1930: From Radicalism to Reaction," *Social Science Quarterly* 59, no. 1 (1978); Paulo-Tarso Flecha de Lima, "Liberalism Versus Nationalism: The Prodevelopment Ideology in Recent Brazilian Political History (1930-1997)," *Presidential Studies Quarterly* 29, no. 2 (1999).

[3] These two institutions were connected and operated under the same administration until after the end of the Radical Movement. During the period considered in this chapter, therefore, it is important to be reminded that events that affected the College also affected the Seminary and vice versa.

[4] José Antonio Gonsalves de Mello, *Tempo Dos Flamengos* (Recife: Governo do Estado de Pernambuco 1978); Mário Melo, *A Guerra Dos Mascates Como Afrimação Nacionalista* (Recife: Governo do Estado de Pernambuco, 1984); José da Costa Porto, *Os Tempos Da Praieira* (Recife: Secretaria do Estado de Pernambuco, 1981).

[5] Sydney E. Ahlstrom, *Religious History of the American People* (New Haven: Yale University Press, 1972), 895-917.

[6] Bill Leonard, *Baptists in America* (New York: Columbia University Press, 2005), 34-35.

[7] Pamela R. Durso and Keith Durso, *The Story of Baptists in the United States* (Brentwood: Baptist History and Heritage Society, 2006), 172-73; Smith, *Fundamentalism, Fundraising, and the Transformation of the Southern Baptist Convention, 1919-1925*, 40-60. Smith shows how the Seventy-Five Million Campaign was a response to both post-War nationalism and the perceived harmful tendencies of the Interchurch World Movement and other ecumenical and potentially internationalizing influences. The Seventy-Five Million Campaign was, as Smith shows, a manifestation of SBC concern with disseminating its theocultural tendencies

macro-societal dynamics within both Brazil and the United States, there-fore, set the stage for the clash between Brazilian nationalist sentiments and SBC denominational confidence as well as for the continuation of the missionary illusion of superiority. When missionaries got involved in the controversies that led to separation, there was little indication that they would not be able to finance the denomination and "starve out" the radi-cals. Missionary resistance to local autonomy was heavily informed by mis-sionary White supremacy—which continued to shape the general South-ern imagination in the first half of the twentieth century both in the US and abroad.

The Radical Movement and
Missionary Racial Imagination

The Radical Movement erupted as a reaction against missionaries whose racial imagination was mostly formed in an environment where White cul-tural domination was maintained through performances that ranged from White supremacist standardized education to ritualized practices of vio-lence and exclusion.[8] In terms of Christian practice, "white southern reli-gion all but unanimously supported the imposition of white supremacy rule and for a very long time offered very scant resistance to its continua-tion."[9] These dispositions were not aggressively challenged by a Brazilian dominant culture that had its own forms of White supremacist tenden-cies,[10] and SBC missionaries in Brazil reenacted their racial sensibilities in their strategies of denominational control while generally maintaining public performances that gave most locals the impression that missionaries imagined the possibility of equality. The Radical Movement challenged missionary domination, and although racial dynamics were not always ex-plicit in the Brazilians/missionaries disputes energized by the movement, it informed the attitudes and decisions of both missionaries and locals.

---

more effectively through missions and education that was energized in a reactionary response to post-War anxieties.

[8] Kristina DuRocher, *Raising Racists: The Socialization of White Children in the Jim Crow South* (Lexington: University Press of Kentucky, 2011), 7–8.

[9] Mark A. Noll, *God and Race in American Politics: A Short History* (Princeton University Press, 2010), 71.

[10] Skidmore, *Black into White*; Telles, *Race in Another America*; Silva and Paixão, "Mixed and Unequal: New Perspectives on Brazilian Ethnoracial Relations."

In the 1920s and 1930s, when the Radical Movement came about, Southern Baptist leaders and missionaries continued to reveal their White supremacist tendencies broadly and to reflect the general sensibility of Southern culture. Southern Baptist missionary literature is full of examples that illuminate the shape of missionary whiteness in the first decades of the twentieth century. One way in which the racial sensibilities of White southerners appeared in SBC missionary literature was through a romanticized slavery nostalgia that praised the "Negro" commitment to the Confederacy. Praise for faithful slaves was common in pro-Confederate publications between the mid-1890s to as late as 1930, and articles containing praise for slave faithfulness were also printed in Southern Baptist missionary literature.[11] An imagination that opened room for Afro-descendant support for the Confederacy sustained a commitment to both the illusion of the objective morality of the antebellum South and the racial violence of their post-bellum present. "In the past," Home Mission Board missionary Richard Carroll wrote, "the Negro proved himself loyal not only to the United States flag, but to the Confederate flag. He fed at the front, threw up breastworks and took care of their wives and children."[12] For Dallas pastor J.B. Cranfill, the support slaves gave to the Confederate cause was so special that "human annals furnish no parallel to this remarkable epoch in Southern history."[13] W.P Price agreed, saying in the 1926 Annual Meeting of the Baptist Convention of Louisiana that slave courage, loyalty, and devotion to the Confederacy "has never been seen among the children of men."[14] O.L. Haley argued that views of slavery as evil were distorted, and such distortions were exacerbated by post-emancipation narratives. During slavery, Haley argued, slaves had access to the Gospel and worshiped with Whites in an array of Black and White spaces.[15]

The appreciation for the "faithful Negro" of the South, however, was

---

[11] David W. Blight, *Race and Reunion: The Civil War in American Memory* (Cambridge: Belknap Press, 2002), 285.

[12] Richard Carroll, "The Negro Exodus to the North," *Home and Foreign Fields* 1, no. 11 (1917): 29.

[13] J.B. Cranfill, "Our Brother in Black," *Home and Foreign Fields* 8, no. 8 (1924): 23–24.

[14] W.P. Price, "The Minsitry of the Home Mission Board," *Home and Foreign Fields* 10 no. 1 (1926): 10.

[15] O.L. Haley, "Our Debt to the Negro," *Home and Foreign Fields* 8, no. 8 (1924): 9.

not always extended to Afro-descendants in Brazil. In a section entitled "Quotable Items About South America," *Home and Foreign Fields* published the following quote: "There are over six million Africans among the thirty millions of people in Brazil, and many of them are the crudest type of Negro on the American hemisphere."[16] Appreciation for African Americans on the part of White southerners was contingent upon the former's alleged approximation to Southern White culture and support of the system that oppressed them—Afro-Brazilians met neither condition. In the White supremacist imagination of Southern Baptists, there was room—ample room—for authentic Christian love for the "Negro" and support for oppressive spaces legitimized by a racial orthodoxy informed by a distorted self-perception that misrecognized evil as good. As a matter of fact, in the minds of many White Southern Christians, Christianity supported their racist imagination and Christian commitment often encouraged White southerners to support White supremacy. Southerners often used explicitly biblical and Christian justifications to support their arguments for White supremacist structures.

Connections to the Confederacy and the antebellum South were not imagined by Southern Baptist Whites as malicious commitments and continued to be sustained during the time when the most significant struggles for Brazilian Baptist identity took place. Confederate connections, therefore, were not to be forgotten, but celebrated. For example, when Kathleen Mallory, then the corresponding secretary of the Woman's Missionary Union, celebrated J.B. Gambrell's life, she did it by listing his most honorable activities in life: "Even so upon every remembrance of him—Confederate soldier, teacher, preacher, friend of the Mexicans, state secretary, seminary professor, writer, president of the Southern Baptist Convention—our Union will give thanks. Of him it may be well said: 'A just man made perfect after he had served his own generation according to the will of God.'"[17] W.B. Crumpton advertised the seventy-five million dollar campaign by comparing it to "the Old Confederate way" of battling.[18] In 1921, R.A. Clifton, a missionary in Brazil, told *Home and Foreign Fields*

---

[16] "Quotable Items about South America," *Home and Foreign Fields* 10, no. 4 (1926): 39.

[17] Kathleen Mallory, "W.M.U. Items," *Home and Foreign Fields* 5, no. 8 (1921): 21.

[18] W.B. Crumpton, "The Greatest Program Ever Undertaken," *Home and Foreign Fields* 2, no. 12 (1918): 4.

of how William Buck Bagby was helped by a "Confederate soldier" who lived in Brazil during his 1882 arrival.[19] A few years later, L.L. Conner praised the construction of the Stone Mountain memorial that celebrated the Confederacy, saying that "When this magnificent work is completed there will be nothing like it in the world. Nor there has been; and people will come from afar to behold this tribute to undying heroism by a loving and loyal people."[20] Rituals of memorialization such as the construction of monuments were central to the maintenance of Lost Cause mythology. Praise for Confederate idols, Robert E. Lee the greatest among them, was also important to the maintenance of White supremacist ideologies of the South. The moral and military infallibility of Lee was a central tenet of Lost Cause mythology.[21] In Brazil, appreciation for Lee on the part of Southern Baptist missionaries was not unknown, and missionary Rosalee Mills Appleby was one of Lee's most vocal supporters.

Rosalee Mills Appleby was not shy about her admiration for Confederate heroes, and she openly praised Lee to both her Brazilian and United States audience. Appleby became a celebrated figure in Brazilian Baptist circles and was a major introducer of charismatic tendencies into Brazilian Baptist life. Lee was one of her archetypes for unblemished morality. In *Rainbow Gleams*, a book of pamphlets and speeches printed in Portuguese and English, Appleby went as far as comparing Robert E. Lee positively to Moses and David. In one of her essays, after showing how Moses and David engaged in sin, Appleby wrote:

> Robert E. Lee, however, realized an unusual triumph, an unblemished success in life. Though defeated at last as a general, he succeeded as a man. His manhood was greater than his generalship. Though he spent many years in strife, he never lifted his voice against the enemy. Broken in fortune and health, his shining character never tarnished. He refused to sell his unsullied name for money even though poor and needy. History may record Lee's work a failure, but the verdict of hearts that appreciated his blameless life is different. His spirit is a challenge to every young man who wants

---

[19] R.A. Clifton, "God's Hand in the Beginning of Baptist Work in Brazil," *Home and Foreign Fields* 5, no. 9 (1921): 8.

[20] L.L Conner, "To Doubt Would Be Disloyalty; to Falter Would Be Sin," *Home and Foreign Fields* 13, no. 4 (1929): 24–25.

[21] Blight, *Race and Reunion*, 264.

to attain an unsullied triumph and a reproach to any who would take a short cut to vulgar success.[22]

Twelve years later, in *Orchids and Edelweiss*, Appleby wrote:

A goodness with no tinge of weakness belonged to Robert E. Lee. He was tender as a son, affectionate as a father, wise as a general, charitable as an opponent. This matchless citizen and Christian writes a noble page in American history.[23]

Lee was, for Appleby, a modern knight whose perfection presented a model for Spirit-filled humanity. For her, if the United States had Lee as its leader, the country would not be in what she perceived as a decadent state. According to Appleby, "What would our nation not be if all her statesmen carried the white, unsullied soul of a [Robert] Lee or a [William Jennings] Byran... These men compose our modern knighthood."[24] Not only race and nationality, but also gender biases are clear in Appleby's praise for Lee. For her, what was to be admired was, simultaneously, Lee's White superiority, his Confederate commitments, and his exemplary manliness. Although herself an unusually independent woman in a world dominated by men, Appleby reifies Southern gender hierarchy in her public appreciation for the Confederate icon.

The commitment to male, White supremacist dispositions present in narratives of slave support for the Confederacy and in the process of memorialization of Confederate morality was part and parcel of the Southern imagination in general, and Southern missionaries globalized these dispositions in their religiously legitimized performances. The way they showed love for other races was not through arguments for equality, but through the preaching of a gospel that they conceptualized according to their racial imagination. If the qualified love they showed other races was already complicated by their White supremacist commitments, their sentiments toward a particular being whose heretical creation was a result of too much approximation between distinct races—the person of mixed blood—was even more problematic. Latin America is a highly miscegenated region,

---

[22] Rosalee Mills Appleby, *Rainbow Gleams* (Nashville: Sunday School Board, 1929), 17.
[23] Rosalee Mills Appleby, *Orchids and Edelweiss* (Nashville: Broadman Press, 1941), 34.
[24] Appleby, *Rainbow Gleams*, 36.

and if the humanity of the "Negro" was already diminished by the violent self-aggrandizement of Southern Whites, the person of mixed blood stood as an aberration that was even less human, if human at all.

In the first decades of the twentieth century, Southern Baptist ideas regarding people of mixed race were varied, but most institutional leaders and intellectuals were avid defenders of their segregationist agendas that saw racial intermingling—especially sexual contact—as an aberration and disgrace. White commitment against interracial relationships in general, of course, was not uncommon in US law, and legal efforts to curb miscegenation go back to at least seventeenth-century legislative decisions made in Colonial Virginia.[25] Antagonism toward people of mixed race, however, gained new steam in the South after Reconstruction as the possibility of racial intermingling became more pronounced with the abolition of slavery and redeemed states acting to sharpen the boundaries of racial difference. The growing preoccupation with miscegenation in the first decades of the twentieth century is evident in the fact that the term "Mulatto" was dropped after the 1920 Census and the term "Negro" was used in the 1930 Census to name anyone with African American blood. The implementation of the "one drop rule" represented the imposition of racial labeling that aimed not only to discourage miscegenation but also to render people of mixed blood invisible not only to others but also to themselves.[26] The general dispositions of Southern Baptists, therefore, were heavily informed by national and regional dynamics that in turn reinforced missionary racial imagination.

If the sensibilities toward mixed races and convictions of Southern Baptist missionaries to Brazil were mostly voiced privately given the mostly mixed population of Brazil, US missions periodicals often made such dispositions public, given its consumption by a predominantly White Southern audience. Such segregationist mentality—that was concerned by social proximity and terrified by sexual contact—was legitimized by religious, historical, and pseudoscientific frameworks articulated by Southern

---

[25] Tyrone Nagai, "Multiracial Americans Throughout the History of the US," in *Race Policy and Multiracial Americans*, ed. Kathleen Odell Korgen (Bristol: Policy Press, 2016), 13.

[26] Jon M. Spencer, *The New Colored People: The Mixed-Race Movement in America* (New York: NYU Press, 2000), 1–5.

Baptist practitioners and intellectuals.[27] B.C. Hening, then Home Mission Board's superintendent for Foreigners, Indians, and Negroes, argued in 1923 that the "Negros" themselves admitted to their inferiority and that the "truth must be burned into our very consciousness that the well being of both races is best subserved by a clear recognition of the strong demarcation between them, and a strict and cheerful acquiescence in the inevitable decree of nature and her God everywhere and all the time."[28] The difficulty that "Negroes" may have had in accepting this truth was, according to Victor Masters, partially a result of the "northern negrophile's"— that is, the northern Negro of mixed blood—influence.[29] Intermarriage and the mixed-blood progeny that such an arrangement would produce was resisted by Southern Baptists not as articulations of unreasonable superiority complexes, but as an expression of love and concern for all races. Editor G.S. Dobbins made this disposition clear when he argued that

> The Negroes have as much to lose in intermarriage as the whites, and should be as bitterly opposed to it on biological and racial grounds. To be a pure-bred Negro is something for the black man to be as proud of as to be a pure-bred Caucasian is for the white man. The solution of the problem of living together is NOT that of amalgamation by intermarriage, and every illegitimate mulatto child is the evidence of some white man's shame.[30]

Dobbins was well aware of the extent of intermarriage in Latin America, and he used the region—of which Brazil was the most important Baptist beachhead—as an example of the disasters of blood mixing. This Latin American disaster, in turn, served as an example that supported the US segregation system. He wrote:

---

[27] Here, again, Southern Baptists are reflecting and reinforcing White southern culture in general. See Greg Carter, *The United States of the United Races: A Utopian History of Racial Mixing* (New York: NYU Press, 2013), 108–13; Noll, *God and Race in American Politics*; John Lee Eighmy and Samuel S. Hill, *Churches in Cultural Captivity: A History of the Social Attitudes of Southern Baptists* (Knoxville: University of Tennessee Press, 1987).

[28] B.C. Hening, "The Separation of the Races," *Home and Foreign Fields* 7, no. 2 (1923): 29.

[29] Victor I. Masters, "The South's Human Problems," *Home and Foreign Fields* 2, no. 8 (1918): 15.

[30] G.S. Dobbins, "Race Prejudice," *Home and Foreign Fields* 13, no. 3 (1929): 17.

The dread of social equality is the source of greatest bitterness toward the Negro on the part of multitudes of white people. The thought of inter-marriage and consequent negroid progeny is utterly repugnant to any right-thinking white man. One has only to go to certain Latin-American countries where this has occurred to be convinced of the terrible disaster which is involved. The standards of both races are lowered, the purity of the racial stock is destroyed, and irreparable harm done to both peoples. No catastrophe to the human race could be quite comparable to the loss of racial integrity of the American white people.[31]

C.E. Maddry, corresponding secretary on the Foreign Mission Board who was resisted by a number of FMB missionaries in Brazil for his progressive disposition toward the locals—as I will show later—assured his audience that among Baptist missionaries in foreign fields, an ideology of racial purity was upheld. "Of course," he wrote, "there is no social intermingling or intermarriage between folk of different color. It is for the integrity of the white and brown and yellow and black and red races that the race stock should be kept pure."[32] When Southern Seminary luminaries William Carver and John Sampey went to Brazil, they immediately noticed the racial differences between Brazil and their country of origin. Sampey confessed that a Black man hugged him for the first time in a Brazilian Baptist church, which left him quite uneasy.[33] Carver, upon his arrival in Bahia, noticed that "when illiteracy is around 80 per cent and 80 per cent are of Negro and Mulatto blood, the problems are not few or easy."[34]

The underlying anxiety in Southern Baptist commitment to racial separation and its supporting ideologies was the superiority of the Anglo-Saxon race. Being Anglo-Saxon was, for a number of Southern Baptists, being simultaneously racially and culturally superior to other peoples. In missionary publications, the ideology of Anglo-Saxon superiority appeared

---

[31] Dobbins.

[32] Charles E. Maddry, "One Solvent for the Race Issue," *The Commission* 2, no. 10 (1939): 346.

[33] John R. Sampey, "The People of Brazil: Potentialities, Problems, and Needs of This Great Growing Nation," *Home and Foreign Fields* 10, no. 1 (1926): 12–13.

[34] William O. Carver, "Trailing Twentieth Century Apostles: From Rio to Pernambuco," *Home and Foreign Fields* 6, no. 12 (1922): 11.

in a number of contexts. African Americas, for instance, should be thankful for slavery's instrumentality in teaching Anglo-Saxon culture and for the fact that the African American "speaks the splendid and virile Anglo-Saxon as his native tongue."[35] The foreigners in the United States, on the other hand, threatened the Anglo-Saxon purity of US Southern culture. J.R. Jester argued that

> More than 5000 foreigners are now farmers in the South. In the past our cities have been kept afloat by the pure, virile blood from the country and through accessions from country churches religious work in the great centers has been kept going. With the settlement of foreigners in the country places this flow of Anglo-Saxon blood and Protestant religion to the cities will cease and "A blood peasantry—a country's pride—when once lost, can never be supplied."[36]

When missionaries wanted to highlight their appreciation for a particular people group, they sometimes called them their region's "Anglo-Saxons,"[37] and Anglo-Saxon domination of particular regions was taken by Southern Baptists as a step forward in the direction of progress and true Christianity.[38]

Southern racial convictions continued to inform the imagination of Southern Baptist missionaries in Brazil during the phase of the Radical Movement. Most times, these convictions were kept private and manifested themselves more structurally than individually, but when Brazilians were made aware of how these cultural sensibilities informed the opinion of FMB missionaries regarding their country, culture, and race, the consequences could be disastrous. The revolt of students and Brazilian faculty of the South Brazil Baptist Theological Seminary (SBBTS) that led to the resignation of Frank Purser, illustrates the tension that could result from

---

[35] O.L. Hailey, "Do the Negro Need Our Help?," *Home and Foreign Fields* 10, no. 4 (1926): 14.

[36] J.R. Jester, "The Challenge and Opportunity of Home Missions," *Home and Foreign Fields* 9, no. 7 (1925): 6–7.

[37] J.R. Saunders, "A New Mission to the Hak-Kas," *Home and Foreign Fields* 5, no. 3 (1921): 20–21; A.R. Gallimore, "The Hakkas, the Anglo-Saxons of China," *Home and Foreign Fields* 11, no. 4 (1927): 5–7.

[38] H.C. Wayman, "Palestine and the Near East as a Mission: Some Intensely Interesting First-Hand Observations and Conclusions," *Home and Foreign Fields* 6, no. 2 (1922): 10–12.

the public knowledge of the White supremacist ideology that dominated missionary imagination. Purser wrote a derogatory article to *Home and Foreign Fields* soon after he arrived in Brazil in 1923—which showed a form of the cultural shock that many missionaries went through. Breaking from the practice of not writing explicity damaging things about Brazilians in Southern Baptist periodicals, Purser wrote to *Home and Foreign Fields* that

> In the book "Brazilian Sketches," the author, Dr. T.B. Ray, says that the people who live in Brazil are the "descendants of the Caesars—of the race that ruled the world for fifteen centuries"—Yes—but the majority of the members of the Baptist churches in Rio de Janeiro are also descendants of a mixture of races, which includes a strong element of blood from the blackest of negroes. And many of them still have far to go up the ladder of civilization.[39]

In addition, Purser criticized Brazil for being a country of cynics and dirty people, and seminary students and local teachers, who had access to the article through a translation provided by the *Jornal do Rio*, threatened to leave the institution if Purser was not removed. In A.R. Crabtree's report to FMB secretary J.F. Love, he explained the issue partially in terms of the frankness of Americans—as opposed to the allegedly delicate and ceremonial spirit of Brazilians—and in terms of the malicious translation of the article by the *Jornal do Rio*, which framed Purser's comments in terms of racial and religious discrimination. In the same report, however, Crabtree stated that a committee compared the Portuguese and English versions and agreed that the translation was generally accurate.[40]

Purser resigned and was assigned to a different field so that Brazilians would not revolt further, but it is interesting to note that both Purser—due to his unguarded frankness in English—and Crabtree in his attempt to defend his missionary friend, essentialized Brazilianess and Americanness and gave the latter the higher moral ground. For both Purser and Crabtree, American honesty and morality was emphasized in contrast to

---

[39] Frank Purser, "Away From Theory, Up Against Facts," *Home and Foreign Fields* 7, no. 7 (1923): 15.

[40] From A.R. Crabtree to J.F. Love, September 15, 1923. The report sent to Love was twelve pages long and included information about several elements of the controversy.

Brazilian dishonesty and indirect style of communication.[41] Brazilians were "cynic and dirty" for Purser, and, in Crabtree's euphemistic explanation, they were just "more delicate and ceremonial"—and presumably not prone to express themselves in the ideal, frank style of the American South. Purser learned the hard way what other SBC missionaries already knew: that if racially charged sentiments were expected to be performed publicly by Whites in the South vis-à-vis the cultural pressures of a Jim Crow society,[42] they would not be easily tolerated among local Baptists in 1920s and 1930s Brazil.

The White supremacist dispositions of Southern Baptist missionaries, therefore, were central to the resistance they showed in giving more autonomy to their local cooperators. Although they denied being discriminatory repeatedly, the way in which Southern culture affected the denomination in the US and SBC missionaries abroad shows that when the Radical Movement appeared, racist distortions of superiority were intrinsic to White Southern ideological and practical commitments. The reaction against the racially-informed, dominating tendencies of SBC missionaries undergirds the Radical Movement and is most clearly demonstrated in a pamphlet that was being distributed in 1923 in Recife, capital of the state of Pernambuco and heart of the North Brazil Mission. W.C. Taylor, a leading missionary who was scandalized by the public advertisement of what he saw as a rabid anti-missionary sentiment, transcribed the full pamphlet and correctly framed it as a fair representation of the spirit of the Radical Movement:

> To the Public: The people should not mistake as evangelicals the group of Americans that want to start, in the Zumby neighborhood, a pseudo-Baptist church.
> Americans W.C. Taylor, E. Hayes, and L.L. Johnson were kicked out of the Baptist churches to which they were affiliated.
> They abused the proverbial hospitality of their Brazilian hosts and began to treat (local) Baptists as if they were slaves, and because these protested against this abuse of their liberty, they offered desperate resistance.

---

[41] From A.R. Crabtree to J.F. Love, September 15, 1923.

[42] James Cobb, *The Brown Decision, Jim Crow, and Southern Identity* (Athens: University of Georgia Press, 2005), 45–46.

They rebelled against the Regional Convention, legitimate representative of the Baptist churches in the states of Pernambuco, Paraiba, and Rio Grande do Norte; they followed an identical procedure toward the administrative boards of the American Baptist School and the Baptist seminary in this city because they were not allowed to fire three Brazilian professors of the institution of theological education. They closed the seminary building and left the administrative board and the students on the street.

… We need foreigners who will come to help us grow our beloved country, but whoever wants to de-nationalize us in order to dominate us will be resisted; let these Americans know that we do not sell ourselves.

To react against these false preachers of the Gospel, these nosy Americans, is not to react against evangelical religion, but it is a patriotic duty.

Unfortunately, there are Brazilians who are fooled and follow them, however, they will soon open their eyes and see what these individuals really want.[43]

Brazilian nationalism is clearly represented in the pamphlet, but it is a nationalism that reacted against a missionary disposition committed to Anglo-Saxon rule of Brazilian denominational activity. Sympathizers of the Radical Movement were not always aware of or willing to name the racist culture that informed the missionary drive for domination, but a Southern White who was not racist in the first decade of the twentieth century—foreign missionary or not—was an exception, and exceptions didn't hold institutional power in 1920s Brazil.

D.L. Hamilton, Local Leadership, and Radicalism

The specific, direct issues that led to the public phase of the Radical Movement began in 1918, when missionary D.L. Hamilton was in the United States caring for his wife, who had to leave Brazil in order to undergo surgery. Hamilton was Director of the Pernambuco Baptist College in Recife under the general leadership of H.H. Muirhead. During Hamilton's stay in the United States, however, Muirhead not only centralized the power over education initiatives in the northern region under his rule but

---

[43] "Ao Publico," *Correio Doutrinal* 1, no. 2 (1923): 18–19.

also made decisions—both as treasurer of the North Brazil Mission and as President of the educational institution—that irritated local pastors, students, and faculty. The specific issues surrounding Muirhead's decisions regarding the direction of the Pernambuco Baptist College and the NBBTS in Recife and Hamilton's positions vis-à-vis the missionary establishment in north Brazil reveal central aspects of the dynamics of Brazilian resistance against missionary domination. Hamilton was the only missionary who sided with the locals in the dispute, but, unlike missionaries told the FMB, Hamilton followed, rather than led, the revolt. The fact that Hamilton used his connections and skills in order to assist the Brazilians, therefore, does not reveal that the Radical Movement had its roots in Hamilton himself; rather, Hamilton's qualified resourcefulness and position in the movement is a manifestation of both his commitment to local autonomy and of Brazilian use of strategic friendships.

Although the relationship between Hamilton and the majority of the other missionaries was clearly damaged by Hamilton's stance after his return from the United States in 1919, the public and private antagonism between him and the missionary establishment characterized his whole missionary career. Over a decade before the public phase of the Radical Movement broke out, Hamilton complained often to his mother about a number of missionaries who he thought were unprepared, opportunistic, and power-hungry.[44] Trusting in his mother's discretion, Hamilton confessed less than one year after his arrival in Brazil that

> Our school has been running two weeks. With the exception of some awfully bad management on the part of missionaries, I am pleased with prospects. But a part of the original charge here must be changes; and while it will come like drawing teeth to some missionaries, I am determined on the change. I want this to be private. But there are missionaries here, who I suppose never made any money at home, who take advantage of the liberality of the Mission Board to live better than they ever did at home. In fact, I firmly believe there are missionaries here who came because they were not

---

[44] Hamilton's personal correspondence was made available to me by Marconi Monteiro. These letters were not found in the archives of the International Mission Board, and Monteiro got them from family members in Recife during his own master's thesis research on the Radical Movement.

capable of commanding a decent job at home.[45]

Hamilton faced some resistance from fellow missionaries but passed financial regulations that would provide more efficiency for the mission in general. When he was contemplating leaving the state of Bahia for Pernambuco because of his constant conflicts with Mrs. Taylor, Z.C. Taylor's second wife, he wondered if his efforts to get the mission in the state of Bahia out of debt would be upheld.[46] Hamilton did not appear to hold the competency and character of his fellow missionaries in high regard. He was discreet and kept many of his opinions private, but he often confessed to family members his frustrations. "It is not well for everybody to know this," he wrote his mother, "but it is a fact that foreign missionaries have no wings. Some have the same inordinate ambitions that cripple the usefulness of so many good preachers at home."[47]

Hamilton also clashed with missionaries soon after the Brazilian Baptist Convention was created. He was disappointed in missionaries in the South of Brazil because they tried to monopolize theological education in the Southern part of the country and used questionable methods to undermine Hamilton's theological school in north Brazil and the seminary in Pernambuco. He wrote in 1908:

> For about 7 years there was seminary work carried on in Pernambuco....They discontinued the work and moved to Rio de Janeiro, the capital of the Republic. Not only this but they tried to take my students. I was surprised at the methods used. I told my boys they could do as they pleased, that I never came to Brazil to compete with politicians, that I had done such things many times and had never lost a battle, but that in the name of religion I absolutely refused. Notwithstanding the crowd in the South offered more money as support than I was paying, the boys absolutely refused to go. It was even hinted that they should have my allowance cut off, and that they (the students) would be left without support. They replied that they would stay with me and work their way.[48]

Hamilton, who had been president of Liberty Herman and Business

---

[45] From D.L. Hamilton to Lydia Hamilton, February 17, 1906.

[46] From D.L. Hamilton to Lydia Hamilton, January 24, 1908.

[47] From D.L. Hamilton to Lydia Hamilton, January 24, 1908.

[48] From D.L. Hamilton to Lydia Hamilton, January 24, 1908.

College and Superintendent of Education of Williamson County when he
was in Texas, was convinced that most of his fellow missionaries were utterly incompetent to lead theological education, and called their decisions
"school boy absurdities."[49] Hamilton also told his mother that he operated
differently from other missionaries in ministerial leadership strategies.
While other missionaries worked in order to embellish their missionary
reports, even if that meant sidelining local leaders, Hamilton opened space
for Brazilian visibility and agency.[50] Hamilton also witnessed a number of
splits in churches and denominational schools that he attributed to missionary leadership,[51] and these issues gave him the impression that he
would have a hard time getting along with his fellow workers. He wrote
W.H. Smith over a decade before his public antagonism against the missionary establishment and confessed: "I love all the missionaries here, but
cannot work conscientiously and in peace with one. We do not agree, and
never will, and it seems impossible for me to have my work to myself."[52]
The troubles between locals and missionaries abound in Hamilton's correspondence and he often emphasized the need to allow locals a greater
level of freedom in order avoid a schism between Brazilians and missionaries.[53] This stance of course informed Hamilton's turbulent relationship
with his fellow missionaries to an extent that Hamilton never seemed satisfied in his field of work. Soon after he arrived in Bahia, he wanted to
leave for Pernambuco, and after a few years in Pernambuco, he wanted to
go to Pará. In 1918, referring to his relationship with missionaries in Pernambuco and the reason he wanted to leave, Hamilton wrote T.B. Ray
saying: "I like them, and they tolerate me. But we do not always agree."[54]

Hamilton, however, not unlike most of his fellow Southern Baptist
missionaries, was inhabited by the prejudices of the Jim Crow South. As a
White son of the South, Hamilton imagined sharp differences between
races. He highlighted what he saw as the ignorance of mixed-race locals,
pointed out the unsophistication of Afro-Brazilians, showed more interest

---

[49] From D.L. Hamilton to Lydia Hamilton, January 24, 1908.
[50] From D.L. Hamilton to Lydia Hamilton, January 24, 1908.
[51] From D.L. Hamilton to W.M. Smith, September 6, 1907.
[52] From D.L. Hamilton to W.M. Smith, September 16, 1907.
[53] From D.L. Hamilton to T.B. Ray, July 6, 1914; From D.L. Hamilton to T.B.
Ray, March 24, 1915.
[54] From D.L. Hamilton to T.B. Ray, September 21, 1918.

in evangelizing and recruiting White Brazilians, and even praised his children when they reenacted White supremacist sensibilities.[55] At the same time, Hamilton often clashed with his fellow missionaries in favor of local interests and concerns. In 1921, for example, he was intentional about taking action against a male missionary who was involved in an inappropriate relationship with a local woman. On this particular matter, once again, it was Hamilton versus the missionary establishment:

> One of our missionaries recently got into trouble about women, and the natives involved called on me to stand by them in the investigation. It was a very delicate undertaking. All the other missionaries were against me. So it turned out that I was on one side with all the natives, and all the missionaries, practically all, were on the other side with the offender. Every effort was made to cover up the matter, but I was armed with documents of which they knew nothing. So I forced them to uncover the thing.[56]

The missionary in question left his field—although he was later reassigned to the same field—and the missionaries in general were thoroughly disappointed in Hamilton, who did not allow them to cover up the incident. From the very beginning of his work in Brazil, therefore, Hamilton was the thorn in the crown of the missionary establishment and his confrontation with fellow workers included a number of issues such as local autonomy, educational strategies, handling of sexual misconduct, and administrative disputes.

Because of his identification with local issues and concerns, Hamilton was a favorite of Brazilian leaders in north Brazil. He was considered a patron of theological education in north Brazil, educated a number of leaders in the region, and was trusted by Brazilian leaders in north Brazil to an

---

[55] The letters Hamilton sent his family and the Foreign Mission Board are full of his impressions about Brazilian society and culture. In his correspondence, it is clear that Hamilton favors White Brazilians over non-Whites. For some examples see: From D.L. Hamilton to Lydia Hamilton, December 20, 1905; From D.L. Hamilton to Fuller Hamilton, January 14, 1906; From D.L. Hamilton to Lydia Hamilton, December 15, 1906; From D.L. Hamilton to Lydia Hamilton, August 16, 1909; From D.L. Hamilton to the FMB, August 20, 1906; From D.L. Hamilton to R.J. Willingham, December 7, 1912; From D.L. Hamilton to T.B. Ray, December 26, 1913; and From D.L. Hamilton to T.B. Ray, December 19, 1919.

[56] From D.L. Hamilton to Lydia Hamilton, July 3, 1921.

extent that other missionaries were not. In the midst of the regional phase
of the Radical Movement dispute, João Jorge de Oliveira, then missionary
to Portugal, wrote a tribute to Hamilton for an English-speaking audience
saying that

> Rev. D.L. Hamilton in North Brazil has the esteem and devout love
> and unlimited confidence of native preachers and churches. We
> have heard him called the "kind old man," the "man that loves us,"
> and the "man we love." The esteem and consideration Brother
> Hamilton has in all North Brazil is due to his sacrifice on behalf of
> Brazilians and his great devotion to Brazilians. He would be always
> ready to give counsel, go anywhere, or make a true sacrifice in behalf
> of white and black. As a missionary he felt that the Lord called him
> to Brazil to give his life to the Lord on behalf of Brazilians.[57]

Oliveira was a personal friend of Hamilton, and was aware of what
was happening in northern Brazil. When he went to Brazil for the annual
meeting of the Brazilian Baptist Convention in 1922, he stayed in Hamilton's home, and Hamilton often talked about him to his mother in his
personal correspondence.[58]

Hamilton seems to be the missionary who was most deeply affected
by Brazilian poverty and by issues central to local Baptists. In turn, local
Baptists in northern Brazil fostered an uncommon personal bond with
him. Hamilton, however, seemed to be puzzled by what he perceived as
the special regard Brazilian Baptists had for him. "I cannot tell why" he
wrote, "but when these people have any difficulty or disappointment, they
bring their troubles to me. And of course I do all for them I possibly can."
He continued to say that J.F. Love, when he visited Brazil, asked him "why
it was that I had more friends among locals than any other missionary."[59]
Hamilton confessed that this was a source of tension between other missionaries and himself. According to Hamilton, Brazilians told him that it
was precisely his identification with locals that gave him a special place
among them. "I really do not know why these conditions exist," he wrote
in 1923, "but they do exist. I have never courted the people, but I have

---

[57] John J. Oliveira, "The Fruits of Wisdom and Sacrifice," *Home and Foreign Fields* 8, no. 1 (1924): 9.
[58] From D.L. Hamilton to Lydia Hamilton, June 3, 1922.
[59] From D.L. Hamilton to Lydia Hamilton, December 1, 1922.

tried to treat them right, that and nothing more. Their version of the matter is that they want a missionary who will weep with those that weep and rejoice with those that rejoice."[60]

Despite Hamilton's consistent and long-lasting reservations regarding the competence and character of his fellow missionaries, the missionaries who worked with Hamilton praised his teaching abilities before the Radical Movement. H.H. Muirhead, who would be one of Hamilton's archrivals in the controversy, wrote to FMB corresponding secretary R.J. Willingham in 1909 saying that Hamilton was a better teacher than Muirhead himself.[61] Appreciation for Hamilton on the part of other missionaries, however, diminished as time progressed. When the cablegram sent by W.C. Taylor to H.H. Muirhead on November 11, 1922, while the latter was in Fort Worth pursuing a doctorate degree, arrived, Hamilton was already perceived as an adversary, and local leaders were perceived as auxiliaries in a Hamilton-inspired plan. The cablegram said: "Grave antimissionary movement led by Orlando, Bernardo, Mesquita. Hamilton pastors refuse salaries from Mission. Systematic campaign begun by pastors throughout Brazil. Hamilton aborting. All other missionaries a unit."[62] A few months later Muirhead would write to Willingham's successor, T.B. Ray, to say that the root cause of the Radical Movement was Hamilton and he had to be removed from the mission.[63] Muirhead's wife, Alyna, was even more explicit in a letter she sent to J.F. Love. She said:

> That case in Pernambuco is just like an extreme case of appendicitis. The pus is Hamilton, the doctors to operate are our brethren of the FMB. The doctors can operate or they can fail but I believe the results would be terrible if they failed to cut out the pus.[64]

But Hamilton was not the only concern. By the later phase of the movement, missionaries were also frustrated with highly educated Brazilian Baptists such as Orlando Falcão, Adrião Bernardes, and Antonio Mesquita—all graduates of SBC schools in the US. After hearing the missionary establishment's version of the story, T.B. Ray confessed to Muirhead

[60] From D.L. Hamilton to Lydia Hamilton, January 9, 1923.
[61] From H.H. Muirhead to R.J. Willingham, July, 31, 1909.
[62] From W.C. Talyor to H.H. Muirhead, November 11, 1922.
[63] From H.H. Muirhead to T.B. Ray, March 17, 1923.
[64] From Alyna Muirhead to J.F. Love, April 3, 1923.

that "If I had my way about it, I never would encourage a single one of them to come to the United States for education. ... The American trained ones ninety-nine times out of a hundred gives us trouble."[65] The presence of well-trained and well-connected leaders was crucial for the success of the Radical Movement. The SBC leaders knew it and, after the movement, deliberately undermined such training and connections until they regained the stable control of the denomination.

Strong, foreign-trained local leaders such as Adrião Bernardes, Orlando Falcão, and Antonio Mesquita gave the movement moral and ideological support.[66] These Brazilian leaders were strongly praised by missionaries when they were perceived as faithful followers of missionary strategy. Missionaries who worked with Bernardes offered profuse public praise for his role in pre-Radical Movement Brazilian denominational life. M.G. White saw in Bernardes the makings of a great editor and denominational leader when Bernardes edited the regional periodical *A Mensagem*.[67] His preaching was widely celebrated and praised by W.C. Taylor.[68] When his role leading the Brazilian arm of the seventy-five million dollar campaign was highlighted, Solomon Ginsburg called him "one of the most eloquent and able" local leaders.[69] Missionary John Mein named Bernardes "our foremost Brazilian evangelist."[70] Pauline White saw him as an indispensable factor in the revival of north Brazil.[71] H.H. Muirhead not only agreed

---

[65] From T.B. Ray to H.H. Muirhead, June 26, 1931.

[66] It must be noted that, although missionaries often misspelled Portuguese names and words, there are considerable variations in the ways in which the names of Bernardes and Falcão appear in missionary correspondence and literature. Bernardes is often reffered to as "Bernardo," and Falcão appears as "Falcon" and "Falcoa" several times.

[67] M.G. White, "Notes of Interest from Brazil," *Home and Foreign Fields* 4, no. 1 (1920): 27; M.G. White, "In and Around Bahia, Brazil," *Home and Foreign Fields* 4, no. 5 (1920): 32.

[68] W.C. Taylor, "Missionary Notes," *Home and Foreign Fields* 1, no. 12 (1917): 19.

[69] Solomon L. Ginsburg, "Is Catholicism Loosing Its Hold?," *Home and Foreign Fields* 6, no. I (1922): 9.

[70] John Mein, "Beating the Catholics at Their Own Game," *Home and Foreign Fields* 7, no. I (1923): 17.

[71] Pauline White, "The Campaign in North Brazil," *Home and Foreign Fields* 4, no. 4 (1920): 30.

with Mein that Bernardes was Brazil's greatest evangelist but was also proud to emphasize that he was a product of the institution that Muirhead himself presided, the Baptist College in Pernambuco.[72] Antonio Mesquita and Orlando Falcão were also celebrated,[73] and both Bernardes and Mesquita authored pieces featured in *Home and Foreign Fields*.[74] Generally speaking, despite the fact that missionaries understood Brazilians who opposed missionary domination as "Hamilton pastors," it was actually Hamilton who was a locals' missionary.

H.H. Muirhead was aware of the delicate balance of the denomination in Brazil well before the public phase of the controversy, and, when his intentions coincided with that of the locals, he highlighted Brazilian competence. In 1918, he wrote to T.B. Ray saying that

> The Board must not overlook the fact that they are not dealing with an ignorant and heathen people. The native leadership here, especially in the North, is composed of leading businessmen and strong pastors—men whose position and ability would make them leaders in any country. They could occupy with dignity a place on any of the boards of the Southern Baptist Convention. These men have been patient and fully appreciate the cooperation of the Foreign Board, but of late were growing skeptical and impatient. They are not revolutionists. They are simply Baptists of the New Testament quality and know what democracy and autonomy are.[75]

His appreciation for Brazilian capacity, however, was still paired with an apparent obsession for missionary control. In the following year, he

---

[72] H.H Muirhead, "The Pernambuco College as an Evangelizing Agency," *Home and Foreign Fields* 5, no. 9 (1921): 15.

[73] "Progress in Pernambuco," *Home and Foreign Fields* 4, no. 3 (1920): 30; White, "The Campaign in North Brazil"; "Missionary Miscellany," *Home and Foreign Fields* 6, no. 9 (1922): 34–35; T. B. Ray, "Missionary Miscellany," *Home and Foreign Fields* 10, no. 7 (1926): 38–39.

[74] Adrião Bernardo, "Bibles! Bibles! Give Us Bibles!," *Home and Foreign Fields* 4, no. 7 (1920): 30; Anônio Neves de Mesquita, "How the Rua Imperial Baptist Church Built Its New House of Worship," *Home and Foreign Fields* 5, no. 9 (1921): 17.

[75] From H.H. Muirhead to T.B. Ray, December (illegible), 1918.

complained several times about the incompetence of local teachers and insisted that the Board send him United States personnel to be teachers and deans of denominational schools and seminaries.[76]

In 1918, when Hamilton was still in the United States, locals began to write him about the growing divide between locals and missionaries in the field. This was not, of course, the first time Brazilians and missionaries disagreed, but now the disagreements would grow consistently and eventually result in the creation of an alternative national denominational body. Hamilton wrote T.B. Ray, saying that locals were upset because they found out that funds sent to the North Brazil Mission for evangelization were not invested for evangelization purposes, and because of these perceived irregularities, Brazilians wanted to administer the work themselves. Hamilton thought that the opinion of other missionaries in the field, who were convinced that local resolve would die down, was mistaken, and he counseled Ray to allow Brazilians to manage their evangelization work.[77] A central complaint of Brazilian pastors was that they were being disrespected by missionaries who managed field evangelization. Locals were many times recruited by missionaries to do evangelization work and they understandably got frustrated when their salaries dropped without apparent reason or appropriate warning.[78] Hamilton saw no reason to be alarmed if the situation was addressed appropriately. He wrote: "I know all parties involved, and all are reasonable; there is no motive I can see why the matter should give any trouble. If the missionary brethren will just handle the affair conservatively, the native brethren can be controlled; but if they alienate them, it may really give some trouble."[79]

When Hamilton arrived back in Brazil on December 14, 1919, from a furlough in the US, other aspects of the Brazilian/missionary tension became clear to him. Hamilton noticed that Brazilians were thoroughly

---

[76] From H.H. Muirhead to T.B. Ray, June 3, 1919; and to T.B. Ray, December 12, 1919.

[77] From D.L. Hamilton to T.B. Ray, June 27, 1918.

[78] From D.L. Hamilton to T.B. Ray, June 27, 1918.

[79] From D.L. Hamilton to T.B. Ray, June 27, 1918.

disappointed in Muirhead's tenure as treasurer of the mission,[80] they were uneasy about the role of Alfredo Freyre in the seminary and college—who locals thought was a non-believer and who was accused of consistently inappropriate behavior toward female students,[81] and locals were calling a number of Brazilian-only meetings in order to address their reservations in regard to missionary leadership.[82] Hamilton wrote J.F. Love a little over three months after arriving in Brazil, urging him to go to the country in order to avoid a schism. Then, Hamilton made clear to Love that he was still investigating matters and did not want to ascribe blame, but he was convinced of the gravity of the situation. He wrote: "There is a question at present troubling our Baptist ranks in this immediate field which, if not settled, and that probably soon, will create a breach. I do not pretend to say who is to blame, but I realize the urgent necessity of a speedy settlement."[83] From then on, Hamilton warned the FMB several times of the growing divide and made clear that he was neither aware of all the things that upset the locals nor an insider to their plans. During his first months back from the US, Hamilton saw himself as someone who was trying to hold things together until the FMB could investigate the issue and see for themselves that the locals had legitimate concerns that the FMB needed to address.[84]

The relationship between Hamilton and other missionaries was progressively worsened by Hamilton's qualified mediation of local concerns with the FMB—which he did mostly as an individual and not as a representative of local organizations. Hamilton revealed a number of perceived irregularities in Muirhead's administration, in Taylor's leadership style and demeanor toward Brazilians, and in White's inability to cooperate with locals to locals' satisfaction. From 1920 until his resignation, Hamilton asked fellow missionaries in Brazil and the FMB for an impartial committee to conduct an investigation on Hamilton himself in order to clarify that he was correct and, in turn, that the most influential missionaries in north Brazil were incompetent at best and malicious at worst. It soon became

---

[80] From D.L. Hamilton to T.B. Ray, January 12, 1920.
[81] From D.L. Hamilton to J.F. Love, March 26, 1920.
[82] From D.L. Hamilton to T.B. Ray, February 7, 1920.
[83] From D.L. Hamilton to J.F. Love, March 26, 1920.
[84] From D.L. Hamilton to J.F. Love, March 29, 1920.

clear to Hamilton that he needed to take an explicit side on the Brazilian/missionary divide. Hamilton sided with the locals, against the North Brazil Mission, and eventually against the missionary establishment despite the practical complications that such a stance would encourage.[85]

Siding with the Brazilians meant, for Hamilton, becoming an advocate for Brazilian administration of evangelistic funds, defending local honor vis-à-vis missionary charges of Brazilian financial immorality, becoming involved in the Brazilian plan of building an orphanage,[86] and advocating for changes in local educational institutions. In all of these issues he would face opposition from his fellow missionaries, especially H.H. Muirhead and W.C. Taylor. Regarding the handling of money, Hamilton wrote T.B. Ray:

> A large majority of the native pastors are dissatisfied with his [Muirhead's] administration in everything. The charges which they make against him and which he makes against them are not at all assuring. There is no dodging the issue. Conditions are not good. Some of the best native pastors we have say he uses the money which passes through his hands as means to dominate them. They also affirm that he dispenses favors on those who make themselves subject to his bidding. I do not mean that all make this charge, but a good number do.[87]

Hamilton did not believe in the missionary argument that Brazilians who

---

[85] From T.B. Ray to D.L. Hamilton, July 28, 1920.

[86] In the early 1920s, before the Radical Movement broke out, Hamilton was fully engaged in building an orphanage before he could retire. As a matter of fact, his correspondence suggests that building an orphanage became an obsession for him. Since 1920, he was constantly pressured by his family to retire in the United States, but he kept on affirming that he could not return until an orphanage was built. His commitment to building the orphanage came out of his experience with infant poverty and infant prostitution in northern Brazil. As he organized locals to build an "Orphanage League" in order to raise money for the orphanage, he changed his previous focus from theological education to preaching and evangelizing. Hamilton's plan to build an orphanage, however, was resisted by his fellow missionaries. The opposing missionaries, however, eventually conceded and the Brazilian Baptist Convention of 1921 approved the plan to build the orphanage. This created some tension between Hamilton and the FMB, once Hamilton defied the Board's directive that prohibited missionaries to raise funds for initiatives of poverty alleviation.

[87] From D.L. Hamilton to T.B. Ray, July 14, 1920.

made these charges were themselves seeking bribes. As time progressed, Muirhead used his position as treasurer to make things increasingly difficult for Hamilton, who was elected Corresponding Secretary of the local evangelistic association by Brazilian pastors. This situation increased the unrest between Brazilian pastors and the North Brazil Mission. Brazilians began considering taking funds from educational initiatives to support evangelistic work in January of 1921. Hamilton promised he would try to fix things and pleaded with them not to change their disposition regarding educational work.[88] As the unrest increased, so did Hamilton's warnings of an imminent schism:

> Now suppose a separation should come, would we not feel that a mistake had been made somewhere? Prevention is the only safe cure for these troubles. And they can be prevented. But they cannot be by trying to force these people into conformity with a regime that in no way coincides with their ideas of justice and Christian ethics. And that is exactly what they believe is being done.[89]

Hamilton also believed this to be a matter of justice, as he wrote a few days later again to T.B. Ray:

> While in the States, long before I knew at all about the original split, I wrote you, if my memory serves me right, that in case of encountering a division upon my return I would go with the native pastors. This was my opinion in advance, because I know these men intimately, and have great confidence in them. I do not mean I have no confidence in my colleagues, but I mean I prefer to confide in the judgment of the native pastors. I have never seen the least particle of excuse for a conflict with them.[90]

In 1921, Hamilton began pressuring the FMB to intervene in Brazil by saying that if Southern Baptist donors knew of the irregularities in the field, they would not approve of the course taken by other missionaries in general and Muirhead in particular.[91] In addition, his confrontation with other missionaries began to go beyond amicable language, and a number

---

[88] From D.L. Hamilton to T.B. Ray, January 5, 1921.
[89] From D.L. Hamilton to T.B. Ray, February 3, 1921.
[90] From D.L. Hamilton to T.B. Ray, February 20, 1921.
[91] From D.L. Hamilton to T.B. Ray, April 2, 1921.

of insults were exchanged between Hamilton and other missionaries, particularly W.C. Taylor. As the exchanges became more heated, missionaries threatened Hamilton with the tarnishing of his future as a missionary, and Hamilton doubled-down on his conviction that he was captive to his conscience and that his conscience was in turn captive to the motives behind local dissent. During the months before the division became clear to all, the FMB did not investigate the issues about which Hamilton complained repeatedly despite his constant requests for an investigation by an impartial committee. Despite the fact that J.F. Love met with Brazilian leaders when he visited Brazil in 1921, the success of his qualified intervention was short-lived. Field missionaries were adamant about not giving locals the autonomy they desired, and Brazilians had their minds set on obtaining unprecedented levels of autonomy.

On October 28, 1922, the missionaries of the North Brazil Mission received a letter from fifteen Brazilian ministers in the state of Pernambuco that would push forward the movement that split the Brazilian Baptist Convention for over a decade. The letter entitled *Memorial dos Pastores Baptistas do Campo Regional aos Missionários Baptistas da Região* (Memorial from the Baptist Pastors of the Regional Field to the Baptist Missionaries of the Region) was the immediate cause for the rupture between the North Brazil missionaries and several Brazilian Baptist pastors in the region. The letter read:

> The Baptist pastors of this region called a meeting to deal with the evangelistic interests of the regional field. These ministers, as servants of the churches—keepers of and responsible for the proclamation of the Gospel—are vitally interested in such evangelization. Therefore, they decided unanimously to present with brotherly affection to the missionary brethren who are collaborators in the same work, the following:
> Considering the great opportunities for evangelization that the field is offering, especially in the large region of the interior of the states;
> Considering that such opportunities are being neglected, especially in the countryside, for lack of an appropriate leadership and as a result of poor planning;
> Considering the urgent need for a greater, friendlier, more intelligent, and impartial cooperation which could result in the use of all resources and efforts;
> Considering, finally, that centralizing the leadership—as it has

clearly been the tendency—of the primary phase of the Baptist work on the missionaries is not productive, rather, it has damaged a balanced distribution of responsibilities;

These ministers suggest:

That the leadership of the evangelistic work be an exclusive responsibility of the Regional Board;

That the funds contributed by the churches as well as those sent by the Richmond Board for evangelism, pastoral support, travel, etc... be administered by the same Board;

That, responding to the "Great Commission," which places a prominent emphasis on the evangelization of the world, in the appropriation requests sent to the Board of Richmond for North Brazil, the evangelization cause in this region receive a fair proportion as compared to the education cause;

That this present memorial be presented to the next Regional Convention for consideration.[92]

The main concerns expressed by the Brazilian leadership of the Regional Convention were strategic and administrative. Brazilian leaders wanted a stronger emphasis on evangelism, rather than education, and they wanted to have more control of the administration of funds in order to ensure that evangelism was prioritized. In order to fulfill their goals, however, local leaders were aware that denominational power had to be shifted from the hand of missionaries to that of locals and that a transition of power was necessary so that the "urgent need for a greater, friendlier, more intelligent, and impartial cooperation" could be achieved.

The missionaries responded quickly and decisively, not only demonstrating clearly their unwillingness to consider the locals' requests, but also pointing out what they saw as the inconsistency of Brazilians, who had denied a similar request from Portuguese Baptists who wanted also more independence from the Brazilian-controlled mission in Portugal.[93] They failed to mention, however, that Brazilian Baptist activity in Portugal was not only informed by FMB influence, but was also a manifestation of Bra-

---

[92] "Memorial Dos Pastores Baptistas Do Campo Regional Aos Missionários Baptistsas Da Região," *Correio Doutrinal* 1, no. 2 (1923): 9–10.

[93] "Aos Pastores Baptistas Do Campo Regional," *Correio Doutrinal* 1, no. 2 (1923): 10–11.

zilian internalization of imported missionary methods. In addition, a number of missionaries already had given Baptists of north Brazil the amount of autonomy they were willing to give. W.C. Taylor, for instance, pointed out that the great majority of pastors in the region were Brazilians, not missionaries, as evidence of the missionary willingness to support local autonomy.[94] Missionary conceptualizations of denominational cooperation abroad, however, were not set on the role of missionary pastoral activity. M.G. White, a missionary in Bahia, shed light on the competing conceptualizations of missionary leadership abroad. He highlighted four theories of self-support that were held by active missionaries: (1) major churches should have missionaries as pastors and such missionaries should have veto power over the deliberations of local pastors of smaller churches; (2) the missionary of a given field is the official pastor of all churches, and local pastors are his assistants; (3) the missionary is not a pastor of a church, but the superintendent of the field and has veto power over Brazilian decisions; and (4) the missionary is a helper and advisor of locals and offers suggestions based on his superior preparation and experience.[95] There were, therefore, different conceptualizations of ideal Brazilian autonomy among missionaries that ranged from more to less explicit forms of domination. Two things problematized the practical implementation of the idea held by supporters of the theory of missions that saw the missionary as "helper and advisor, " such as White. First, as White himself later wrote on a report to the FMB, such a stance was contingent upon missionary perceptions regarding the maturity of locals,[96] and leading missionaries in North Brazil thought of the Brazilian denomination in general as an adolescent denomination.[97] Second, as the history of the Radical Movement shows, when significant missionary suggestions were not well received, missionaries generally implemented them regardless. After the missionary response, the gap between two factions—the radicals, who wanted local autonomy, and the constructives, who resisted the initiatives of the Radical

---

[94] W.C. Taylor, "Amostra Da Propaganda Radical," *Correio Doutrinal* 1 (1923): 5.

[95] M.G. White, "The Dawning of a New Era in South American Missions," *Home and Foreign Fields* 1, no. 11 (1917): 7.

[96] M.G. White, "North Brazil Mission," in *Seventy-Sixth Annual Report of the Foreign Mission Board*, 1921, 245.

[97] S.L. Watson, "Baptist Progress and Opportunity in South Brazil," *Home and Foreign Fields* 9, no. 6 (1925): 24–25.

Movement—would widen until they no longer saw themselves as "collaborators in the same work."

The Widening of the Radical-Constructive Gap

When the fifteen Brazilian leaders who signed the 1922 "Memorial from the Baptist Pastors" met to produce the document, the accumulated frustrations of missionary domination, unmet nationalistic anxieties, perceived mistreatment of Brazilian-favorite D.L. Hamilton,[98] and differences regarding the future of the work took strategic and symbolic form. After lively discussion, the pastors sent the missionaries the document,[99] and although the missionaries denied the locals' requests, the Regional Convention approved the plan they had suggested to the missionaries. Because the locals had no support from the Mission, this only widened the gap between the two factions. When the local Baptists decided to appeal to the FMB in Richmond, they received a response that made clear the FMB's support of the missionaries. The response insisted on a proportionality criterion in the boards of the Brazilian Baptist institutions in which the missionaries should outnumber the Brazilians.[100]

The letter, signed on February 8, 1923, warned against post-war "unnatural and anti-Christian racial pride that would put a stop to the missionary work that we are doing,"[101] but it did recognize explicitly that the administration of the Board's resources should serve missionary interests and the interests "of the freedom of our people here [in the southern

---

[98] D.L. Hamilton was the most respected missionary among those who came to be identified with the Radical Movement. He was the only missionary to stay on the radicals' side. Hamilton had been demoted from his position in the NBBTS in 1920, and, ever since, most locals thought that the other missionaries had done an injustice to Hamilton.

[99] Mesquita, *Historia Dos Baptistas Em Pernambuco*, 216-17; Martins, "O Radicalismo Batista Brasileiro," 23. The original documment is not easily available. Mesquita, who wrote eight years after the event, reproduced the document in its entirety. Martins had access to the document through the personal collection of denominational leader Antônio Simões, and his extended quotation of the document matches Mesquita's version, despite Martins' updating of the language to contemporary Portuguese.

[100] "Resposta Da Junta de Richmond a Junta Regional," *Correio Doutrinal* 1, no. 2 (1923): 12; 15; 17–18.

[101] "Resposta Da Junta de Richmond a Junta Regional," 12.

US]."[102] At the same time, the FMB's response acknowledged that missionaries had written damaging things about Brazilians that were published in American periodicals, and they assured Brazilians that the FMB condemned such actions insofar as they were maliciously written, which they did not think was often the case.[103] The plausibility of such claims, however, is challenged by the continuous White supremacist sensibilities showcased in the missionary publications of the Southern Baptist Convention. On the other hand, for White missionaries and Southern missionary agencies, White supremacy wasn't malice; it was a way of life!

When the Board answered directly the concerns of Brazilians, they reaffirmed the position espoused by missionaries, saying Americans were better prepared to lead, that the funds had to be used efficiently according to American standards, and that the proportion of Brazilian leadership should match the proportion of their financial contribution.[104] The answer was consistent with the North Brazil Mission's decision of creating a new position of Missionary to the Field when the first Brazilian Corresponding Secretary of the Regional Convention—Baylor University graduate Adrião Bernardes—was elected to the position. The Corresponding Secretary was historically the person who managed the evangelization efforts in the North Brazil region, but when a local was elected, the Mission created an overlapping position in order to continue to control evangelistic strategies. The response to the FMB letter and the attitude of the Mission, which missionaries took to be conciliatory, was the expulsion of several missionaries from churches and the disciplining of several others by their local pastors—which led missionaries to start pro-missionary churches. What was once implicit in missionary practice in Brazil became explicit, as missionaries began effectively threatening locals with the withholding of funds in case they cooperated with Brazilian-controlled rather than missionary-controlled institutions. Missionaries began charging local critics of being mercenaries, and absolute loyalty to the North Brazil Mission became the litmus test for missionary assistance. Hamilton, on the other hand, thought that the notion of framing radicals as "local mercenaries" was absurd. He wrote:

---

[102] "Resposta Da Junta de Richmond a Junta Regional," 15.
[103] "Resposta Da Junta de Richmond a Junta Regional," 15.
[104] "Resposta Da Junta de Richmond a Junta Regional," 17–18.

It is unthinkable that these pastors and deacons, and even laymen, want to wrong us in any way. They have always received us with open arms. They are the product of our work during the last thirty years. They are representative preachers of the Gospel, worthy deacons and faithful laymen. The sacrifices they made, financially and otherwise, put us to shame as to our own efforts and fill us with hope for the future of this country. Who then could imagine they had mercenary designs upon our money? I contend that if we had tried as we ought to have done at the proper time we could have established a plan of cooperation safe and sound, practical and Biblical, that would have entirely satisfied every desire of the natives.[105]

The absurdity of missionary charges against locals was, for Hamilton, evident in missionary inconsistency of administrative practices. "Now it is true the Cor. Sec.," Hamilton wrote, "when he was a missionary selected by the Mission, handled all the funds for general evangelization, both the part contributed by the local churches and the part appropriated by the Mission. But when a local was chosen it was declared he wanted to take foreign money and administer it."[106] Rather than doubting the character of the locals, Hamilton suggested that the accounts of the Mission should be audited in order to account for the Mission's mishandlings.[107] When Hamilton went to the US on furlough in 1923, T.B. Ray wrote him a personal letter, asking him to resign.[108] After months of Hamilton's continuous pleads for investigations and audits that remained unanswered to his satisfaction, Hamilton decided to resign, and his resignation went into effect in April of 1924.

Between 1923 and 1925, the antagonism between locals and missionaries grew and the conflict strengthened. This led to further expulsions of missionaries from churches, the planting of new pro-missionary churches, the founding of an alternative theological seminary, the creation of an alternative regional convention, and the establishment of new partisan periodicals.[109] The FMB missionaries did not want to negotiate further with

---

[105] From D.L. Hamilton to J.F. Love, February 17, 1923.
[106] From D.L. Hamilton to T.B. Ray, February 21, 1923.
[107] From D.L. Hamilton to T.B. Ray, February 21, 1923.
[108] From T.B. Ray to D.L. Hamilton, June 20, 1923.
[109] The best treatments of these developments are Martins, "O Radicalismo Batista Brasileiro"; Monteiro, "Radicalism in Pernambuco: A Study of the Relationship between Nationals and Southern Baptist Missionaries in the Brazilian

the Brazilians because they thought the locals' initiative would die anyway
for lack of financial support. The locals, however, were firm in their conviction that "money will not buy us, even because money is not our objective."[110] When the Brazilian National Convention met on January 19th of
1925, the field in the Pernambuco mission was divided between missionaries, with their respective churches, publications, convention, and seminary, and locals, who had their own institutions as well as one retired missionary on their side: D.L. Hamilton.

Despite its multifaceted manifestations, the struggle for the Brazilian
Baptist soul in the 1920s also became a fight for the correct interpretation
of authentic Baptist belief and practice. The pro-missionary side of the
struggle counted with their new periodical, the *Correio Doutrinal*, in order
to disseminate its anti-radical propaganda. The *Correio Doutrinal* was
founded in 1923 and its editor, W.C. Taylor, was invested in the aggressive condemnation of the Radical Movement. One of the main ways in
which the pro-missionary establishment attempted to undermine the radicals was by connecting radical sensibilities to what they thought was a
theopolitical threat to true New Testament Christianity: anti-individualism! This anti-individualism had a number of ramifications and was manifested in the unspoken commitments of radicals and their sympathizers.
In the first issue of *Correio Doutrinal*, an anonymous article argued that
the Radical Movement was founded on the principle of class solidarity,
and that class solidarity was not only "the doctrinal basis and the organiz-
ing principle of this radicalism" but it was "identical to those of other radical movements that bring conflict to religion and civilization everywhere,"
such as Russia.[111] Missionaries and their followers, on the other hand, were
"followers of individualism, paired with a social justice that does not de-
stroy the individual responsibility and sovereignty of conscience or the supremacy of the Spirit over the mind enlightened by Scripture."[112] Pro-mis-
sionaries argued that this anti-individualism, in turn, approximated

---

Baptist Struggle for Autonomy"; Mesquita, *Historia Dos Baptistas Em Pernambuco*;
and Oliveira, *Panorama Batista Em Pernambuco*.

[110] Adrião Bernardes, "Manifesto Aos Baptistas Brasileros (Nossa Atitude),"
(1925): 1.

[111] "O Radicalismo Anti-Missionário Em Pernambuco: Seus Princípios Bási-
cos," *Correio Doutrinal* 1, no. 1 (1923): 3.

[112] "O Radicalismo Anti-Missionário Em Pernambuco: Seus Princípios Bási-
cos," 3–4.

radicals to Roman Catholic sensibilities because the fundamental difference between Roman Catholicism and Baptists was the doctrine of individualism.[113]

The pro-missionary establishment also connected radical dissent from missionary rule to heretical movements from the first century. For instance, an article entitled *O Movimento Anti-Missionário do Primeiro Século* (The Anti-Missionary Movement of the First Century) drew correlations between the Radical Movement and the characters who resisted Paul and John in biblical narratives.[114] Another article compared the radicals with the heretics on Munster, who were disliked by both Protestants and Catholics.[115] In addition, the *Correio Doutrinal* printed a number of articles arguing that the radicals' search for true autonomy was both practically and ideologically futile and unproductive. The articles did this by defining true patriotism along the lines of a love for the nation that focused on cooperation and development, not anti-American sentiments. The pro-missionary establishment argued that radicals adopted the same criticism voiced by Roman Catholics against New Testament Christians and such criticisms were inherently contradictory because they were also informed by foreign forces. Alvaro Reis, a pro-missionary Brazilian, provided the most compelling polemic of this nature, pointing out that the Roman Catholic Church was foreign even in its name. He wrote: "Religion of the foreigners! Religion of the Americans! The Dollar! North American imperialism—these are the cries repeated by the gramophone of romanism."[116] He went on to say that "Any citizen can consult the statistics of the main evangelical denominations and see that NORTH AMERICAN MISSIONARIES ARE IN THE ABSOLUTE MINORITY. The evangelical churches are truly NATIONAL, with legal documentation; with its NATIONAL COUNCILS, without spiritual dependence on foreigners."[117]

---

[113] Orlando Falcão, "O Catholicismo Romano Contrastado Com Os Principios Baptistas," *Correio Doutrinal* 2, no. 6 (1924): 6.

[114] "O Movimento Anti-Missionário Do Primeiro Século," *Correio Doutrinal* 1, no. 2 (1923): 4–5.

[115] José Alves Ribeiro, "Que Patriotas Quereis Acompanhar?," *Correio Doutrinal* 1, no. 9 (1923): 8.

[116] Alvaro Reis, "Religião de Estrangeiros?! Religião de Americanos?!," *Correio Doutrinal* 2, no. 8 (1924): 4.

[117] Reis, 4.

The allegedly false independence sought by radicals was also criticized in the *Correio Doutrinal* in light of the fact that leaders of the radical movement reached out to the Texas Baptist Association for support.[118] An article argued that "Radicalism is bifurcated. Some want to be independent, but cannot. Others want to live from the oppositionist Texas dollars, but are not sure if they can. And radical churches and institutions change pastors and directors faster than the phases of the moon change, and some good people still let themselves be exploited."[119] When the pro-missionary Pernambuco Baptist Convention was formed—in opposition to the radical-dominated Regional Baptist Convention—two main points were raised for the separation:

> The Regional Convention allowed itself to be fooled by a false, violent, and partisan propaganda that is not acceptable to the greatest number of Baptists in this state for the representation of churches that do not approve of its mundane methods....
> The Board of the [Regional] Convention and some churches that cooperate with it already became dissident and tries to be connected with an insignificant North American Baptist group of a similar dissident spirit, therefore being dissociated of almost all Baptist work in Brazil, who cooperate with the Board of Richmond, representative of the largest Baptist convention in the world.[120]

At the national convention of 1925, a new attempt to solve the problem created by the Radical Movement was put in place. A document named "Bases of Cooperation," which was a result of a committee composed of members of both parties—missionaries and radicals—was suggested, revised, and accepted by the BBC. The document focused on highlighting the autonomy of churches and boards as well as the cooperative spirit between the Brazilian Baptist Convention and the Foreign Mission Board.[121] The Bases of Cooperation document did not represent a victory for the radicals. The Bases of Cooperation specified that boards with pre-

---

[118] W.C. Taylor, "A Propaganda Radical Em Texas," *Correio Doutrinal* 2, (March 21, 1923): 2.

[119] "Querem Ser 'Independentes' Mas Não Podem," *Correio Doutrinal* 1, no. 45 (1924): 4.

[120] "Convocação e Manifesto Da Convenção Baptista Pernambucana," *Correio Doutrinal* 1, no. 17 (1923): 10.

[121] Minutes of the Brazilian Baptist Convention, 1925.

determined quotas that were mostly composed of missionaries would govern schools and seminaries, that the radical seminary that was founded in Recife was to be dissolved, and that the editor of the *Jornal Batista* did not have to be Brazilian. Furthermore, the locals who were part of the Radical Movement were not elected or re-elected to any relevant board in the National Convention.[122] Yet, the Radical leaders who attended the convention took the Bases of Cooperation back to their churches and, once they returned, a regional committee was put in place to analyze the proposal.[123] The most powerful radical churches of the region did not accept the proposal; they wanted the excluded members to reconcile with the original churches before accepting the Bases of Cooperation. As a result of the disagreement, in June of 1925 another national body was created: the Brazilian Baptist Association.[124]

The National Phase of the Radical Movement (1925-1938)

The creation of an alternative national denominational body was a symbolic marker of the potential consequences of missionaries' unwillingness to grant the Brazilians the level of autonomy they desired. When D.L. Hamilton returned in 1926 from a time in the United States, he was a part of the Baptist Missionary Association of Texas (henceforth BMAT), a group with strong Landmarkist elements that gave some financial support to the new national convention.[125] The BMAT already had competed with the Brazilian Baptist Convention before. In 1918, the association supported missionary J.B. Parker in São Luiz do Maranhão.[126] The Parkers eventually shifted from the BMAT to the FMB because the first was not reliable in its financial support of their missionaries.[127] Then, in 1922, it

---

[122] Minutes of the Brazilian Baptist Convention, 1925.

[123] Mesquita, *Historia Dos Baptistas Em Pernambuco*, 90.

[124] Monteiro, "Radicalism in Pernambuco: A Study of the Relationship between Nationals and Southern Baptist Missionaries in the Brazilian Baptist Struggle for Autonomy," 104.

[125] Mesquita, *História Dos Baptistas Do Brasil*, 90.

[126] Mário Ribeiro Martins, "O Radicalismo Batista Brasileiro" (master's thesis, Seminário Teológico Batista do Norte, 1972), 33.

[127] L.L. Johnson, "B.M.A.," *Correio Doutrinal*, I (June 8, 1923), 3. Writing to the *Correio Doutrinal*, Johnson states that the Parkers even counted on the help of the North Brazil Mission of the FMB while they were still a part of the BMAT.

recruited missionary to Portugal, João Jorge de Oliveira. Oliveira most likely switched allegiances form the BBC to the BMAT also for financial, rather than theological, reasons. Although there is little indication that Oliveira went through a theological shift, the financial support offered by the Baptist Missionary Association of Texas was substantially better than the one offered by Brazilian Baptists.[128] The examples of movement of missionaries between different Baptist groups, in the Brazilian case, seem to be more motivated by practical financial matters than by ideological shifts on the part of missionaries.

When D.L. Hamilton joined the BMAT, he had already been forced to resign from the FMB and Antonio Neves Mesquita also went to the United States in order to facilitate the negotiations for the involvement of the BMAT in the Brazilian Baptist Association.[129] Both Hamilton and the Brazilian Baptist Association were in urgent need of financial support. David Hamilton's connection with the BMAT may indeed have been informed by his Landmarkist convictions, as Monteiro pointed out.[130] In his correspondence with Lydia Hamilton, David Hamilton connected his commitment to Radical Movement ideals with his defense of "old time gospel as was practiced by Graves and those Landmarkers that were with him."[131] In addition to the financial motive on Hamilton's part, however, Brazilian Baptists did not perceive the participation of the BMAT in the life of the Brazilian Baptist Association as a commitment to Landmarkism. The struggle of the Radical Movement was one for local denominational power, not against denominational centralization, as was the case of full-fledged Landmarkism.[132] In regard to the reach of the dissenting

---

[128] Pereira, *História Dos Batistas No Brasil (1882-1982)*, 117.

[129] Martins, "O Radicalismo Batista Brasileiro," 34.

[130] Monteiro, "Radicalism in Pernambuco: A Study of the Relationship Between Nationals and Southern Baptist Missionaries in the Brazilian Baptist Struggle for Autonomy," 83.

[131] From D.L. Hamilton to Lydia Hamilton, March 17, 1923.

[132] Mesquita, *História Dos Baptistas Do Brasil*, 287; Zaqueu Moreira de Oliveira, *Panorama Batista Em Pernambuco* (Recife: Junta Evangelizadora Batista de Pernambuco, 1964), 32. Mesquita himself, who was an active part of the negotiations that culminated in BMAT involvement with the Brazilian Baptist Association, differed from Hamilton when it came to the reunification of radicals with the Brazilian Baptist Convention. According to Mesquita, who reunited with the BBC, Hamilton never liked the idea of reunification. Yet, given financial struggles and the possibility of local leadership, the overwhelming majority of local dissenters reunited. Zaqueu Oliveira

group, churches in five states cooperated with the Brazilian Baptist Association and its institutions.[133] For thirteen years, the two national denominational bodies operated separately from each other, dividing Brazilian Baptists between two conventions.

The presidential address delivered by Adrião Bernardes during the 1926 annual meeting of the Brazilian Baptist Association sheds light on the consistency of radical criticism against the missionary establishment. Bernades argued that their reaction against foreign rule was the manifestation of the strength of local Baptist work in Brazil, not its weakness.[134] For Bernardes, Brazilian dissent from missionary rule revealed the true intention of the missionary establishment in Brazil. He said that "it now came to light what was already in the feelings and actions of those who, by the power of the gold, wanted to reduce their brothers and companions to a condition of mere robots and imbeciles who do not know how to act and how to direct their lives without foreign direction."[135] Bernardes also drew from his firsthand knowledge of the Southern Baptist Convention to tell his local audience that in the US denominations, churches are normally ruled by astute denominational politicians and that denominations are run like a business. But his grievances were overwhelmingly focused on missionary demand of Brazilian submission. He recognized that missionaries misled Brazilians by their constant allusions to an always-future transition of power. Bernardes claimed that Brazilian Baptists "lived moved by the sweet touch of the confidence in the promises made by those who were leaders by divine right,"[136] but for missionaries, "just unreserved submission"[137] was sufficient. He went on to mock a caricature of missionary self-perception that reflected local perceptions of missionary demeanor toward Brazilians:

---

frames Hamilton as a strange missionary, not fully comprehended by many despite his commitment to the Baptist denomination. If Hamilton indeed thought the Radical Movement to be a Landmarkist-inspired move on the part of Brazilians, he misunderstood the spirit of Brazilian Baptist dissenters.

[133] Mesquita, *História Dos Baptistas Do Brasil*, 90.

[134] Adrião Bernardes, "A Situação Actual Dos Baptistas No Brazil," *Speech at the Meeting of the Brazilian Baptist Association*, July 28, 1926, 3.

[135] Bernardes, 3–4.

[136] Bernardes, 5.

[137] Bernardes, 6.

If they [the missionaries] were human creatures like us, vulnerable to errors, suspicions, misunderstandings, faults, and sins, we would have a common base with which we could work: but they are extraordinary creatures, *sui generis*, infallible, invulnerable, and even imponderable and inaccessible with authority superior to that of the churches of Christ, escaping even their administration. What can we do with such creatures?[138]

Bernades recognized the importance of denominational institutions, but he emphasized what he saw as the exaggerated authoritarianism of SBC missionaries as well as the disrespect with which missionaries approached local dissent. "Our supposed guides," he wrote, "assumed a paternalistic attitude and said: 'come here inexperienced boys, confess that you were wrong. We did nothing. Besides, was it not us who gave you the Gospel?'"[139] Bernardes told his audience that when local dissidents did not reconcile according to missionary terms, missionaries threatened them with financial sanctions and called them "thieves, robbers, players, and liars."[140] He argued that in Brazil the principle of denominational work has been "whoever pays, rules," but they were no longer willing to abide by that principle.

Despite what characterized the clashes between missionaries and Brazilians, the few interpreters of the movement noticed that between 1925 and 1936, when the "New Bases of Cooperation" that led to the unification of national bodies were accepted, "the hostility between the two parties decreased steadily."[141] These interpreters, however, gave no overall satisfactory reason for the noticeable de-escalation.[142] There were, however,

---

[138] Bernardes, 7.

[139] Bernardes, 18.

[140] Bernardes, 19.

[141] Monteiro, "Radicalism in Pernambuco: A Study of the Relationship between Nationals and Southern Baptist Missionaries in the Brazilian Baptist Struggle for Autonomy," 105.

[142] Machado, *Educação Batista No Brasil: Uma Análise Complexa*; Mesquita, *História Dos Baptistas Do Brasil*; Martins, "O Radicalismo Batista Brasileiro"; Monteiro, "Radicalism in Pernambuco: A Study of the Relationship between Nationals and Southern Baptist Missionaries in the Brazilian Baptist Struggle for Autonomy"; Zaqueu Moreira de Oliveira, *Panorama Batista Em Pernambuco* (Recife: Departamento de Educação Religiosa de Junta Evangelizadora de Pernambuco,

a number of factors that contributed to the reunification of the denomination, which was made official once the demands for autonomy originally made by the radicals back in 1922 were by and large met. A major factor for the union between the two factions was the Great Depression in the United States, which affected both the Southern Baptist Convention, which helped fund the Brazilian Baptist Convention, and the Baptist Missionary Association of Texas, which helped fund the Brazilian Baptist Association.[143]

The Great Depression in the United States had a catastrophic impact on the United States in general. When it came to Baptist missions, the FMB was bankrupt in the years that preceded the reunification of competing Brazilian denominational bodies. Writing to missionary H.H. Muirhead, FMB Corresponding Secretary T.B. Ray said that:

> The great debt we have been carrying has finally pressed us right into the corner. It is now so large that the banks say they will not lend us anymore money to tide us over the lean period through which we pass every summer. I don't know where we are going to get money enough to meet our bills or our budget during the next five months.[144]

This situation meant that missionaries who were on furlough would not return to their field of operation for lack of funds. This development, in turn, would diminish significantly the missionary personnel for teaching, preaching, and administrative tasks. Muirhead, who was then president of the SBBTS, was keenly aware of the connection between financial strength and missionary control of the denomination. According to him,

---

1964); and Pereira, *História Dos Batistas No Brasil (1882-1982)*. None of the major works of Brazilian Baptist history analyze the potential reasons for reunification.

[143] The concern for the involvement of the Baptist Missionary Association in Brazilian missions appears in polemical treatises issued in the *Correio Doutrinal*. Also, T.B. Ray shows this concern when he wrote to Muirhead saying that he kept Antonio Mesquita, who visited the FMB in Richmond in 1924, from meeting with representatives of the Baptist Missionary Association. See letter From T.B. Ray to H.H. Muirhead, October 3, 1924; W.C. Taylor, "A Propaganda Radical Em Texas," *Correio Doutrinal* 2 (March 21, 1923); and L.L. Johnson, "B.M.A.," *Correio Doutrinal* (June 8, 1923), 1. Writing to A.W. Luper in 1937, R.S. Jones blames the financial support sent by the Baptist Missionary Association to the Brazilian Baptist Association for the division of Baptist work in Brazil. See A.W. Luper, February 5, 1937.

[144] From T.B. Ray to H.H. Muirhead, May 6, 1932.

"the cuts in appropriation have greatly increased the nationalistic spirit among the native brethren."[145] At times, Muirhead wrote to corresponding secretaries T.B. Ray and C.E. Maddry as if he was convinced that another, stronger, local controversy was going to take place and would be successful. In 1933, he lamented that he "had to put two more Brazilian teachers in the seminary to take [the] place of the missionaries in the homeland."[146]

C.E. Maddry, T.B. Ray's successor as secretary, shared the reluctant spirit of Muirhead when it came to local participation. Considering the FMB's financial burdens, Maddry wrote: "I think for a long time to come we will be compelled to have leaders and directors and teachers from America, but more and more we are going to have to depend on the native Christians themselves for the carrying of the burden of the work in the respective lands."[147] Between 1932 and 1936, Muirhead wrote to several influential individuals warning of the growing anti-missionary spirit in Brazil and asking fellow missionaries and denominational leaders for a more diplomatic stance, given the effects of the FMB's financial vulnerability.[148]

In 1930, W.E. Entzminger wrote an article published in *Home and Foreign Fields* in which he criticized T.B. Ray for not appropriating enough funds for the mission in Brazil and wondering whether Baptists would go out of the foreign mission business.[149] In his section on *Home and Foreign Fields*, Ray consistently acknowledged the difficult financial situation of the FMB, and the minutes of the FMB themselves are a testimony to the desperate struggles that overtook the Board in the early thirties.[150]

If the FMB was in a state of financial upheaval, so was the Baptist

---

[145] From H.H. Muirhead to T.B. Ray, February 17, 1932.

[146] From H.H. Muirhead to T.B. Ray, May 4, 1933.

[147] From C.E. Maddry to H.H. Muirhead, May 13, 1933.

[148] Beyond the letters already mentioned, which include similar arguments, see: From H.H. Muirhead To R.S. Jones, March 12, 1935; From H.H. Muirhead To Jessie Ford, April, 15, 1936; From H.H. Muirhead To C.E. Maddry, September 15, 1935; and From H.H. Muirhead To W.C. Taylor, September 23, 1936.

[149] W.E. Entzminger, "Baptists in Petropolis," *Home and Foreign Fields* (January 1930): 12.

[150] For a few examples, see the Minutes of the Foreign Mission Board from December 11, 1930; October 13, 1931; January 14, 1932; and from March 8, 1934.

Association of Texas, which helped support the Brazilian Baptist Association created by the radicals. D.L. Hamilton returned to the United States in 1933 and, in the same year, there was a strong indication that the Baptist Missionary Association of Texas, pressured by the new financial reality imposed by the Depression, would contemplate reuniting with the Baptist General Convention of Texas and enter the SBC fold.[151] On both sides of the conflict in Brazil, the possibilities of financing a Baptist denomination in an environment where the presence of another Baptist body was competing for more coreligionists in the religious market became unattractive. The missionaries and their supporters, then, between 1925 and 1936, became more willing to accept what seemed inevitable: relinquishing explicit and rigid denominational control. The New Bases of Cooperation represented this shift.

Antonio Mesquita noted that "the 'New Bases of Cooperation' voted in by the BBC in 1936 opened the doors for the return of all churches belonging to the Brazilian Baptist Association."[152] The main points of the New Bases of Cooperation represented a qualified victory for the radicals, who gained a level of official denominational autonomy that was unprecedented in the history of the denomination in Brazil. First, the system of quotas that ensured missionary dominance in the boards of the denomination was eliminated. There was no minimum number of missionaries required for any board. Second, there was no impediment for the nomination of Brazilian leaders to the presidency of major denominational institutions such as seminaries and publishing houses. Finally, an executive commission was created to coordinate, together with the FMB, the strategy of future missionary efforts.[153]

---

[151] BMAT missionary A.W. Luper, a former FMB missionary to Brazil, was a key figure in attempts to reunite the BMAT with the BGCT. His papers includes a 1933 draft of a proposal to bring the BMAT into closer cooperation with the BGCT due, among other things, to the financial advantages of reduced overhead costs. Luper also corresponded with a number of FMB officials, wanting to return to Brazil through the FMB. In 1935, FMB secretary C.E. Maddry wrote to Luper saying: "I am glad to know about the development looking towards cooperation, if not union, between the Baptist groups in Texas" (see From C.E. Maddry To A.W. Luper, October 12, 1935).

[152] Mesquita, *História Dos Baptistas Do Brasil*, 191.

[153] Annals of the Brazilian Baptist Convention, 1936.

When it came to the elimination of the quotas that guaranteed a majority for the missionaries in the boards of the BBC, the commission that delivered the report of the New Bases of Cooperation in the 1936 national meeting was abundantly clear in its strong break with past practices. It read: "The commission proposes the elimination of the percentage between missionaries and Brazilians in the constitution of the boards of the Brazilian Baptist Convention, and all the boards are to be immediately dissolved so that new ones can be elected according to our new resolution."[154] In the meeting, Djalma Cunha, a radical leader who would soon become president of the SBBTS from 1936 until 1945, delivered a speech and a prayer celebrating the victory of the locals. C.E. Maddry, FMB secretary, came to Brazil for the meeting, and the *Jornal Batista* reported Cunha's performance in a jubilant tone:

> Pastor Djalma Cunha presented a report about the New Bases of Cooperation with the FMB, which was unanimously approved as it was written. The same brother, then, in a rapturing prayer, expressed in the name of the Brazilian Baptists the joy for the victory attained, asking Dr. Maddry to convey to the Southern Baptists in the United States the deep thankfulness felt by the Brazilian Baptists for the fraternal and intelligent cooperation that Dr. Maddry, in the FMB's name, will enact in conquering new ideals. With the people standing, Dr. W.C. Taylor offered a prayer of thanksgiving.[155]

Powerful avenues for the reunion of the two national conventions were finally open after over a decade of official separation.

The Beginning of Brazilian Institutional Control: A Conclusion

The boards of the national convention, already in the 1936 meeting, counted on an unprecedented representation of local leadership.[156] After 1936, the NBBTS had its first Brazilian president, and the number of Brazilian professors gradually grew in proportion to the faculty appointments

---

[154] Annals of the Brazilian Baptist Convention, 1936.

[155] "24a Reunião Da Convenção Batista Brasileira," *Jornal Batista* 28 (July 9, 1936): 4.

[156] "Convenção Batista Brasileira," *Jornal Batista* 28 (July 9, 1936).

of missionaries born in the United States. The changes at SBBTS paralleled those in the NBBTS as Brazilian presidents and provosts were appointed. The rate of Brazilian faculty appointments at SBBTS also grew to unprecedented levels. Almost eighty years after the arrival of the first Baptist missionary in Brazil, there was finally the possibility of a Brazilian Baptist Convention actually controlled by locals. When the Brazilian Baptist Convention met in 1938 in Rio de Janeiro, the national competitor of the BBC, the Brazilian Baptist Association, was dissolved.[157] Although there were still regional expressions of the Radical Movement until the 1970s, none would prove strong enough to generate the national division for which the New Bases of Cooperation represents the resolution.

The apparent universal and joyful unions that the official documents conveyed, however, were at odds with the reluctant nature with which the field missionaries approached the new denominational arrangement. The reunion of missionaries and radicals generated their own tensions, and the resolution of these tensions in the following decades would require missionaries to be more efficient and less direct in their strategies of denominational control. The resolution of the Radical Movement controversy did not mean the end of missionary commitment to denominational control; rather, it prompted the missionary reconceptualization of domination. The gains of the Radical Movement in terms of unprecedented Brazilian representation in denominational institutions, therefore, represented a local victory that was followed by a missionary reaction. If it became harder for missionaries to dominate Brazilian Baptists explicitly, the new turn in missionary strategy emphasized the formation of Brazilian leaders who would deploy US evangelical ideologies with little qualifications. It is to this new post-Radical Movement period that this narrative now turns.

---

[157] Oliveira, *Panorama Batista Em Pernambuco*, 33.

CHAPTER FOUR

STRUGGLING FOR HOLY POWER: MISSIONARY STRATEGIES FOR MAINTAINING LEADERSHIP

The shift in Brazilian Baptist denominational structures presented the Brazilian Baptist Convention (BBC) with the possibility of more ideological freedom. Yet ideological freedom had not been a major concern of Brazilian Baptists who organized against Southern Baptist denominational White supremacy in Brazil. Brazilian concerns had been more trivial, strategic, and administrative, and, as such, robust imaginative alternatives to Southern Baptist evangelical conservatism were mostly present in occasional pockets of resistance.[1] In addition, the frustration felt by missionaries because of the denomination's shift toward greater Brazilian institutional inclusivity gave way to strategies that attempted to retract some of the progress that had been made in terms of local denominational control. The strategies adopted by missionaries who led institutions of cultural production after they regained denominational control proved more effective than those that relied on explicit domination. A new generation of Southern Baptist missionaries—some who had been raised in Brazil—would prove to be more concerned with the enforcement and policing of ideological sensibilities than with older forms of missionary domination, which were generally rejected by a number of locals and resisted by the Radical Movement. This shift took place in an environment of exponential growth within the denomination. In 1940, the denomination had fifty thousand members in the country. That number had doubled by 1950,

---

[1] The continuous presence of regional manifestations of radicalism, such as in the case of the divisions in the Pernambuco field, was one form of divergence from Southern Baptist orthodoxy that endured in corners of denominational life. In addition, individual pastors would at times diverge from the theological opinions of the Southern Baptist missionaries. These divergences, however, were generally not threatening to the Southern Baptist-informed ideological status quo.

tripled by 1960, sextupled by 1970, and in 1980 Brazilian Baptists numbered over six hundred thousand members.[2] As the denomination grew, the missionary/Brazilian ratio diminished and, in turn, the strategy of ideological domination of post-Radical Movement missionaries proved to be efficient in the growing denomination. The control of denominational institutions of cultural production meant, in retrospect, the dissemination and maintenance of Southern Baptist orthodoxy in Brazil and, through the influence of Brazilian Baptist missions, in the whole continent.

This chapter focuses on the development of the BBC as a "Brazilian-led" denomination between the reunification of 1938 and the celebration of the 100 years of Baptist presence in Brazil in 1982. I will pay particular attention to what molded denominational identity and thus helped account for the maintenance of Southern Baptist orthodoxy in the country. Here, I continue to give a central place to the correspondence of missionaries as a way to uncover the unspoken reasons for denominational decisions. For the purposes of this chapter, however, I also give priority to the *Jornal Batista* in order to show how central aspects of denominational history, identity, and ideology were being performed more publicly through the denomination's main publication.

A number of factors contributed to the shaping of the Brazilian Baptist Convention in the decades that followed the Radical Movement, and most of them were informed by Southern Baptist sensibilities. The aspects that are indispensable to understanding the development of Brazilian Baptist identity between the reunification of 1938 and the celebration of the Brazilian Baptist centennial in 1982 include the reestablishment of Southern Baptist control of institutions of cultural production—particularly the two major seminaries; the numeric growth and relative success of the denomination in Brazil; the charismatic schism that led to the creation of an alternative national convention, namely, the National Baptist Convention (NBC)—a topic approached with more detail in the following chapter; the growing presence of Brazilian missionaries across the globe, particularly after 1970; and the continuous power of Southern Baptist symbolic presence through denominational publications and events. As regards seminaries, I will show how just a few years after local leadership was established, Southern Baptist control of the two major institutions of

---

[2] Azevedo, *A Celebração Do Indivíduo: A Formação Do Pensamento Batista Brasileiro*, 196.

ministerial training was reasserted. The missionaries who became leaders of the seminaries after the New Bases of Cooperation were put in place used their tenures to consolidate further Southern Baptist ideals, convictions, and methods as the normative standard for training Brazilian Baptist leadership.

The development and relative success of the denomination, which I explore briefly below, did not encourage particular ideological creativity. The growth of the Brazilian Baptist Convention paradoxically paralleled consolidation of Brazilian Baptist ideological dependence on Southern Baptist commitments. As the years went on, the independence and nationalization of the Brazilian Baptist Convention did indeed take place, but not as quickly as the Radical Movement leaders had hoped. Instead, this autonomy came progressively and in unison with Southern Baptist orthodoxy. The clearest manifestation of this independence and growth was the impressive advance of Brazilian Baptist presence abroad. The World Missions Board of the BBC was created simultaneously with the national convention itself, but in the 1970s it grew exponentially, increasing the Brazilian Baptist sense of independence, autonomy, and missionary identity. This growth was combined with a self-understanding that mimicked Southern Baptist strategies and patterns, and was paired with a sense of pride and accomplishment. The Brazilian Baptist Convention used its independence to show how like their Southern Baptist founding fathers the Brazilian Baptists were. Brazilian Baptist autonomy, thus, was most strongly exercised as a freedom to imitate.

The progressive growth of the Brazilian Baptist Convention was not immune to the strength of Global Pentecostalism. The tensions between Pentecostalism and the Brazilian Baptist Convention date back to just a few years past the 1906 Azuza Street Revival that is generally considered to be the genesis of the movement. In the 1960s, however, the presence of pentecostalizing forces within the BBC prompted a number of confrontations that resulted in a schism. Although charismatic tendencies were disseminated in the denomination mainly through a Southern Baptist missionary, this schism energized the BBC toward the strengthening of its stance on Pentecostalism and charismatic practices. The competing presence of the alternative, charismatic Baptist convention in Brazil—the National Baptist Convention, founded in 1967—and the continuous growth of a number of Pentecostal churches were key factors in the development of a denominational identity that was always suspicious of and oftentimes aggressively against Pentecostalism. In addition, the continuous presence of the Southern Baptist Convention and its mainstream ideologies in Brazilian publications ensured that the imagination of Brazilian Baptists remained inundated by issues and anxieties that were typical of Southern Baptists in the United States. Taken together, these issues of the reestablishment of Southern Baptist control of Brazilian Baptist institutions of cultural output, numeric growth, charismatic schism, growing global presence, and captivity to Southern Baptist imagination ensured the continuity of Brazilian Baptist identity along Southern Baptist lines. In general, the Brazilianization of Brazilian Baptists took place as a progressive administrative autonomy that allowed the most powerful expressions of Brazilian Baptist denominational dispositions to be autonomous expressions of Southern Baptist Christianity in Brazil—a testament to the efficacy of Southern Baptist missions and their aggressive strategies of ideological cloning.

The New Bases of Cooperation
and Missionary Whitelash

The reaction of field missionaries against the implementation of the New Bases of Cooperation was almost immediate. This reaction, however, was voiced in intra-missionary exchanges and did not often appear in official documents and public performances. At times, the public performance of missionaries masked their private opinions, revealing the complexities of missionary activity abroad. For example, though publicly someone like A.R. Crabtree could praise the Brazilian Baptist heritage, as he did in his 1937 book on the history of Brazilian Baptists,[3] privately he would, in that same year, confess his regret for returning to the country after a year of furlough because of the challenges presented by what he saw as the nationalist spirit that gave Brazilian Baptists their symbolic independence.[4]

Likewise J.R. Allen saw in the New Bases of Cooperation a new period in Brazilian denominational life. Writing to A.W. Luper, he said that leaders such as W.C. Taylor were alarmed at the new denominational arrangements.[5] The longtime secretary of the Rio de Janeiro Field, J.J. Cowsert also corresponded with Luper, who wanted to return to Brazil as

---

[3] Crabtree, *História Dos Baptistas Do Brasil* 1, 1-2.
[4] From A.R. Crabtree to A.W. Luper, March 16, 1937.
[5] From J.R. Allen to A.W. Luper, March 3, 1937.

a missionary. Cowsert lamented that under the New Bases of Cooperation, he no longer had the political clout to bring Luper to Brazil on a unilateral, missionary decision. Cowsert went on to say that

> We are going through a very radical change in the organization and plans of work in Brazil. Since Dr. Maddry's visit we do not know just where we are. Everything has been turned over to the Brazilian Convention. And unfortunately the political groups are pretty well in the lead. They have things in their hands. They didn't put Watson out of the College but he couldn't stay. They all but put Morgan out of the College in São Paulo and will when he goes home at the end of the year. They really did worst for Johnson in Recife, for they put a man in as vice president to take charge. They are doing all they can to keep Allen from coming back to the Seminary when he returns. They are working to put both Stover and myself out of the Publishing House. Well we are plodding on without much hope to continue to develop what we now have an opportunity to develop with a little more equipment. The only place that a missionary will be able to work from now on will be in some interior place. It may be best and all this may be sent of the Lord, but some of us do not feel that way.[6]

Cowsert also said that there was hope for the reestablishment of missionary control in the event that the new Brazilian leaders failed in their newfound administrative responsibilities.[7] Apparently, he was not praying for his local enemies, as his Lord would have him do! Talking about the changes in Brazilian denominational life, W.C. Taylor told Luper that "Rip Van Winkle did not find physical changes more astounding than the spiritual changes you would find here in Brazil, were you to return."[8] S.L. Watson, who Taylor later called "the troubleshooter for the Baptist denomination in Brazil,"[9] warned Luper along the same lines: "Missionary work in this country is changing to a native orientation, so that you will find that you are coming to a very different situation to that you knew here

---

[6] From J.J. Cowsert to A.W. Luper, March 24, 1937.

[7] From J.J. Cowsert to A.W. Luper, March 24, 1937.

[8] From W.C. Taylor to A.W. Luper, February 15, 1937.

[9] W.C. Taylor quoted by Jerry Key in Key, "The Rise and Development of Baptist Theological Education in Brazil, 1881-1963: A Historical and Interpretive Survey," 50.

years ago. Consequently you may find it not so agreeable as you do your present place in the Kingdom."[10] The public joy of the new cooperative efforts was paired with the private pains of missionary loss of power to locals who were perceived as threats to their plan for Brazilian Baptists. Although the disappointment of field missionaries with regard to the new denominational arrangement was general, the control of the institutions of cultural production—especially the seminaries—became a particular concern in the field.

From the 1930s onward, a number of Baptist seminaries were founded in Brazil,[11] with the result that Brazilian Baptist education became progressively diversified in terms of the places in which pastors were trained. The prominence of the two major seminaries—North Brazil Baptist Theological Seminary (NBBTS) and Southern Brazil Baptist Theological Seminary (SBBTS)—however, is evident in the fact that even today most denominational leaders were trained in these two central educational institutions of the BBC. After the New Bases of Cooperation were implemented in 1936, a new phase began in Brazilian Baptist theological education. Until then, the two major seminaries were connected to denominational K-12 schools. The New Bases of Cooperation, however, included a provision that made the seminaries autonomous[12]—meaning that the seminaries would have an autonomous board of trustees, their own directors, and would no longer benefit from the financial advantages of being connected to the generally more profitable K-12 schools.

Yet despite all the potential advantages of such an organization, a number of powerful missionaries were bitter about the new denominational arrangement that opened space for local leadership in the seminaries. S.L. Watson, for instance, told C.E. Maddry that the fact that Brazilians were taking over the seminaries would make it hard for missionaries to demonstrate true cooperation.[13] Likewise, W.C. Taylor, who taught at the NBBTS and was elected to be FMB's secretary to Latin America, demonstrated a general pessimism about the new arrangement. Writing

---

[10] From S.L. Watson to A.W. Luper, February 26, 1937.

[11] For examples of alternative Baptist theological institutions in Brazil, see Key, "The Rise and Development of Baptist Theological Education in Brazil, 1881-1963: A Historical and Interpretive Survey," 183-202.

[12] Key, 112.

[13] From W.C. Taylor to C.E. Maddry, September 19, 1936.

about some of the reasons for great tension in Brazil, Taylor warned Maddry that

> in a few cases, missionaries who have been "over" administrative posts of great honor and responsibility have come "under" brethren who are nationals, chosen to that same honor and responsibility. In other cases the administrative unity has been divided and an even harder "side-by-side" relationship exists, as if two engineers, one foreign, another national, had their hands upon the throttle of one engine.[14]

The FMB had to be proactive in trying to dissuade field missionaries in Brazil from sabotaging Brazilian leadership. Writing to Jessie Ford, Taylor said that Maddry

> was both informed of much which one could hardly believe if another told it to him and got in some plain words by correspondence which may curb some of the destructive maneuvers by missionaries who are entrenched in positions of power and do not want the status quo disturbed, so were planning an Al Smith stunt of nullification of all that had been agreed upon between Brazilian Baptists and Dr. Maddry, so far as it affected their ambitions.[15]

As time went by, FMB officials such as Maddry and Taylor, who were initially protective of the New Bases of Cooperation, shifted toward a stance that was less friendly toward the locals. But the first years of implementation of the New Bases of Cooperation were tense and, at times, revealed the disagreements between an FMB that wanted to make the deal work and field missionaries who wanted it to fail.

Orlando Falcão, in one of his numerous letters to W.C. Taylor, told him that many missionaries in Brazil openly criticized Maddry and the direction he was giving to the FMB, even calling him a dictator.[16] Taylor was well aware of the tension and had told Maddry that there were missionary "cliques" in Brazil who were not in line with the FMB's initial hope for true cooperation soon after the New Bases of Cooperation went into

---

[14] W.C. Taylor, "Long Distance Call." Although this piece was not dated in the IMB archives, there are clear indications that it was written no sooner than 1936 and no later than 1937.

[15] From W.C. Taylor to Jessie Ford, August 2, 1936.

[16] From Orlando Falcão to W.C. Taylor, March 30, 1940.

effect.[17] Taylor often wrote to Maddry suggesting that Southern Baptist missionaries in Brazil made public propaganda for nationalization but secretly worked against such a move.[18] The missionary resistance against the New Bases of Cooperation, as Taylor later revealed to Maddry, came because missionaries never wanted to cooperate; rather, they wanted the FMB to give them the ability to form a different convention in 1936 instead of trying to make peace with nationals.[19]

Theological education was at the center of this struggle, and Taylor told Maddry that the seminaries were going to "continue to be the worst whirlpool of denominational politics on this continent."[20] Denominational politics did play out in the seminaries, and by the second half of the twentieth century, the winners of the political games spoke Portuguese with a Southern US accent. By the time Brazilian Baptists celebrated their centennial, Southern Baptists either had direct control of the major seminaries or had already established a seminary organizational culture that consolidated Brazilian theological education along the lines of Southern Baptist orthodoxy.

The North Brazil Baptist Theological Seminary

After the denominational shift of 1936, a number of students enrolled in the NBBTS still maintained a significant nationalistic stance. In addition, many of the Southern Baptist missionaries thought that the FMB had committed an injustice to the centers of theological training in accepting the Brazilians' request of separating the seminaries from the schools, giving them independence.[21] Former radical leader Orlando Falcão, who saw the independence of the seminaries as a positive approximation of Brazilian institutions to the two great seminaries of the United States—"the seminaries at Louisville and Fort Worth"—celebrated the new direction of the seminaries in the *Jornal Batista* in 1936:

> [We now have] seminaries independent from the schools, not mere theological departments; independent seminary boards, not people

---

[17] From W.C. Taylor to Jessie Ford, June 25, 1936.
[18] W.C. Taylor, "Another Tuesday," June 2; To C.E. Maddry, June 25, 1940.
[19] From W.C. Taylor to C.E. Maddry, June 26, 1940.
[20] From W.C. Taylor to C.E. Maddry, September 25, 1936.
[21] Key, "The Rise and Development of Baptist Theological Education in Brazil, 1881-1963: A Historical and Interpretive Survey," 154.

who are not invested in its vital interests; professors that do not have to divide and subdivide their time, but actual seminary teachers; a seminary with its own buildings and its own life, offering a curriculum of culture and erudition necessary for an efficient ministry. These are ideals that show a change in emphasis.[22]

That shift did not mean that all the tensions had disappeared from the northern part of the country. Oliveira, for instance, reported a number of articles published in the late 1930s that showed a resistance to SBC missionary leadership coming from students of the seminary.[23] The conflicts in the leadership and faculty of the newly independent seminary ended up provoking further division in the state of Pernambuco where the seminary was located.

The national unification after the New Bases of Cooperation did not end the animosity in the state of Pernambuco. In 1939, after visiting the NBBTS, Firmino Silva painted a picture of what he saw: "I saw seminarians hating each other with mortal hate. I saw an extremist and agitated group who were against the missionaries. This group combats the missionaries systematically, and wants to neutralize missionary activity completely in the north of the country."[24]

In 1940, the state of Pernambuco was divided between the newly formed Pernambuco Baptist Evangelizing Convention, led by the missionaries and their local supporters, and the Pernambuco Baptist Convention.[25] This state-level division lasted until the 1960s and affected the NBBTS negatively. The division, however, assured that local leadership of the seminary established in 1936 would only last for four years. The missionaries strongly resisted Orlando Falcão's 1937 leadership of the NBBTS on the grounds of his positive stance toward secular education and his radical sympathies. When the seminary board decided to elect Munguba Sobrinho to the directorship in 1938, fights over the directorship of the seminary led to the FMB withholding funds for the institution. In addition, the FMB threatened to repossess the NBBTS properties if the institution did not go in an acceptable direction according to the

---

[22] Orlando Falcão, "Mudança De Emphase," *Jornal Batista*, no. 44 (1936): 7.

[23] Oliveira, *Ousadia E Desafios Da Educação Teológica: 100 Anos Do Stbn*, 67-68.

[24] Firmino Silva, "Onde Estamos, E Para Onde Vamos," *Jornal Batista* 16 (1939): 5.

[25] Oliveira, *Ousadia E Desafios Da Educação Teológica: 100 Anos Do Stbn*, 70.

FMB's standards.[26] When the seminary board once again elected Orlando Falcão to the directorship in 1940, the BBC intervened in the matter because of the tensions surrounding the NBBTS in the state of Pernambuco and, as a result, a Southern Baptist missionary led the seminary for four decades. After a few years of short administrations, John Mein led the NBBTS from 1942 to 1952 and David Mein, John Mein's son, assumed leadership from 1953 to 1984.[27]

With the intervention of the BBC, which resulted in the appointment of John Mein as the senior officer of the seminary, things became more stable in the seminary administration and classroom. By 1945, the faculty of the NBBTS was comprised of three Brazilians and three missionaries.[28] A particular difficulty that Brazilian theological education faced throughout its first decades however, was adequate pay for Brazilian faculty. While the missionary professors had an easier time focusing on their teaching duties, the first local to teach full-time was Lívio Lindoso, who acquired this status in 1954, over half a century after the founding of the NBBTS.[29]

John Mein had been director of the K-12 school in Recife and of the NBBTS from 1930 until 1935. Soon after the New Bases of Cooperation were established, Mein, together with a number of missionaries and FMB officials, began planning to take over the leadership of these institutions from the newly appointed local leadership. In 1940, Mein was elected president of the school by beating a local contender. The quick re-establishment of missionary leadership was cause for celebration in Recife as well as in Richmond. Writing to C.E. Maddry, Mein rejoiced saying that his election "is counted among the [missionary] brethren as a big victory for the right, and has instilled new hope into their thinking. It means that the College is out of their [Brazilian] hands, saved for the constructive

---

[26] Monteiro, "Radicalism in Pernambuco: A Study of the Relationship between Nationals and Southern Baptist Missionaries in the Brazilian Baptist Struggle for Autonomy," 115-26.

[27] Oliveira, *Ousadia E Desafios Da Educação Teológica: 100 Anos Do Stbn*, 193; Mário R. Martins, *Missionários Americanos E Algumas Figuras Do Brasil Evangélico* (Goiânia: Kelps, 2007), 70-71.

[28] Key, "The Rise and Development of Baptist Theological Education in Brazil, 1881-1963: A Historical and Interpretive Survey," 160.

[29] Key, 172.

[missionary] work."[30] Not only was the missionary establishment determined to take the institutions of cultural production back from Brazilian hands soon after the New Bases of Cooperation were accepted, it interpreted the shift of power back towards them as a divine act. God willed the crusade for missionary power, in Mein's imagination. In the same celebratory letter he sent to Maddry to let him know of his election, Mein said: "As I wrote you, some even thought that I should take some drastic step if need be to wrestle the institution from the hands of the radicals. But thank the Lord that was unnecessary. HE WORKED IT OUT FOR US, as I believe HE is going to do at the National Convention in Rio."[31] For Mein, the college was important in and of itself, but in the great scheme of things it was only one battle in a national crusade for God in a broader struggle against Brazilian competition.

When the radicals lost some ground in the 1941 national convention in Rio de Janeiro, the missionaries moved to take over the NBBTS and annul the influence of Orlando Falcão, who, as a director, tried to nationalize the seminary. When S.L. Watson became interim director of the seminary for one year, he immediately prohibited faculty and staff of the NBBTS from discussing denominational matters.[32] In addition, C.E. Maddry wanted Falcão gone from the NBBTS faculty as a condition of FMB financial support, and when Mein educated Maddry about Brazilian labor laws, Maddry revealed that he wanted to entice Falcão into suing the denomination so that he would lose influence with Baptist nationals. Maddry wrote:

> I believe it would be very wholesome for the Conservatives and for Baptist unity throughout Northern Brazil for Mr. Orlando to sue the seminary, and, if necessary, sell the building for funds for the payment of his pension. I think it would show him up before his own people as an unworthy Judas Iscariot. The mission could then either buy the property in the sale, if the price were right, or they could let it go and proceed to organize a new seminary and erect a new building. You would then be rid of Mr. Orlando.[33]

---

[30] From John Mein to C.E. Maddry, January 14, 1940.

[31] From John Mein to C.E. Maddry, January 14, 1940.

[32] S.L. Watson, "Seminário Batista Do Norte," *Jornal Batista* 41, no. 6 (1941): 5.

[33] From C.E. Maddry to John Mein, March 26, 1941.

Maddry's resolve was informed by the dealings of the FMB in other countries, where nationals were also reacting against the missionary establishment. Eventually Maddry wanted a compromise in the Falcão case and told Mein that although he saw no justice in Falcão's insistence in reciving the pension he claimed was legally owed, he would not object if Mein could buy off Falcão "for a small sum."[34] Falcão eventually received a sum of money from Mein and signed off all of his claims on denominational institutions, and without his nationalizing presence, the way was cleared for missionary leadership.[35] Maddry was intentional in the direction he wanted denominational institutions in Brazil to go. He told Mein: "Please do your very best to see to it that we never take on another national in Brazil in any of our institutions who will turn against us and sue us. This kind of people deserves the contempt of all good people."[36] For Maddry, denominational institutions were "our institutions," and their agendas ideally would be directed by missionaries with the possible mediation of local surrogates, as long as they behaved.

When Mein was appointed director of the NBBTS in 1942, he stepped down from the presidency of the K-12 school, but not before the board of the school was made pro-missionary.[37] He also played a key role as an influential strategist for the North Brazil Mission. As director of the seminary, Mein struggled to keep and appoint new missionary personnel for administrative and teaching posts at NBBTS. However, in addition to the foreign policy difficulties involved in securing missionary visas to Brazil, the FMB appointed many more missionaries to the South of the country. New missionaries did not want to go to the north of Brazil, partially because they perceived the region as being anti-missionary and, according to Mein, the South Brazil Mission intentionally enticed missionaries to move South.[38] Throughout Mein's administration, his language and that of FMB officials indicate their desire to flood strategic institutions in Brazil with missionary leadership, although money, denominational politics, and international relations kept this ideal from ever being fully realized.

---

[34] From C.E. Maddry to John Mein, May 21, 1941.

[35] From John Mein to C.E. Maddry, August 14, 1941.

[36] From C.E. Maddry to John Mein, September 9, 1941.

[37] From John Mein To C.E. Maddry, February 7, 1942.

[38] From John Mein to Everett Gill, Jr., April 9, 1943; From Everett Gill, Jr. to John Mein, October 5, 1943; From Everett Gill, Jr. to John Mein, October 23, 1943; From John Mein to Everett Gill, Jr., n.d.

Mein's time as president of the school, director of the NBBTS, and a leader in the North Brazil mission was effectively invested in skewing Brazilian Baptist power dynamics toward a pro-missionary stance. Despite the fact that he operated out of Recife, a hotbed for radical local Baptists, he succeeded in maintaining control of key denominational institutions. Mein wrote Everett Gill, Jr. in 1951,[39] a little over a decade after his direct influence could again be felt in two of the major Baptist educational institutions in the country, celebrating the fact that the north Brazil field itself had turned to a more pro-missionary stance.[40] Mein was a key player in these developments, and when Gill found out that Mein, his wife, and his son were elected to denominational leadership positions once held by locals, he celebrated this development with surprise: "The turn in missionary leadership is tremendously interesting, and is quite a change from what I saw ten years ago when I first visited Recife. The fine Christian spirit of you missionaries has won out in the long run."[41] Implicit in Gill's language is the latent conviction that Brazilians who opposed missionaries did so out of unchristian sensibilities, and that the successful strategizing for power by field missionaries was a demonstration of their "fine Christian spirit."

John Mein opened the doors to the seminary's administration to his pupil and son David, who in time would be director of the seminary for nearly three decades. David Mein had a set of characteristics that set him up for success at NBBTS. First, he had been raised in Brazil and spoke fluent Portuguese without the characteristic United States accent and speech patterns that pervaded traditional missionary communication. He was also highly educated and held degrees from different United States universities and seminaries. He was young, energetic, and had experience in leadership positions in state-level and national-level denominational structures—including as first vice-president of the BBC.[42] David Mein

---

[39] Gill's own White supremacist dispositions can be seen in his books on foreign missions. For example, he was excited about missions to Russia because Russians were White, and he emphasized Brazilian "Negro" humorous nature and Native stoicism as natural attributes, reserving attributes of competence to the White population. See Everett Gill, *Europe and the Gospel* (Richmond: Foreign Mission Board, 1931), 22; Everett Gill, *Pilgrimage to Brazil* (Nashville: Broadman Press, 1954), 7–11.

[40] From John Mein to Everett Gill, Jr., November 10, 1951.

[41] From Everett Gill, Jr. to John Mein, December 6, 1951.

[42] "Seminário Teológico Batista Do Norte," *Jornal Batista* 53, no. 5 (1953): 3.

was a rare instance of the possibility of missionary leadership and plausible double-identification given his unique fluency in two cultural repertoires. A White male, born in the United States but raised in Brazil, educated in both countries, the son of a longtime power player in missionary institutional politics who wanted to become an FMB missionary and was willing to follow in his father's footsteps did not come along very often. David Mein was the perfect missionary storm, and rain in the north of Brazil he did.

David Mein, as any other Southern Baptist missionary in Brazil of the mid-1900s, had his deep disagreements with locals who identified with the Radical Movement. Mein, however, differed from any other Southern Baptist seminary president whose tenure was before or during his time at NBBTS in the sense that he took with unprecedented seriousness the need to establish local leadership. He accepted a position to teach at NBBTS in 1948[43] and by 1950 he was already serving as interim director while the official director, his father John Mein, was in the United States.[44] Both before and during his time as interim director, David Mein was no less critical of the radicals' nationalizing presence than his predecessors had been. He was, however, less concerned with the preservation of missionary representation in denominational institutions than with the maintenance of Southern Baptist ideological control.

The way forward, for Mein, was to implement an efficient pipeline of pro-missionary nationals who would go to the Southern Baptist seminaries in the United States and return to teach in Baptist seminaries in Brazil. There were, of course, already US-trained, pro-missionary Brazilians in important denominational positions in Brazil. After the Radical Movement, however, the FMB became more cautious in terms of supporting locals for US-training, once the most powerful leaders of the Radical Movement were also trained in the Southern United States. Soon after being elected president of NBBTS, Mein wrote Everett Gill saying that

> I am of the opinion that if possible we should choose Brazilians who seem to show some qualities of being professors and train them as much as possible. That leads me to say that at present we have two men in our seminary who seem to be future professors....I am trying

---

[43] From David Mein to Everett Gill Jr., February 13, 1948.
[44] From David Mein to n/a, January 27, 1950.

to see if it is possible to arrange scholarships for them in our seminaries in the U.S. that they might go and prepare themselves better to help us as future professors. In a case like this do you think that the Board in Richmond would be willing to give some assistance?[45]

He was, however, aware of the concerns raised by US-training of locals in the past:

Of course I realize that in the past some men have gone to the U.S. and have not panned out so well. I feel though that the spirit in Brazil has changed. I know that the spirit here in the seminary is 100 percent better than it used to be. I believe that these two young men could be trusted, and I don't think that they would give us any trouble in the future.[46]

Gill agreed to begin to finance Brazilian students who aimed to do graduate work in the United States, but this time the FMB wanted a stricter selection process and the assurance that such students would return to teach at the sending seminaries. Gill—and, through him, the FMB—wanted the candidates to be recommended by the missions, by the board of trustees, and by the faculty. In addition, the candidates were expected to have been tested in ministry and in the classroom.[47] In other words, the FMB wanted to make sure that no student that might go rogue got a scholarship from the Board.

Despite the stricter approach to selecting and recommending Brazilian students for theological work, Mein was intentional about sending a significant number of students to the United States with the understanding that these students would be future faculty members at NBBTS. At times, Mein tapped his personal network to secure financial help for Brazilian students studying in the United States, framing investment in a Brazilian student in the South as a missionary investment in Brazilian Baptist theological education.[48]

By all indications, David Mein's approach to the implementation of Southern Baptist ideological control in Brazil through theological education was not as antagonistic to local voice as the approach of those who

---

[45] From David Mein to Everett Gill Jr., January 16, 1953.
[46] From David Mein to Everett Gill Jr., January 16, 1953.
[47] From Everett Gill Jr. to David Mein, January 31, 1953.
[48] From David Mein to Miss Bryant, May 11, 1954.

preceded him, but it was more effective in its indoctrinating anxieties. He did realize the shortcomings of previous generations of missionaries in regard to their condescending treatment of Brazilian workers,[49] and condescension was not a part of his general *modus operandi*. He did, however, have a zeal for effective ideological dissemination. He wrote books and articles, organized conferences, preached frequently, and, in a number of cases, defended Brazilians by advocating with the FMB for more financial and logistical support for Brazilian-led initiatives. His concern with effective ideological dissemination, however, is clear in his sporadic mentions of the specter of nationalist radicalism among local Baptists. Ultimately, Mein wanted a smooth transition of power that would shift toward more local representation in denominational institutions. Of course the growth of the denomination itself already assured this transition to some extent, but Mein was intentional about setting in motion a schema that would ensure that theological education in the north of the country would be done by Brazilian bodies with Southern Baptist minds.

David Mein's legacy in the north of Brazil is impressive. He was given the title of Citizen of Recife in 1974, pastor emeritus at the Baptist Church of Cordeiro in 1982, professor and rector emeritus of NBBTS in 1984, FMB emeritus missionary in 1985, and emeritus president of the Brazilian Baptist Convention in 1994.[50] A monument in his honor was erected at NBBTS at the front of the David Mein Chapel. His students remember him as an open-minded leader with a loving character but a dictatorial tendency. He invited people such as R.Q. Leavewell, T.B. Maston, K.S. Lattourette, and Orlando Costas to give lectures at the school. He taught classes at Southern Baptist Theological Seminary, Southeastern Baptist Theological Seminary, New Orleans Baptist Theological Seminary, and Southwestern Baptist Theological Seminary. Though he received many offers to join the full-time faculty of the most important Southern Baptist institutions of theological education, he stayed at NBBTS until his retirement in 1984.[51] Under David Mein, the seminary grew in size and in the

---

[49] From David Mein to Frank Means, November 16, 1958.

[50] Oliveira, *Ousadia E Desafios Da Educação Teológica: 100 Anos Do Stbn*, 85.

[51] Mein wrote a book in which he narrated the contributions of the Southern Baptist Convention to Brazil, although by and large he omitted denominational controversies. See David Mein, *O Que Deus Tem Feito* (Rio de Janeiro: JUERP, 1982). Earlier, Ben Oliver had already published his version of the presence of the SBC in

number of courses it offered, being able to offer a Masters degree in theology in the 1970s. By 1984, when he stepped down from the leadership of the seminary, the school had fourteen buildings, many of them dedicated to Southern Baptist missionaries who worked in Brazil.

Partially due to the influence of John and David Mein, not only had the prominent Brazilian leaders incorporated into their worldview the core of the theocultural understandings of Southern Baptists, they also thought of theological knowledge as theological knowledge *in English*. Lívio Lindoso, a professor at NBBTS, manifested this reality when writing to the NBBTS's internal bulletin about the necessity of knowing English. He stated: "The seminary student who does not possess the key to this wealthy language [English] stays outside this palace of erudition, dies of thirst of knowledge at the foot of the spring, looks at the great crystal mirror but from the wrong side."[52] In the imagination of Brazilian Baptists, very often theological knowledge was valid and profitable only if measured positively by the orthodoxy of Southern Baptist knowledge in the original language of the missionaries.

Yet the strengthening of the NBBTS did not translate into the production of local theological contributions. What former missionary faculty Jerry Key wrote in the 1960s in his doctoral dissertation is still very much characteristic of Brazilian Baptist theological education: there is no emphasis on scholarly research, the Brazilian context is generally neglected, there is no adequate literature in Portuguese for extensive theological research in the language, and Baptist theological institutions in the country do not pay their local faculty an adequate salary.[53] Writing in the early 1960s, Key predicted that missionary ideological control and financial support was necessary for the effective continuation of theological education in Brazil until at least the late 1980s.[54] In retrospect, his prediction was actually quite optimistic.

---

the country. See Ben A. Oliver, *Baptists Building in Brazil* (Nashville: Broadman Press, 1942).

[52] Lívio Lindoso, "Porque Exames Vestibulares?," *Boletim do Seminário Teológico Batista do Norte do Brasil* 16, no. 3 (July 1956).

[53] Key, "The Rise and Development of Baptist Theological Education in Brazil, 1881-1963: A Historical and Interpretive Survey," 242-67.

[54] Key, 242-67

The South Brazil Baptist Theological Seminary

Field missionaries also perceived the independence of the SBBTS from the Baptist school in Rio negatively. They saw in the unified schools an easier path to accomplishing the dream of former longtime director, J.W. Shepard: developing a university with a superior theological department.[55] The seminary, however, became independent, and Djalma Cunha was elected as its first Brazilian director.[56] Cunha led the seminary from 1937 to 1945, when a feud with four faculty members led to the intervention of the BBC, which resulted in Cunha's firing and the re-establishment of missionary leadership for the next two decades. In 1945, four out of seven faculty members—Walter Kaschel, Antonio Mesquita, Reynaldo Purim, and Manuel Avelino de Souza—refused to teach, alleging Cunha's authoritative methods and his treatment of Mesquita and Souza as reasons for the rebellion.[57] In 1946, A.R. Crabtree was appointed as the new director of the SBBTS.[58] Crabtree's administration is key for understanding the development of SBBTS after the New Bases of Cooperation. His administration was responsible for shifting the institution away from the nationalist tendencies of many Brazilian Baptists at that time.[59]

In his history of the SBBTS, author Edgard Hallock called Crabtree's administration a "time of consolidation."[60] His tenure, however, consoli-

---

[55] Key, 114.

[56] Hallock and Ferreira, *Historia Do Seminario Teologico Batista Do Sul Do Brasil: 1908 a 1998*, 39.

[57] Walter Kaschel et al., "Decalração Necessária Aos Batistas Do Brasil " *Jornal Batista* no. 14 (April 5, 1945): 3; Hallock and Ferreira, *Historia Do Seminario Teologico Batista Do Sul Do Brasil: 1908 a 1998*, 46-47.

[58] "Flagrantes Da Convenção Batista Brasileira," *Jornal Batista* 46, no. 10 (1946): 2. Djalma Cunha attacked the seminary board for replacing him with A.R. Crabtree at the 1946 national convention. He planned on making a statement in his defense at the 1946 national convention but gave up on the idea.

[59] Sebastião Ribeiro and Pedro de Melo, "Comunicação Da Junta Do Seminário Do Sul," *Jornal Batista* 12, no. 3 (1946). The official communication of Crabtree's appointment in the *Jornal Batista* comes with the additional news that the whole faculty was remade by the new administration. Crabtree already had enough power and influence in the denomination in order to make this change in partnership with the pro-missionary board.

[60] Hallock and Ferreira, *Historia Do Seminario Teologico Batista Do Sul Do Brasil: 1908 a 1998*, 49-57.

dated much more than what Hallock emphasized, namely, the entire campus structure and financial health of the seminary. Crabtree's tenure also reestablished the organizational culture of the seminary as a missionary-oriented institution. Despite the fact that Hallock narrated the history of Crabtree's leadership exclusively in terms of his accomplishments in construction and enrollment, a period of missionary resurgence also marked Crabtree's tenure. A decade after the New Bases of Cooperation were negotiated, missionaries were coming back to the leadership of the central denominational institutions in Brazil, and they were keenly aware of the importance of consolidating themselves as the normative leaders of such bodies.

Crabtree had been involved in the controversies surrounding the Radical Movement since the early 1920s. Although he operated in the South of Brazil, and thus away from the more radical manifestations of Brazilian Baptist nationalism, several times he asked for FMB intervention in order to stop nationalistic tendencies in the denomination.[61] Before the implementation of the New Bases of Cooperation, Crabtree warned FMB secretary C.E. Maddry that the FMB "ought to be safeguarded against the promotion of selfish interest in the name of nationalism."[62] Brazilian nationalism was a strong concern for Crabtree, and the development of the denomination into a Brazilian-led body heightened a sense of need for missionary unity and organization. When it came to the leadership of SBBTS, Crabtree thought that J.W. Shepard's administration failed to foster missionary unity in the institution. According to Crabtree, Shepard often played missionaries against one another in order to keep power over the institution.[63] By contrast, Crabtree's administration, informed by the new institutional arrangements that favored local power, fostered missionary unity and organization.

Crabtree was named director of the seminary in 1946, but he was already involved in the institution's leadership during Djalma Cunha's administration. Soon after the independence of the seminary, it became clear that without foreign financial support the seminary would not be finan-

---

[61] See From A.R. Crabtree to T.B. Ray, April 15, 1923; From A.R. Crabtree to (illegible), May 12, 1923; From A.R. Crabtree to J.F. Love, September 25, 1923; and From A.R. Crabtree to C.E Maddry, December 2, 1935.

[62] From A.R. Crabtree to C.E Maddry, December 2, 1935.

[63] A.R. Crabtree, "Report on Dr. Muirhead's Resignation as President of Rio Baptist College and Seminary of Rio," (n.d.).

cially stable. In 1937, Crabtree therefore asked C.E. Maddry to send financial support to the seminary confidentially, for it was clear that the local leadership would not ask for money and, without foreign money, Crabtree thought the seminary would die.[64] In 1938, when Cunha went to the United States to study at the Southern Baptist Seminary in Louisville, Crabtree filled the position, serving as interim director. Crabtree was concerned that his leadership would alienate local churches that expected a national to fill the position, but Cunha wanted to receive a full salary when in the United States, and he could not do so unless a missionary—whose salary was paid by the FMB—was named temporarily in his place. Cunha pledged to use the *Jornal Batista* to appease the churches before he left to the United States in order to avoid any strong reaction against Crabtree's appointment, and the board of trustees wanted Crabtree to cover for Cunha while he was gone.[65] By 1939, Crabtree was already openly asking for FMB financial support as interim director of the SBBTS,[66] and planning ways by which to annul the New Bases of Cooperation.[67]

Despite missionary resistance, there was a qualified growth in the number of nationals in denominational institutions. This growth in the nationalization of institutional leadership left the FMB concerned about the property and the intellectual formation of Baptists in the country. Crabtree and Maddry's correspondence show that they were considering voiding the New Bases of Cooperation deal, but more strongly trying to exempt the Publishing House, the Church Loan Board, and the Property Holding Group from the arrangement. Maddry wrote:

> We ought to work out a special statue for these three agencies so that they will remain in the control of the Foreign Mission Board for ten years, and longer if found necessary. I believe that such a move on the part of our Board would indicate to the radicals in the Brazilian Convention that we mean business, and if they do anymore of the wild talking that was done in the last Convention, this Board itself will take the initiative and declare null and void this agreement.[68]

---

[64] From A.R. Crabtree to C.E. Maddry, April 5, 1937.
[65] From A.R. Crabtree to C.E. Maddry, May 19, 1938.
[66] From A.R. Crabtree to C.E. Maddry, February 25, 1939.
[67] From A.R. Crabtree to C.E. Maddry, April 14, 1939.
[68] From C.E. Maddry to A.R. Crabtree, May 4, 1939.

He called for the missions to unite on this matter, both in the north and in the South. Crabtree did not see danger in the nationalization of the property-holding boards, but the Publishing House was a concern for him.[69] But Crabtree knew that power and money guided institutional politics. Although radicalism was still perceived as a threat to the missionary conception of proper institutional functioning, Crabtree was convinced that "even the most radical Brazilians become pro-missionary when they get in positions of leadership where they need support of the Foreign Mission Board."[70]

Crabtree rightly thought that the FMB sometimes acted as if they thought that the missionaries wanted the institutions under Brazilian leadership to fail because of their jealousy of newly appointed local leaders. He recognized that missionary jealousy indeed existed, but did not agree that it went as far as a desire for Brazilian failure.[71] While Cunha was still in Louisville, Crabtree asked the FMB for more missionary faculty for SBBTS. He emphasized to the Board that it was through the seminaries that the missionaries had the greatest influence. Ideological formation, Crabtree recognized, is where true power lies.[72] Consequently, before the return of Djalma Cunha in 1941, Crabtree had already used his interim director status to lay the groundwork for greater missionary influence in the seminary in particular, but also more generally throughout the denomination.

When Crabtree was elected director of the SBBTS in 1946, not only was the denomination more pro-missionary than it had been a decade before, but the country had become more pro-American than it had ever been. Between the late 1930s and the end of the Second World War, the intentional efforts of the United States Government and private initiatives to seduce Brazil away from a pro-Germany stance and toward a pro-American disposition had succeeded. Brazilian popular culture had become pro-American within a decade, and despite the ongoing instances of Baptist Brazilian-missionary tension, Crabtree became director in a cultural environment that had never been more pro-American in the history

---

[69] From A.R. Crabtree to C.E. Maddry, May 25, 1939.

[70] From A.R. Crabtree to Jessie Ford, November 9, 1939.

[71] From A.R. Crabtree to Jessie Ford, November 9, 1939.

[72] From A.R. Crabtree to the Foreign Mission Board, March 31, 1941.

of the country.[73]

Crabtree's administration solidified the culture of Baptist theological education in the SBBTS, and his pro-missionary policies were unapologetic. Already in his first year, 1946, Crabtree wanted to substitute a number of Brazilian faculty with missionary personnel.[74] In addition, Crabtree was concerned with maintaining a missionary lineage of seminary leaders in the SBBTS. Writing to secretary Everett Gill, Jr., Crabtree said: "We need to get the seminary firmly established, and we need to have a good young man, preferably a missionary, in training to take my place six or seven years from now."[75] Crabtree imagined theological education and ideological formation as the last holdout of missionary influence in the country. He was constantly concerned with recruiting missionaries for faculty positions and in establishing a pipeline of missionary teachers to replace outgoing missionary faculty, and he often lamented when he had to hire Brazilian faculty members.[76]

In a climate in which Brazilians increasingly were taking over leadership positions in the Brazilian Baptist Convention, Crabtree was concerned about the strategic power of missionary ideological control, which was exercised through the seminaries and literary production. The nationalization of the Presbyterian seminary worked together with the unprecedented Brazilian presence in denominational leadership in intensifying Crabtree's anxieties concerning seminary control. He wrote:

> I plead for new missionaries for the seminary, where I am sure their position and influence will count for most. If we cannot get mis-

---

[73] See Moniz Bandeira, *A Presença Dos Estados Unidos No Brasil (Dois Séculos De Hisória)* (Rio de Janeiro: Civilização Brasileira, 1973); Frank D. McCann, *The Brazilian-American Alliance, 1937-1945* (Princeton: Princeton University Press, 1973); Antonio Pedro Tota, *The Seduction of Brazil: The Americanization of Brazil During World War II* (Austin: University of Texas Press, 2009). The change in the stance of Brazilians in general toward American immigrant in Brazil was also noticed by missionaries. Appleby, Crabtree, and John Mein mention explicitly that Brazilians treated United States missionaries better after the Brazilian Army joined the allies in the Second World War.

[74] From A.R. Crabtree to M.T. Rankin, November 27, 1946.

[75] From A.R. Crabtree to E. Gill, Jr., August 25, 1947.

[76] From A.R. Crabtree to E. Gill, Jr., October 13, 1947; From A.R. Crabtree to E. Gill, Jr., December 10, 1951.

sionaries for the seminary, the Administrative Board will put Brazilians in this strategic institution, and missionary influence in general will decline even more rapidly, as it has so rapidly declined among Presbyterians, a denomination which has an all-Brazilian Faculty in their seminary, and are now obliging American missionaries to work in the interior.[77]

Despite Crabtree's sporadic mention of his alleged desire for local leadership, whenever his strategy for the seminary and the denomination was described, it was paired with an imagination that correlated Brazilian leadership presence with missionary obsolescence—and missionary obsolescence with damage to the Gospel message.

Crabtree's tenure as director of SBBTS was frankly dedicated to an intentional overturning of Brazilian-informed tendencies in Brazilian theological education, both in terms of administrative roles and ideological formation. The FMB could never fulfill all of his desires for missionary personnel, but Crabtree changed the culture of theological education back to its original, missionary-friendly disposition and paved the way for future leadership that he had nurtured. When he stepped down, he recommended that his pupil, Ben Oliver, be appointed in his stead. The Board of Trustees obliged and at the end of 1955, Oliver was elected director of SBBTS.[78] Crabtree stepped down with a sense of mission accomplished. The seminary had new buildings, record enrollment, and a renewed sense of the common missionary ideological control. Crabtree was named Emeritus Director of the SBBTS, a measure of the lasting imprint he left on Brazilian Baptist theological education.[79]

As planned, Ben Oliver's term was a continuation of the establishment of missionary ideological control. His recollection of his first day as president of the SBBTS illustrates his self-understanding at the beginning of his tenure:

---

[77] From A.R. Crabtree to E. Gill, Jr., August 31, 1949.

[78] From the Board of Trustees of the South Brazil Seminary, December 7, 1955. Starting with Oliver's adminstration, the nomenclature of the title of the main officer of the seminaries changed from "director" to "rector." For the sake of simplicity, however, I will keep using the title "director" for the purpose of this piece.

[79] "O Seminário Do Sul Tem Novo Reitor," *Jornal Batista* 55, no. 52 (1955): 4.

It was with a bit of fear and trembling [that] I occupied the chair and office which Dr. A.R. Crabtree, my worthy and honored predecessor, had left. I remember how I felt the first time I sat at his desk: I had entered alone into his office, and felt the need of his mantle to be thrown about my shoulders, so that I might have a double portion of that spirit of wisdom, sympathy and courage that I knew I should need so very much.[80]

From the outset, it was clear that Oliver would follow the trajectory set by Crabtree, as indeed he did. From his earliest times in Brazil, Oliver had been a staunch critic of nationalist tendencies among Brazilian Baptists. He came to Brazil at the height of the disputes over the correct interpretation of the New Bases of Cooperation, and he was so upset with national assertiveness in regard to denominational representation that, after his 1939 confrontation with locals, he considered never again attending meetings of the national convention.[81]

In 1954, before assuming the official directorship of the SBBTS, Oliver went to the United States to teach a history of missions course at Baylor University and to investigate what was being done in Southern Baptist theological education—so that he could transplant Southern Baptist methods to SBBTS. In December 6, 1955, when he was already director, Oliver informed the seminary board that the SBBTS had decided to adopt the Abstract of Principles that was followed by the Southern Baptist Theological Seminary in Kentucky. Werner Kaschel was elected dean of the SBBTS.[82] Out of the fifteen new faculty appointments made under Oliver, ten were missionaries.[83] Oliver shared Crabtree's conviction that the seminaries were the most important strategic institutions of Brazilian Baptist life and, not unlike his mentor, he acted in favor of missionary ideological control.[84] Like David Mein, he did, however, send a number of locals to be trained in Southern Baptist institutions and return to teach at SBBTS.[85]

---

[80] Ben Oliver, Annual Report to the South Brazil Mission, n.d.

[81] From Ben Oliver to C.E. Maddry, April 19, 1939.

[82] Hallock and Ferreira, *Historia Do Seminario Teologico Batista Do Sul Do Brasil: 1908 a 1998*, 59-60.

[83] Key, "The Rise and Development of Baptist Theological Education in Brazil, 1881-1963: A Historical and Interpretive Survey," 144.

[84] Atas da Convenção Batista Brasileira, 1957, 95.

[85] From Ben Oliver to Frank Means, March 22, 1967.

Of course, missionary control was paired with United States money and symbolic power. When it came to finances, throughout Oliver's tenure, for example, the FMB paid for an average of sixty percent of students' tuition.[86] When the SBBTS inaugurated two new buildings in 1960, the director of the *Jornal Batista* wrote an editorial piece thanking "the brothers of the other América" for raising the money for the project and chided Brazilians for not contributing as much as Baptists in the United States to the Baptist educational cause in the country.[87] Missionaries such as Mein, Crabtree, and Oliver were not ill-intended people; they were simply well intentioned advocates of the famous capitalist adage: you get what you pay for!

The symbolic power of imagined United States standards of education was also important throughout the history of missionary activity in Brazil, and it had become the golden theological standard in unprecedented ways in post-war Brazil. Reporting on a conference of the two major seminaries in 1956, Paulo Silva celebrated the standards of Brazilian theological education by saying that "the Brazilian Baptist seminaries have followed the progress of United States theological education, and this is reason for celebration, because such education provides the leaders of our 'School of the Prophets' a broad vision of a well-prepared ministry."[88] In this and many other instances, the country's most widely read Baptist publication openly celebrated ideological americanization.

In 1967, Dr. João F. Soren, a pro-missionary Brazilian who was a graduate of Southern Baptist Theological Seminary, was elected director of the SBBTS. Yet students opposed Soren's administration and there was some tension between faculty and students. By 1970 Soren already wanted to leave his appointment as director, but the board of the seminary asked him to stay a while.[89] The financial issues that undergirded the tensions

---

[86] Ben Oliver, "Carta Aberta Aos Pastores Batistas Do Brasil," *Jornal Batista* 56, no. 9 (1956): 8. Oliver did try to enhance the cooperation of local churches for the SBBTS's finances. He initiated scholarship programs as well. During his term, however, the FMB still carried the heavy load of seminary expenses.

[87] Almir Gonçalves, "O Seminário Não Pode Parar," *Jornal Batista* 55, no. 50 (1960): 2.

[88] Paulo Wailler da Silva, "O Seminário Do Norte E O Do Sul Em Proveitosa Conferêmcia," *Jornal Batista* 56, no. 25 (1956): 1.

[89] Hallock and Ferreira, *Historia Do Seminario Teologico Batista Do Sul Do Brasil: 1908 a 1998*, 76-78.

faced by Soren, however, did not go unnoticed by David Mein, who went beyond his boundaries as president of the NBBTS to advocate for his Brazilian colleague. Mein's defense of Soren reveals that Mein was perceptive in regard to a popular Brazilian criticism of the Southern Baptist missions in Brazil, namely, that the missions only sent appropriate financial support to institutions led by Southern Baptist missionaries. Mein wrote Secretary Frank Means, saying

> I'm sure that you are acquainted with what is happening in the South Brazil Seminary financial wise. So I won't go into that part. My concern is that should nothing be done to get the seminary out of the situation in which it finds itself we might have a repercussion in a far greater scale and consequences of the 1923 and 1940 nationalist movement among Baptists. It has always been voiced abroad in Brazil that when a Brazilian is head of an institution the Missions do not give them sufficient funds to administer the institutions with; but that when a missionary is head of the institution money flows. When Dr. Djalma Cunha (who recently passed away) was president of the South Brazil Seminary money was hard to be had; then Dr. Crabtree and Dr. Oliver followed him, and during their administrations buildings were built, etc...; and now with Dr. Soren as president apparently they are having a hard time making ends meet. About six weeks ago I had a letter from a pastor in Rio in which he made the statement: the situation of the Rio Seminary is a clear evidence that when Brazilians are in administrative positions the missions do not help them financially.[90]

Mein went on to say that either the FMB had to intervene and help the SSBTS or they would have a new, stronger form of the Radical Movement on their hands. Frank Means denied that the missions treated Brazilians differently, and tellingly Soren did not last in the leadership of SBBTS.

In 1971, the president of the seminary board, David Malta Nascimento, assumed the directorship of the SBBTS. During Soren's and Malta's terms, the enrollment of students had grown to unprecedented figures and some new buildings had been added. The number of courses

---

[90] From David Mein to Frank Means, November 16, 1970.

offered also increased. The imprint of missionary ideological control, however, was still noticeable by the end of Malta's directorship in the mid-1980s, and direct FMB financial support for the institution as well as support in the form of missionary faculty salary was still fundamental for the functioning of the SBBTS.[91]

The Brazilianization of the Brazilian Baptist Convention

At the national level, the perceived radical victory of 1936 was also short-lived. At the 1941 national convention, there was a major win for the pro-missionary side of Brazilian Baptist life, and local and FMB personnel were appointed to key denominational positions. From the perspective of the pro-missionary side, the result of the 1941 national convention signified the resolution of the "radical problem" at a national level, and from that point on radicalism became more an imagined than a real threat to the pro-missionary establishment.[92] The presidency of the BBC, for example, from 1946 until 1970 was held most notably by two pro-missionary leaders who often alternated in the post, namely João F. Soren and Rubens Lopes.[93] Soren was president six times during the decades that followed the reunification and Lopes held the post thirteen times. Munguba Sobrinho, another pro-missionary local, held the post four times in twenty years.[94]

Despite the efforts and qualified success of Southern Baptist missionaries in implementing ideological control among Brazilian Baptists through theological training, literary production, and financial dependence, the growth of Brazilian Baptists ensured the increasing presence of Brazilians in denominational organizations. A number of organizations and initiatives were implemented as the national reverberations of Brazilian Baptist nationalism waned. Brazilian Baptists stopped meeting in a national convention between 1942 and 1945 because of the Second World War. When the BBC began meeting again, anti-missionary nationalism was not as much of a threat as it had been ten years earlier. In 1949, the Youth National Congress began its biannual meetings, a rhythm that

---

[91] Anais da Convenção Batista Brasileira (1981-1985).
[92] Pereira, *História Dos Batistas No Brasil (1882-1982)*, 144-45.
[93] Pereira, 155.
[94] Pereira, 156.

lasted until 1981.[95] Evangelistic crusades sponsored by the Brazilian National Mission Board of the BBC also ensured exponential growth in the denomination.[96]

The mid-to-late-1950s were key for the development of the Baptist denomination in Brazil. In 1955, the BBC became fully recognized by the Brazilian government and became the legal owner of denominational properties.[97] In the same year, the BBC decided to begin a Baptist Bank, which was led by Antonio Mesquita until its dissolution less than three years after its establishment.[98] Despite its short existence, its initial approval by the BBC had signaled the development of a spirit of administrative boldness that was unprecedented among local Baptist leaders. In 1958, a new cooperative financial plan was established. From then on, the churches were to send a minimum of ten percent of their budgets to the state convention. The state conventions then sent forty percent of the received contributions to the Executive Board of the BBC and the BBC distributed the moneys according to the needs of denominational institutions.[99]

The institutions that benefited the most from this cooperative plan were the National Mission Board, the World Mission Board, and the two major seminaries. By 1981, twenty percent of the budget went to the National Mission Board, nine percent to the World Mission Board, and thirteen percent to each of the two major seminaries.[100] In 1959, the demands of the 1923 radicals were finally met without any notable disturbance. During that year, in a meeting with FMB's secretaries Frank Means and Baker James Cauthen, new cooperative measures were taken. Two major measures of this new deal were of particular and substantial value: that the financial contributions of the FMB to Brazil—which by then were not as significant proportionately as they were during the Radical Movement—

---

[95] Pereira, 166.
[96] Joe Underwood, "O Idealizador Das Campanhas Simultâneas De Evangelização No Brazil," *Jornal Batista* 65, no. 42 (1965).
[97] Pereira, *História Dos Batistas No Brasil (1882-1982)*, 164.
[98] Anônio Neves de Mesquita, "Marcha Pra Campanha Pró Banco," *Jornal Batista* 55, no. 26 (1955); Silas Botelho, "Carta a Um Jovem Ministro," *Jornal Batista* 55, no. 26 (1955); and Pereira, *História Dos Batistas No Brasil (1882-1982)*, 166-67.
[99] Anais da Convenção Batista Brasileira, 1958.
[100] Anais da Convenção Batista Brasileira, 1981.

were administered by local Brazilian state conventions, and that the properties of major denominational institutions, such as the seminaries and the publishing house, became properties of the Brazilian Baptist Convention.[101]

The symbolic strength of the Baptist denomination in Brazil was clearly manifested in 1960 with the meeting of the Baptist World Alliance in the country. João Pereira, who was an organizer of the meeting, celebrated Billy Graham's closing event, which packed a stadium in Rio de Janeiro, not only as the first countrywide demonstration of evangelical strength but as the most important Protestant occasion in twentieth-century Brazil.[102] João F. Soren was, in the same year, elected the first Latin American president of the Baptist World Alliance. Yet only a few years after the joys of the Baptist World Alliance historic meeting, a major issue once again brought division to the Brazilian Baptist denomination—a topic dealt with in more detail in the next chapter.

Brazil as a Missionary-Sending Nation

Brazilian Baptists began sending missionaries to foreign nations early in the history of the BBC. Already in 1908 the Brazilian Baptist Convention had a missionary presence in Chile, and Portugal followed in 1911.[103] In 1918, the FMB took responsibility for the work in Chile, and the BBC remained responsible for the administration of the work in Portugal.[104] New fields of work emerged systematically only after the 1970s. Before the 1970s, only Bolivia (1946) and Paraguay (1964) became additional foreign fields of the BBC. From 1970 until 1982, the World Mission Board of the BBC (WMB) included thirteen new fields in its efforts towards world evangelization: Mozambique (1970), Angola (1973), Azores (1974), Uruguay (1975), Argentina (1976), Rhodesia (1976), Venezuela (1977), France (1977), Spain (1977), Canada (1978), South Africa (1980), the United States (1981), Peru (1982), and Ecuador (1982).[105]

The rapid growth of a Brazilian Baptist presence in the world after

---

[101] Pereira, *História Dos Batistas No Brasil (1882-1982)*, 171-72.

[102] Pereira, 180-81.

[103] Mesquita, *História Dos Baptistas Do Brasil*, 116–17.

[104] Mesquita, 116–17.

[105] The *Jornal Batista* is the best tool to trace when the BBC entered each country.

the 1970s is, no doubt, the fruit of the financial and numeric success attained by the denomination in the previous decades. It is also the result of Brazilian early appropriation US missionary methods. The WMB was created together with the BBC, and although in 1907 there were only around four thousand Baptists in Brazil, the urge to evangelize the world was institutionalized as soon as the national convention was created.[106] When the *Jornal Batista*, in 1967, celebrated the sixtieth anniversary of Brazilian Baptist global expansion, there were already fifty churches in Portugal and thirty ordained Portuguese pastors. In Bolivia, in 1967, there were twelve churches, a seminary, and two primary schools—and the new work in Paraguay was also bearing fruit.[107]

The BBC denominated the second Sunday of March as "Foreign Missions Day," and the tenth and eleventh issues of the *Jornal Batista* were usually directed toward the celebration and advertisement of the work of the WMB as well as toward fundraising. In the tenth issue of the *Jornal Batista* of 1971, soon after the WMB entered Africa, a note on the front cover highlighted the spirit of evangelization and administrative independence attained by the BBC:

> Next Sunday is Foreign Missions Day. It must be a day of joy, enthusiasm, and inspiration. Now we have twenty missionaries in Portugal, Bolivia, Paraguay, and Africa! They are Brazilian Baptist missionaries and not of the Foreign Mission Board, because it rests on the Brazilian Baptists the responsibility of giving these missionaries material support and all spiritual help. We need to know their names, the places where they are serving, the work that they are doing, so that we can better pray for them. May all Brazilian Baptists unite in prayer and contribute generously, so that our goal may be fulfilled.[108]

By the 1970s, Brazilian Baptists had developed a strong denominational organization and were able to think about themselves as a missionary denomination that was an independent but close daughter of Southern Baptist missionaries.

---

[106] "O Campo é o Mundo: Sessenta Anos de Missões Estrangeiras," *Jornal Batista* 67, no. 10 (1967): 1.

[107] "O Campo é o Mundo: Sessenta Anos de Missões Estrangeiras," 1.

[108] Note on the front page of the Jornal Batista, March 7, 1971.

The *Jornal Batista* faithfully supported the foreign missionary cause and individual missionaries were constantly showcased in the periodical. Some issues of the *Jornal Batista* went as far as publishing the birthdays and addresses of all the missionaries in the countries with Brazilian Baptist presence.[109] In the 1970s, Brazilian Baptists also began to think about expanding their reach into North America, which was not on the Board's radar until the denomination noticed the mass migration of Portuguese people to the continent. A prominent missionary object of the BBC, the Portuguese Catholic, was the object that inserted North America into the BBC's missionary imagination. In 1974, editor J. Reis Pereira talked about Brazilian Baptist missionary presence in the world as follows:

> Someone could say that it is pretentious of Brazilian Baptists to speak of world missions when the world is so big and the Brazilian Baptist community so small. Well, we can, as William Carey said, have the world in our hearts even though we have not yet reached the ends of the earth. What is important is the ideal. However, it is proper to remember that we have missionaries in Portugal, Bolivia, Paraguay, Mozambique, and Angola. That is, we have missionaries in Europe, South America, and Africa. The Board already received a call coming from Asia. The growing Portuguese community in Australia can become a challenge for us in the near future and some are already saying it is time for us to thank those who brought us the gospel and send missionaries to North America.[110]

The missionary imagination of Brazilian Baptists grew increasingly ambitious in the 1970s, and a number of countries in the developing world began to appear on the denominational radar.[111]

---

[109] J. Reis Pereira, "Dia de Aniversário e Endereço Dos Missionários," *Jornal Batista* 83, no. 10 (1973): 3. A similar article also appeared in the tenth edition of the *Jornal Batista* in 1975 and, in other years, the *Jornal Batista* mentioned just the names of every missionary asking for nationwide prayer and financial support.

[110] J. Reis Pereira, "Dia de Missões Mundiais," *Jornal Batista* 74, no. 10 (1974): 3.

[111] Talking about Global South Christians in Europe, Jenkins noted that missionaries often have a sense of repaying obligations to European missionaries who reached them. This is certainly true of Brazilian Baptists and their relationship to the SBC. See Jenkins, *God's Continent*, 90.

The cover page of the *Jornal Batista* of March 14, 1976 printed a map showing the future plans of the Board. The ambitious plans of the WMB regarding the appointment of missionaries to global nations become more explicit in that issue. In addition to Ecuador, Venezuela, Peru, and Indonesia, the Board planned to enter Canada, Spain, and France. In regard to Canada, the article noted that "there is an enormous Portuguese colony in Canada and representatives of Canadian Baptists established contact with us in regards to sending missionaries for working with that group of Portuguese people. Because there is no language barrier, it would be a good advantage for the start of this evangelizing effort."[112]

The rationale for thinking about going to France initially mentioned the Portuguese, but it focused on the possibility of reaching French people: "There are, according to some, around one million Portuguese people in France. ... The president of the Baptist French Federation manifested his desire for Brazilian Baptists to go to France to preach for the French people."[113] A year later, when the *Jornal Batista* reported the appointment of missionary Paulo Sória and his family to France, the focus was on reaching the French people, but the Portuguese people in France was also a factor.[114] It is, thus, in the 1970s that the plan of reaching Latin America, Lusophone Africa, and the Portuguese people abroad began to be set in motion by a national convention that was becoming increasingly autonomous in administrative terms, even if not in ideological ones.

In their global enterprise, Brazilian Baptists thought of themselves as faithful and proud imitators of English and United States missionaries. Mentions of figures such as William Carey, Judson Taylor, and a number of Southern Baptist missionaries who had gone to Brazil abound in the *Jornal Batista*, bearing testimony to the lineage that Brazilian Baptists wanted to emulate. Answering criticisms that the BBC was an explicit imitator of Southern Baptist strategies and goals, J. Reis Pereira wrote:

> We received the Gospel from the United States. It was natural, therefore, for us to use their methods of evangelization and religious education. We gave thanks to God for these, because, humanly

---

[112] "Avançando Pelo Mundo Até Os Confins Da Terra!," *Jornal Batista* 76, no. 11 (1976): 1.

[113] "Avançando Pelo Mundo Até Os Confins Da Terra!," 1, 4.

[114] "Primeiro Missionário Dos Batistas Brasileiros a França," *Jornal Batista* 77, no. 29 (1977): 5.

speaking, practicing these methods is one of the reasons why we grew.[115]

When the *Jornal Batista* decided to pay tribute to the fifteen single women who were doing missionary work in six countries, it honored them by comparing the missionaries with a United States Baptist figure:

> In this day of foreign missions, we pay tribute to the young Baptist women who are dedicating their lives to missionary work. We have been focusing on the almost twenty missionary couples, but today we thought convenient to celebrate the single young women who left everything here in Brazil in order to go to their fields. They are our Lottie Moon.[116]

The pictures and names of the young single women were printed on the periodical's front cover. Three of them were in Europe, two in Africa, and ten in Latin America—icons of the Brazilian success in replicating the faith of Southern Baptist fathers and not-so-submissive mothers.

The fundraising for Brazilian foreign missions in the 1970s went better than planned. From 1970 to 1978, the yearly financial goal had been surpassed every single year. The progressive increase of the financial goal in the 1970s was also positive, even considering inflation. In 1970, the goal was four hundred thousand *cruzeiros*, and in 1978 the goal was up to eleven million *cruzeiros*, a growth of over twenty-six hundred percent over the course of eight years.[117] From 1976 to 1977, the goal grew seventy-one percent—from three and a half to six million *cruzeiros*—and it was surpassed. From 1977 to 1978, the new increase was eighty-one percent;[118] the eleven million *cruzeiros* that were raised would help to fund new missionaries in several fields. According to the director of the *Jornal Batista*, among the new expenses was the beginning of the project of expanding missionary work to reach Portuguese immigrants in developed countries. Pereira wrote that "it is possible that as early as July we send a couple to Canada, in order to listen to the appeal of Canadian Baptists who want a

---

[115] J. Reis Pereira, "Métodos Norte-Americanos," *Jornal Batista* 74, no. 15 (1974): 13.

[116] "As Moças Missionárias: Quinze Moças Batistas Brasileiras Estão Dando Suas Vidas a Pregação Do Evangelho Em Terras Distantes," *Jornal Batista* 77, no. 11 (1977): 1.

[117] J. Reis Pereira, "O Alvo de Missões Estrangeiras," *Jornal Batista* 78, no.11 (1978): 3.

[118] One must keep in mind, however, the high inflation of 1970s Brazil. In 1978, for instance, inflation was close to forty percent.

Brazilian missionary working in Toronto, where there are 300,000 Portuguese people."[119] Later in 1978, the WMB sent Carlos and Glaucia Keidann to Canada along with two other missionaries to Spain.[120] It was the investment in the Portuguese in Canada that provided a model and an encouragement for sending Brazilian missionaries to the United States in 1981. By then, the financial goal had grown to ninety million *cruzeiros*, once the currency fluctuation had become a bigger issue given the presence of Brazilian Baptists in North American and European nations.[121]

The *Toronto Star* published an article on January 27, 1979, highlighting the work of Brazilian Baptist missionaries among the Portuguese population in Canada.[122] The *Jornal Batista* published a copy of the headline and the picture published in the Canadian newspaper, showing Brazilian missionary Carlos Keidann alongside a Portuguese entrepreneur inside his seafood store. The caption to the picture, as published by the *Toronto Star*, read "Rev. João Carlos Keidann, right, talks to parishioner Amador Fernandez in Fernandez's fish store on Dundas St. W."[123] *Toronto Star* contributor, Leslie Tarr, observed that the church to which the Brazilian missionaries went was Olivet Baptist Church, a church that formed in 1901 and now found itself surrounded by Portuguese immigrants. Tarr wrote that, according to Keidann, around two thousand Portuguese families lived in the area around Olivet Baptist Church, and he planned to try to evangelize all of them, despite the presence of the seventeen Roman Catholic priests that gave assistance to Portuguese Catholics in the city.[124] In 1981, missionaries Humberto Viegas Fernandes and Marilena Andreoni Fernandes—the first and most historically significant WMB missionary couple sent to the Untied States—appeared on the front cover of the *Jornal Batista* together with the other missionaries of the WMB along with the new financial goal for the year: 220 million *cruzeiros*.[125]

---

[119] Pereira, "O Alvo de Missões Estrangeiras," 3.

[120] J. Reis Pereira, "Lembremos de Nossos Missionários," *Jornal Batista* 79, no. 10 (1979): 3.

[121] "Hoje é Dia de Missões Mundiais," *Jornal Batista* 81, no. 10 (1981): 1.

[122] Leslie K. Tarr, "Growing Portuguese Population Brings a Missionary from Brazil," *Toronto Star*, January 27, 1979, sec. G, 6.

[123] "Nosso Missionário No Canadá é Notícia," *Jornal Batista* 79, no. 11 (1979): 1.

[124] Tarr, "Growing Portuguese Population Brings a Missionary from Brazil," 6.

[125] "Nossos Missionários No Exterior," *Jornal Batista* 82, no. 11 (1982): 1.

Southern Baptist Symbolic Presence

Brazilian Baptists watched the administrative, social, and theological developments in Southern Baptist life closely[126]—usually siding with the most conservative elements within the SBC[127]—and, in Brazil, resisted a

---

[126] Direct reporting on SBC events grew as the number of Brazilian Baptists studying and working in the United States began to serve as correspondents of the *Jornal Batista*. This tendency increased exponentially in the 1970s. See Joelcio Rodrigues Barreto, "Um Comentário," *Jornal Batista* 70, no. 42 (1970): 12; Elias M. Gomes, "A Convenção Batista Do Sul: Últimos Flashes," *Jornal Batista* 72, no. 33 (1972): 8; Elias M. Gomes, "A Convenção Batista Do Sul," *Jornal Batista* 73, no. 29 (1973): 8; Elias M. Gomes, "A Convenção Batista Do Sul: Fatos E Personalidades Que Impressionam," *Jornal Batista* 73, no. 33 (1973): 8; Benilton Carlos Bezerra, "Os Batistas Da Convenção Batista Do Sul Dos Estados Unidos Tomam Posição Face Aos Problemas Sociais," *Jornal Batista* 68, no. 40 (1968): 1; Elias M. Gomes, "A Convenção Do Sul Em Fatos E Figuras," *Jornal Batista* 74, no. 30 (1974): 12; Elias M. Gomes, "O Primeiro Preto Em 129 Anos: A Nova Diretoria Da Southern Baptist Convention," *Jornal Batista* 74, no. 29 (1974): 8; Elias M. Gomes, "The Southern Baptist Convention: Dallas—Texas—11 a 13 de Junho," *Jornal Batista* 74, no. 28 (1974): 8; Elias M. Gomes, "Um Preambulo Espetacular (A Convenção Do Sul - 1974)," *Jornal Batista* 74, no. 27 (1974): 8; Elias M. Gomes, "Chales Colson - Um Testemunho Inolvidável," *Jornal Batista* 75, no. 29 (1975): 8; Elias M. Gomes, "Ressoa O Sino Da Liberdade: A 188a Asembéia Da Convenção Do Sul," *Jornal Batista* 75, no. 28 (1975): 7–8; "A Maior Convenção Batista Do Mundo," *Jornal Batista* 76, no. 30 (1976): 1; "A Maior Convenção Batista Do Mundo II," *Jornal Batista* 76, no. 31 (1976): 1; "A Maior Convenção Batista Do Mundo III," *Jornal Batista* 76, no. 32 (1976): 8; "A Maior Convenção Batista Do Mundo IV," *Jornal Batista* 76, no. 33 (1976): 2; "A Maior Convenção Do Mundo Reuniu-Se Em Kansas City," *Jornal Batista* 77, no. 31 (1977): 1–2; J. Reis Pereira, "Linha Conservadora Vence Na Convenção Batista Do Sul," *Jornal Batista* 80, no. 28 (1980): 3; J. Reis Pereira, "Lições Da Convenção Do Sul," *Jornal Batista* 81, no. 15 (1981): 3; J. Reis Pereira, "Oremos Pela Conveção Do Sul," *Jornal Batista* 81, no. 22 (1981): 3; J. Reis Pereira, "Oremos Pela Conveção Do Sul II," *Jornal Batista* 81, no. 23 (1981): 3; J. Reis Pereira, "Os Batistas Do Sul Continuam Crescendo," *Jornal Batista* 81, no. 12 (1981): 3; J. Reis Pereira, "Paz Na Convenção Do Sul," *Jornal Batista* 81, no. 28 (1981): 3; J. Reis Pereira, "Uma Visita ao 'Baptist Standard' I," *Jornal Batista* 81, no. 39 (1981): 3; J. Reis Pereira, "Uma Visita ao 'Baptist Standard' II," *Jornal Batista* 81, no. 40 (1981): 3.

[127] Gomes, "A Convenção Batista Do Sul: Últimos Flashes," 8; Elias M. Gomes, "Fatos Memoráveis: A 188a Assmbléia Da Convenção Do Sul," *Jornal Batista* 75, no. 30 (1975): 12; J. Reis Pereira, "A Eleição de Adrian Rodgers," *Jornal Batista* 79, no. 29 (1979): 3; "O Novo Presidente Da Convenção Batista Do Sul Dos EUA," *Jornal Batista* 79, no. 28 (1979): 1.

number of theological issues that were first introduced to Brazilian Baptists due to their prominence in the Southern Baptist imagination, such as the rise of Darwinism and woman ordination.[128] Theologically, there was little doctrinal difference between the Brazilian Baptist leadership and the conservative corners of Southern Baptist life. One of the ongoing features of the *Jornal Batista* was its dissemination of Southern Baptist theological anxieties, and a number of theological responses to the social issues in the United States made to the pages of the journal.

The *Jornal Batista* was, for instance, the stage for a campaign for prohibition in Brazil. Several articles condemning the use and legalization of alcohol were printed by the periodical. In a 1925 front cover of the journal, then director S.L. Watson made it clear that following the example of the United States—to which he referred only as "a great nation"—would mean increasing the Christlikeness of Brazilian society. He wrote

> Death to King Alcohol! A great nation was able to hurt this enemy of humanity, making it illegal and persecuting it restlessly with the power of law: it was the Christian spirit, through Sunday schools and evangelical churches, that achieved this victory. Evangelical churches and Sunday schools in Brazil must also join the fight against King Alcohol.

In the news section of the journal, a number of news articles relating alleged moral and financial gains of prohibition also appeared.[129]

The Scopes Trial also spurred several anti-evolutionist articles in the *Jornal Batista*. This Baptist tension with scientific evidence is ongoing in both Brazil and the United States, but was introduced to the Brazilian Baptist audience through Southern Baptist lenses. The first article directed specifically to the Scopes Trial appeared in June of 1925 and looked to Southern Baptist statements for a correct interpretation of the events. After a long diatribe about the evils of evolutionary theory, the article asked:

---

[128] Harold Wilson Bertrand, "Se Minha Mãe Fosse Pastora...," *Jornal Batista* 76, no. 46 (1976): 5; José Ednaldo Cavalcanti, "A Posição Da Mulher Na Igreja," *Jornal Batista* 76, no. 36 (1976): 3; José Ednaldo Cavalcanti, "Pastores Do Novo Testamento," *Jornal Batista* 76, no. 37 (1976): 5; Silas Melo, "A Posição Do Homem e Da Mulher No Universo," *Jornal Batista* 76, no. 39 (1976): 2;7; Russel P. Shedd, "E Bíblica a Ordenação de Mulheres?," *Jornal Batista* 76, no. 35 (1976): 2; 11.

[129] "De Toda a Parte," *Jornal Batista* 25, no. 25 (1925): 2; "De Toda a Parte," *Jornal Batista* 25, no. 26 (1925): 2.

"Would it be fair that citizens pay their taxes for a public school that corrupts their sons' ideas? Or where they teach them dishonestly mere theories as established facts? Certainly not."[130] The author then published the creationist declaration put together by "six of the greatest Baptists, namely, Drs. E.Y. Mullins, S.M. Brown, W.J. McGlothlin, E.C. Dargan, L.R. Scarborough, and Z.T. Cody" that supported creationism boldly.[131]

The major social, political, and theological developments that took place in the United States were translated into Southern Baptist idioms for the Brazilian Baptist audience. At times, there was a qualified level of ideological diversity, as in the case of Martin Luther King Jr.'s legacy. The most prominent Civil Rights leader was remembered sometimes as a fighter for peace and sometimes as a misguided radical,[132] but Baptists often interpreted his fight for civil rights as a secondary distraction to what they considered the most important Christian exercise: evangelism.[133] When it came to the controversies that culminated in the division of the Southern Baptist denomination in the United States, Brazilian Baptists were also keenly aware of what was at stake, and by and large they were as scared of the alleged theological liberalism as the conservative wing of Southern Baptist life claimed to be.[134]

In 1970, Joelcio Barreto wrote for the *Jornal Batista* about the controversy of the Broadman Bible Commentary. Barreto, who was studying at Southern Seminary in Louisville, had a copy of the Genesis volume, written by G. Henton Davies, and was reprimanded by a friend of his who was a pastor in Texas.[135] He let the Brazilian Baptist audience know of the dangers that the SBC saw in the commentary, despite the fact that he intended to keep his copy. In 1972, Elias Gomes wrote that a new edition

---

[130] T.R.T., "O Evolucionismo e a Bíbila," *Jornal Batista* 25, no. 30 (1925): 3.

[131] T.R.T., 3.

[132] "Martin Luther King Jr, O Apóstolo Da Paz, Morto Pela Violência," *Jornal Batista* 68, no. 15 (1968): 1.

[133] João José Soares Filho, "Martin Luther King, Um Visionário a Menos," *Jornal Batista* 68, no. 23 (1968): 8.

[134] For two of the finest assessments of the controversies in the Southern Baptist Convention, see Nancy Tatom Ammerman, *Baptist Battles: Social Change and Religious Conflict in the Southern Baptist Convention* (New Brunswick: Rutgers University Press, 1990); and Bill Leonard, *God's Last and Only Hope: The Fragmentation of the Southern Baptist Convention* (Grand Rapids: Eerdmans, 1990).

[135] Barreto, "Um Comentário," 12.

of the Genesis volume was already under way to reflect a more conservative viewpoint. He highlighted the tensions surrounding conservative denominational leaders' charges of liberalism in the SBC seminaries.[136] J. Reis Pereira celebrated the ability of the SBC to keep a conservative stance after controversial leader Adrian Rogers stepped down from the presidency of the SBC. He reported that Adrian Rogers' presidential address championed the centrality of the Bible. Pereira celebrated the conservative leader's position saying that Rogers "in his presidential address, reaffirmed his commitment to the Bible as the infallible word of God, without error, and appealed for unity among Baptists."[137] In 1981, Pereira wrote editorials asking for prayers for the SBC, once there was an aggressive resistance from some "liberals" in the denomination who opposed the conservative committees of the denomination.[138] This tendency of following the SBC in its conservative manifestations was evident in the 1980s and was by and large maintained throughout the years. With the exception of the BBC's recent tolerance of local and sporadic ordination of women—which is sanctioned or discouraged depending on local chapters of the Brazilian Order of Pastors and still raises acute nationwide disagreements—today there are no pronounced disagreements between the latest version of the Confession of Faith of the Brazilian Baptist Convention and the most recent Southern Baptist doctrinal statement, namely, the Baptist Faith and Message 2000.

The Brazilianized Shift and a General Denominational Diagnostic: A Conclusion

In the forty-four-year period between the end of the national manifestation of the Radical Movement and the beginnings of Brazilian Baptist presence in Brazil, the identity of Brazilian Baptists had shifted from an initial excitement about the increase of national denominational participation to the surrender of denominational institutions of cultural production to Southern Baptist control. After the 1938 reunification, locals controlled the seminaries for only a few years before Southern Baptist missionaries such as A.R. Crabtree and John Mein took control of the seminaries again

---

[136] Gomes, "A Convenção Batista Do Sul: Últimos Flashes," 8.

[137] Pereira, "Linha Conservadora Vence Na Convenção Batista Do Sul," 3.

[138] Pereira, "Oremos Pela Conveção Do Sul," 3; Pereira, "Oremos Pela Conveção Do Sul II," 3.

and, now fully aware of the dangers that nationalization posed to the missionary status quo, consolidated a pro-missionary organizational culture that outlived them. The *Jornal Batista* was central in shaping the memory of missionaries once fully engaged in denominational control as unqualified heroes of God's work in Brazil.[139] In contrast, leaders of the Radical Movement were remembered in the *Jornal Batista* almost exclusively for their denominational contributions unconnected to the controversy over missionary control[140] and when mention of the controversy was made, it was portrayed as something completely irrelevant to the present.[141] As the centenary of the BBC approached, a hymn for the hundred-year celebration published in the *Jornal Batista* made no equivocation when it came to the memory of missionary presence. Among several mentions of missionary accomplishment, two sections stood out:

> Faithful Missionaries, the holy and courageous men of God,
> The believers in the Lord, the new converts,
> Worked tirelessly, with zeal and strength;
> They left us, therefore, examples of piety:
> Preaching their sermons, living in holiness,
> They did their best for the good Savior.

---

[139] David Gomes, "Sinto Saudades de W.C. Taylor," *Jornal Batista* 71, no. 22 (1971): 6; Tiago Lima, "Cadê O Bombeiro: Reminiscências Do Dr. W.C. Taylor," *Jornal Batista* 71, no. 22 (1971): 7; Anônio Neves de Mesquita, "Doutor W.C. Taylor, O Maior Batista Do Brasil," *Jornal Batista* 71, no. 22 (1971): 6; "W.C. Taylor, O Teólogo Dos Batistas Brasileiros," *Jornal Batista* 71, no. 15 (1971): 1–2; Almir Gonçalves, "William Carey Taylor: Um Príncipe Em Israel," *Jornal Batista* 71, no. 22 (1971): 7; Ebenezer Gomes Cavalcanti, "William Carey Taylor: Umas Memórias," *Jornal Batista* 72, no. 37 (1972): 9; "W.E. Entzminger, Fundador Djornal batista," *Jornal Batista* 76, no. 2 (1976): 1; "David Mein: Missionário Pastor Durante Vinte E Cinco Anos Na Mesma Igreja," *Jornal Batista* 76, no. 29 (1976): 1; 5. W.C. Taylor was by far the most celebrated Southern Baptist missionary in the pages of the *Jornal Batista* because of his many theological books and articles. All of the major Southern Baptist missionaries, however, were given praise in the pages of the publication.

[140] Moysés Silveira, "Dr. Adrião Bernardes, O Rouxinol Emudecido," *Jornal Batista* 70, no. 2 (1970): 1; "Djalma Cunha," *Jornal Batista* 70, no. 39 (1970): 1; "Um Príncipe Em Grande Israel: Djalma Cunha," *Jornal Batista* 70, no. 40 (1970): 2.

[141] Anônio Neves de Mesquita, "Dr. Adrião Bernardes," *Jornal Batista* 70, no. 4 (1970): 7.

I greet these brothers, Brazilian Baptists,
Very faithful heirs of the pioneers of old
Who knew how to do their best for the Lord!
I greet the North American missionaries
Who did not measure their losses and suffered great pain
In order to proclaim here Jesus, the highest good![142]

The numeric growth of the Brazilian Baptist Convention, however, ensured the increasing presence of Brazilian Baptists in denominational administration. As the number of Brazilian Baptists grew in the nation, the BBC progressively nationalized in terms of the make-up of denominational boards and institutions. Efforts toward national missions, youth recruitment, and evangelistic crusades were successful in increasing the number of Baptists in the country. By the mid-1950s, the BBC was already the official owner of a considerable number of denominational properties once owned by the Southern Baptist Convention and wanted to start its own bank—a demonstration of its self-confidence and administrative boldness. The cooperative plan of the 1950s also contributed to denominational financial independence, a move that gave the BBC the ability of increasing its support of educational and evangelistic institutions, and by the end of the decade locals were already responsible for the administration of FMB funds sent to the nation. The denomination went through turmoil in the 1960s given the Charismatic Schism, but the steady growth of the BBC continued well after the division.

Theologically, by 1982 the BBC had been through a schism involving alleged irreconcilable differences with charismatic Baptists. That schism forced the denomination to clarify its stance on issues such as the doctrine of the Holy Spirit and Pentecostal practices such as healing, speaking in tongues, and prophesying. Since the beginnings of Pentecostal presence in Brazil, Baptists had competed with them, and the schism of 1965 helped to shape the leadership of the BBC as intentionally anti-Pentecostal.

Between the 1930s and the 1980s, the BBC became a truly global enterprise, exporting a polyglot Southern Baptist orthodoxy to a number of countries in Latin America, Africa, Europe, and back to North America. The BBC was engaged in what missiologists sometimes call "reverse

---

[142] José Brito Barros, "Salve o Centenário Dos Batistas Brasileiros!," *Jornal Batista* 82, no. 37 (1982): 9.

missions" as early as 1911, when Portugal became an official mission field, although BBC missions in general is better characterized as multidirectional as soon it went to countries in many parts of the globe.[143] But the reverse mission project of the Brazilian Baptist Convention picked up steam between the 1970s and the early 1980s, when missionaries were sent to France, Spain, Canada, and the United States. In the case of Canada and the United States, the Portuguese were the intended object of Brazilian Baptist foreign missions. Portuguese migration to places like Canada and the United States became the avenue through which Brazilian Baptists expanded their global brand into North America. Brazilian Baptist global expansion, despite signaling denominational administrative and financial independence, also showed how the methods and convictions of Southern Baptists were deeply appropriated by Brazilian Baptist leaders.

The growth and continuous autonomy of the BBC did not mean the denomination's isolation from the dynamics of the Southern United States. What happened in the Southern Baptist Convention generally left a mark in Brazil through publications of theological conflicts and tensions that may not have been introduced to Brazilian Baptists if not for their connection with Southern Baptists. Brazilian Baptists, however, were made keenly aware of the conflicts that took place in the SBC and in United States culture in general and were generally presented the assessments of social, political, and theological issues from the conservative Southern Baptist wing. As such, the presence and appropriation of a conservative Southern Baptist imagination was a constant element of Brazilian Baptist theocultural development.

In 1982, the BBC had the SBC as the gold standard for ideological convictions. Administratively, however, the BBC reached unprecedented levels of independence. It grew exponentially, became the legal owner of a number of denominational properties, expanded its global reach, started administering the funds sent by the FMB, and developed a self-perception that was articulated in terms of full independence. When the first Brazilian

---

[143] I am indebted to Afe Adogame for the idea of multidirectional missions as a more appropriate term for the Brazilian Baptist missionary endeavors. His Austin Presbyterian Seminary's Settles Lecture, entitled "Rethinking Reverse Mission Dynamics Within World Christianities," convinced me of the usefulness of the term, despite perceived minor differences in terms of the importance of labor migrations to the presence of Global South Christians in the United States.

Baptist missionary came to the United States, he was a product of a Brazilianized BBC, which had achieved significant levels of administrative autonomy but was ideologically captive to SBC orthodoxy. In 1982, to be a poster child of the BBC one would have to ascribe to the tenets of SBC orthodoxy, be socially conservative, have an anti-Pentecostal disposition, and emphasize missions as the most pronounced characteristic of Christian action. In sum, despite sporadic challenges to denominational ideological hegemony, the progressive nationalization of the BBC was one that manifested itself in terms of unprecedented financial and administrative autonomy and not in terms of an ideological creativity that encouraged locals to distance themselves from the SBC brand. That is not to say that there was no development, but only that ideological development among Brazilian Baptists of the BBC was often prescribed in and by Christian Dixie. There were, however, digressions from the main tendencies within the BBC, and despite the fact that such digressions never represented a majority, they were, at times, significant. Two issues stand out as the most divisive among the many Baptist digressions: Pentecostal/charismatic practices and the qualified ecumenism they engendered.

CHAPTER FIVE

THE SCHISM OF THE SPIRIT:
THE PENTECOSTAL DIGRESSION
AND THE BREAKING OF
INSTITUTIONAL UNITY

In the 1950s, the unity of the Brazilian Baptist Convention was upset by the Spirit. In Brazilian Baptist history there were, of course, many digressions from missionary and missionary-controlled activity by Brazilians, but the only doctrinal issue that split the denomination was the Pentecostal/Charismatic digression. For over half a century—and counting—the National Baptist Convention operated as the charismatic alternative to the Brazilian Baptist Convention and became the institutional sign of the inability of Baptists in Brazil to maintain a cooperative fellowship while disagreeing on aspects of the doctrine of the Holy Spirit. For Baptists in Brazil, defining the work of the Holy Spirit became a contention about acceptable articulations of true Baptist identity, and on both sides of the issue, the influence of the Southern Baptist convention was so significant that it put into question the extent of the indigeneity of the Pentecostal/Charismatic digression.[1] In other words, if, in the first century of Baptist history in Brazil, Baptist consensus was guided and defined by missionary influence, so was Baptist doctrinal dissent.

Global dynamics and demographic shifts provided the broader context for the charismatic turn within Brazilian Baptist circles. More specifically, the expansion of Pentecostalism in the Global South informed the

---

[1] In regard to the controversy about differing approaches to the doctrine of the Holy Spirit in Brazilian Baptist life, language can be confusing. During the controversy, Brazilian Baptists and missionaries did not use language of "Spirit-filled" or "charismatic" to describe those who wanted to remain Baptist while practicing the gifts of the Spirit. Rather, Baptists who wanted to practice the gifts of the Spirit and remain in the denomination were more often called "Pentecostals" or "Pentecostalizers" by their opponents within the Brazilian Baptist Convention. In order to reflect the fluidity in the language used in the sources, I did not trace a clear distinction between terms such as "charismatic," "Pentecostal," and "Spirit-filled."

dynamics of Baptist resistance and acceptance of charismatic belief and practices.[2] In Brazil, Pentecostalism began to grow rapidly in the 1950s, and its growth was influenced by internal migration as well as post-war industrialization and urbanization.[3] According to André Corten, who studied Pentecostalism in Brazil, the number of Pentecostals in Brazil tripled during the years of the Charismatic Schism in the BBC.[4] Baptist concern with this growth was evident in Southern Baptist literature. Lester Bell, for example, wrote in his 1965 book entitled *Which Way In Brazil* that "Brazilian Baptists have a doctrinal problem. Pentecostalism is flourishing in most countries in South America, and especially in Chile and Brazil."[5] Bell was correct in noticing the flourishing of Pentecostalism in Brazil, a country where Pentecostalism was so successful that Robert Hefner called it "the Capital of Pentecostalism in the Global South,"[6] and most of this success was due to effective recruiting from traditional Protestant denominations and the Roman Catholic Church.[7]

It is also important to note that history of Pentecostalism in Brazil is inseparable from the history of Baptists in the sense that the Swedish immigrants who formed what became the largest Christian denomination in the country—the Assemblies of God—began their Brazilian journey in a

---

[2] For more on the specifics of the growth of Global Pentecostalism from different perspectives see Donald E. Miller, Kimon H. Sargeant, and Richard Flory, eds. *Spirit and Power: The Growth and Global Impact of Pentecostalism* (Oxford University Press, 2013); Philip Jenkins, *The Next Christendom: The Coming of Global Christianity* (Oxford: Oxford University Press, 2007); and Mark A. Noll, *The New Shape of World Christianity: How American Experience Reflects Global Faith* (Downers Grove: IVP Academic, 2009).

[3] Zwinglio Mota Dias and Rodrigo Portella, "Apresentação" in *Protestantes, Evangélicos e (Neo) Pentecostais: História, Teologias, Igrejas e Perspectivas*, eds. Zwinglio Mota Dias, Rodrigo Portella, and Elisa Rodrigues (São Paulo: Fonte Editorial, 2014), 19-20.

[4] André Corten, *Pentecostalism in Brazil: Emotion of the Poor and Theological Romanticism* (New York: St. Martin's Press, 1999), 47.

[5] Lester C. Bell, *Which Way in Brazil?* (Nashville: Convention Press, 1965), 112.

[6] Robert W. Hefner, "Introduction: The Unexpected Modern—Gender, Piety, and Politics in the Global Pentecostal Surge," in *Global Pentecostalism in the 21st Century*, ed. Robert W. Hefner (Bloomington: Indiana University Press, 2013), 18.

[7] John Lynch, *New Worlds: A Religious History of Latin America* (Yale University Press, 2012), 339.

Baptist church.[8] The connection between these two groups is so significant that Gedeon de Alencar, in the latest academic history of the Assemblies of God in Brazil, argued that "the Assemblies of God, in its ecclesiastical and historic origins were Baptist and, therefore, congregational, but it also has in its DNA a strong need to deny this fact, given that its biggest enemy is precisely the Baptist denomination."[9] According to both Alencar and Laura Premack, who studied the early Baptist-Pentecostal interactions in Brazil, the animosity between Baptists and Pentecostals can be understood more in terms of their resemblances as direct competitors in the religious market than in terms of their differences. The congregational, loosely democratic, and voluntary qualities of Baptist churches and denominational work, together with the Baptist language of freedom of the individual in interpreting scriptures, made the Baptist fold especially susceptible to Pentecostal influence in general. Pentecostal influence indeed came noticeably in the second half of the twentieth century.

The inroads of Spirit-filled movements into Baptist circles also had a long history in the English-speaking world. Douglas Weaver's book *Baptists and the Holy Spirit* maps the lively exchange between Baptists and Holiness-Pentecostal-Charismatic movements and demonstrates the general animosity with which the majority of Baptists resisted these movements. Weaver's assessment of the common Baptist stance in regard to Spirit-filled movements in the United States is also applicable to the Brazilian situation. As in the United States, most Brazilian Baptists and Baptist missionaries in Brazil were cessationists, and consequentially "Baptist cessationism was widespread and clashed with the minority of Baptists open to the power of biblical miracles, especially a full gospel that emphasized speaking in tongues and divine healing in the present age."[10] A form of

---

[8]For a history of early Pentecostalism in Brazil and Baptist polemic against Pentecostals in the first decades of the movement in Brazil, see Laura Premack, "'The Holy Rollers Are Invading Our Territory': Southern Baptist Missionaries and the Early Years of Pentecostalism in Brazil," *Journal of Religious History* 35, no. 1 (2011): 1–23.

[9]Gedeon Alencar, *Matriz Pentecostal Brasileira: Assembleias de Deus, 1911–2011* (Rio de Janeiro: Novos Dialogos, 2013), 137.

[10] C. Douglas Weaver, *Baptists and the Holy Spirit: The Contested History with Holiness-Pentecostal-Charismatic Movements*, (Waco: Baylor University Press, 2019), xv

anti-Pentecostal militancy based on Southern Baptist cessetionism manifested itself in a number of countries, as the Brazilian and French examples illustrate.[11] The memory of the previous clash with Pentecostals in earlier decades of Baptist history in Brazil—when members of a church pastored by Swedish-born missionary Eric Nelson became Pentecostal—provided an additional historical argument that Baptists in Brazil used to resist the influence of Spirit-filled movements. In addition, Baptists who resisted charismatic tendencies frowned upon the perceived ecumenicity of Baptists who were influenced by or open to charismatic expressions of worship. To a lesser but significant extent, this issue also became a point of contention in Brazilian Baptist history.

The turn of a number of prominent Brazilian Baptists toward a charismatic stance in the second half of the twentieth century, however, was not completely disconnected from missionary figures of authority. Rather, it was heavily informed by missionary activity. Among Brazilian Baptists, the Spiritual Renewal Movement of (*Renovação Espiritual*)—led by Southern Baptist missionary Rosalee Mills Appleby and her Brazilian mentees—was the most important means by which the Spirit was translated, introduced, and sustained. Most Baptist leaders in Brazil, both local and foreign, fiercely resisted the practices usually associated with Pentecostalism during most of the denomination's history in the country.[12] It was in the tension between an affirmation of traditional Baptist dispositions by some and the particular manifestations of the perceived need for spiritual renewal by others that the first nationwide doctrinal schism happened among Brazilian Baptists.

Rosalee Appleby and the Spirit in Baptist Tradition

The turn to charismatic expressions of Christian worship among Brazilian

---

[11] Sebastién Fath describes a very similar scenario in contemporary France, where some Baptists were open to charismatic beliefs and practices but most were aggressively against charismatic tendencies. See Sébastien Fath, "The Impact of Charismatic Christianity on Traditional French Baptist Identity," in *Baptist Identities: International Studies from the Seventeenth to the Twentieth Centuries*, eds. Ian M. Randall, Toivo Pilli, and Anthony Cross (Milton Keynes: Paternoster, 2006), 90.

[12] A look at the *Jornal Batista* from the early 1900s until the end of the twentieth century presents readers with a number of polemic tracts against pentecostalisms of all stripes.

Baptists was periodically raised in local churches, but it was through the influence of Southern Baptist missionary Rosalee Mills Appleby that a charismatic tendency was systematically introduced into the denomination. Appleby was a direct influence on two local pioneers of charismatic tendencies among Baptists in Brazil, namely, José Rego do Nascimento and Enéas Tognini. Tognini's narrative of the charismatic tendencies among Brazilian Baptists goes far beyond the story traditionally told by denominational historians affiliated with the BBC. Unlike BBC historians, Tognini traced the genealogy of pentecostalizing tendencies within Baptist ranks not to the 1960s disagreements that resulted in the schism more directly, but to the dispositions and practices of pioneering Southern Baptist missionaries—on that, he followed in the footsteps of his mentor, Rosalee Mills Appleby.[13]

Appleby went to Brazil in 1924 and worked as a missionary there for thirty-six years. She was a prolific writer in Portuguese and English, a church planter, and a host for a radio show that bore the name of what became a contentious movement within Brazilian Baptist circles, namely "Spiritual Renewal."[14] It is interesting to note that Appleby thought that she did not need to adapt her books and articles between her Brazilian and

---

[13] Enéas Tognini, *História Dos Batistas Nacionais: Documentário* (Brasília: Convenção Batista Nacional, 1993), 17–19.

[14] For a few examples of Rosalee Appleby's published works, see Rosalee Mills Appleby, *The Queenly Quest* (Philadelphia: Judson, 1933); Rosalee Mills Appleby, *Rainbow Gleams* (Nashville: Sunday School Board, 1929); Rosalee Mills Appleby, *The Life Beautiful* (Nashville: Broadman, 1936); Rosalee Mills Appleby, *Orchids and Edelweiss* (Nashville: Broadman Press, 1941); Rosalee Mills Appleby, *Flaming Fagots* (Nashville: Broadman Press, 1943); Rosalee Mills Appleby, *Wings against the Blue* (Nashville: Broadman Press, 1942); Rosalee (Mills) Appleby and Stela Câmara Dubois, *A vida vitoriosa*, (Rio de Janeiro,1954); Rosalee (Mills) Appleby, *Melodias no alvorada* (Rio de Janeiro: Casa Publicadora Batista, 1954); Rosalee (Mills) Appleby, *Filhas do rei*, (Rio de Janeiro: Casa Publicadora Batista, 1946). For more on the life and ministry of Rosalee Appleby, see João B. Chaves, "Disrespecting Borders for Jesus, Power, and Cash: Southern Baptist Missions, The New Immigration, and the Churches of the Brazilian Diaspora" (PhD diss., Baylor University, 2017); Stela Câmara Dubois, *Rosalee Mills Appleby* (Lapa, São Paulo, SP: Edições Enéas Tognini, 1991); João Leão dos Santos Xavier, *Colunas da renovacao: Rosalee Appleby, José Rego do Nascimento, Enéas Tognini, Achilles Barbosa, Rosivaldo de Araújo, Ilton Quadros, Renê P. Feitosa, Achilles B. Júnior* (Belo Horizonte, MG: Lerban, 1997).

United States audience significantly. Sometimes she wrote books in Portuguese first and then translated them into English. Her publications, in this sense, were transnational. She kept a continuous presence in both Brazil and the United States through books, articles, and public speaking. In 1941, she wrote to C.E. Maddry about one of her writing projects:

> This is just a note added to a letter mailed to you last week. I wanted to make an explanation to you personally, that a new book to be out soon, ORCHIDS and EDELWEISS, is more or less the same as one in Portuguese ready for the press: O SEGREDO DA VITO-RIA.[15]

Appleby told Maddry about the adaptability of her publications so that he would know that she was not investing all her time in writing books and pamphlets as well as to let him know that she was hoping to raise extra funds for her work through the selling of her books. In his response, Maddry was emphatically supportive:

> With reference to the publications of the book, it is perfectly all right and I hope you will get a lot of extra funds out of it for your mission work. If at any time the Foreign Mission Board could get behind the publication of books from your pen, if it would help them to sell, we would be very glad to do it.[16]

Appleby expected to have her book on display at the SBC national meeting in 1941[17] and the potential for fundraising represented by her books went beyond just book sales—exposure created potential for gifts. Appleby's transnational fame was so significant that her use of financial gifts without the approval of the mission was the source of some discomfort between her, other missionaries in Brazil, and FMB officials.[18] Appleby was extremely popular, and FMB officials were glad to capitalize on her popularity, as long as they could control it.

---

[15] From Appleby to Maddry, January 14, 1941.

[16] From C.E. Maddry to Rosalee Appleby, February 6, 1941.

[17] From Rosalee Appleby to C.E. Maddry, March 17, 1941.

[18] See correspondence from Rosalee Appleby to Everett Gill Jr., September 1, 1944; from Everett Gill Jr. to Rosalee Appleby, September 15, 1944; and from Rosalee Appleby to Everett Gill Jr., March 5, 1945.

The Keswick[19] influence in Appleby's language—focusing on the power of the Holy Spirit for service—together with her proto-ecumenism and her criticism of the growing formalism of the Baptist denomination in Brazil was responsible for generating significant tension between her and fellow Southern Baptist missionaries in Brazil.[20] It is unclear how and when Appleby incorporated Keswick language into her writing and speaking, but by the mid-1930s she was already writing about abundant and powerful life in the Holy Spirit.[21] In 1941, emphasizing the importance of the power of the Holy Spirit over the role of denominational institutions, she wrote in her book *Orchids and Edelweiss* that "the power is not in the organ nor in the organization; it is transmitted by endued men quickened by the Holy Spirit. God never breathed the breath of life into systems or things but into men."[22] Soon afterwards, in *Flaming Fagots*, a book in which Appleby advocates for missionaries with "hot hearts," Appleby wrote that "to give radiance to our anemic Christianity, it must be re-energized by divine power."[23] Appleby was not happy with her impression of the current state of traditional Protestant Christianity, and she was not worried about keeping her dissatisfaction a secret.

The language of spiritual revival and the Holy Spirit also became more prominent in Rosalee Appleby's correspondence in the early 1940s. Her concern with what she saw as the unnecessary rigidity of Baptists was later repeated by both her mentees, Tognini and Nascimento. Appleby was convinced that after the Second World War there would be a great revival in Brazil, and she was enthusiastic about what was happening in

---

[19]The Keswick Holiness Movement was a movement that initiated in England during the second half of the nineteenth century but had great influence in the United States. For Keswick-inspired Christians, the baptism of the Holy Spirit was a second religious experience seen as the Spirit's enduement of power for evangelism and missions. Appleby and other FMB officials and missionaries also used Keswick language, but the lines between Keswick and charismatic language and experiences were not always clear, as the story of Appleby and her Brazilian mentees narrated in this chapter illustrates.

[20]Chaves, "Disrespecting Borders," 137–42.

[21] Rosalee Mills Appleby, *The Life Beautiful* (Nashville: Broadman, 1936), 30 and 101.

[22] Rosalee Mills Appleby, *Orchids and Edelweiss* (Nashville: Broadman Press, 1941), 29.

[23] Rosalee Mills Appleby, *Flaming Fagots* (Nashville: Broadman Press, 1943), 47.

the state of Minas Gerais where she was serving as a missionary.[24] She wrote C.E. Maddry in 1942, saying

> After this war, I believe the doors will be wider. There should be a more liberal [illegible] more open mind. We do long to prepare spiritually for greater things. Everywhere in Brazil, folks are praying and thinking about a great religious revival. We feel it especially in Minas and pray daily for its coming. The TASK is His and unless he works through us, all our efforts will be in vain. It is a serious thing to be the representative of a spiritual KINGDOM and yet build an earthly kingdom; to substitute man-made plans and material conquest for spiritual victories.[25]

Writing to both C.E. Maddry and Everett Gill, Jr. in 1943, Appleby made clear her criticisms of the denomination in Brazil:

> All over Brazil there are those who pray for a great religious revival. … Brazil has never been blessed with a revival such as [those that] swept and blessed other countries. We need it now in this changing time when the Light is breaking through the crust of centuries-old fanaticism. Our hearts long to see this blessing, and a spiritual Christianity with power and strength to heal, to renew, to reconstruct, to break the force of evil. … Someone rightly said of the Christianity of the past: "Ours is a Christianity without force, passion, or effect; a suburban piety, domestic and kindly, but unfit to cope with the actual moral case of the world. We cannot deal to any purpose with the deep damnation of the race. Our word is but a lovely song the people hear it, but do not fear, they are enchanted but unchanged. Pentecost is our need."[26]

The quotation came from British theologian P.T. Forsyth, whose works included an emphasis on holiness in Christian practice.

Despite the numerous letters penned by Appleby to Maddry and Gill emphasizing the language of spiritual renewal and the doctrine of the Holy Spirit, until direct confrontation with Appleby became inevitable, their responses tended to focus mostly on the administrative elements of their interactions rather than doctrinal matters. The responses she got from FMB

---

[24] From Rosalee Appleby to C.E. Maddry, October 14, 1942.
[25] From Rosalee Appleby to C.E. Maddry, October 14, 1942.
[26] From Rosalee Appleby to C.E. Maddry and Everett Gill, Jr., July 28, 1943.

that reflected their stance in regard to her revivalist language, however, were generally supportive. Her writings that emphasized the need for the power of the Holy Spirit were never censured by FMB officials, and when FMB officials responded directly to her emphasis on the need for more power from above, they were positive. For example, in a response to one of Appleby's letters, Gill wrote:

> We join with you in that prayer for a great religious revival which would sweep Brazil and all of Latin America. To me it is their only hope. They have resources, a glorious history and a wonderful people, but lack the inner power to realize their mission. That power and change of character can only come from the one whom we try to represent.[27]

Language of spiritual power and religious revival, however, would prove hard to manage. Appleby's movement for spiritual renewal developed into charismatic sensibilities that tried to claim similar Baptist sources and genealogies to the majority, anti-charismatic faction who came to resist it. Keswick language itself opened the possibility for a number of interpretations regarding the work of the Holy Spirit. In other words, the foundational Keswick element of the enduement of power given to believers by the Holy Spirit as a second blessing could be easily translated—as it was by some in Brazil—into an endorsement of Pentecostal/charismatic practices. When the controversy over the issue of Pentecostal influence in Brazilian Baptist circles became public in the late 1950s, the potential for different articulations regarding the language of Holy Spirit power and spiritual revival/renewal used by Appleby since the 1930s became a point of contention.

Appleby's expectation and work for a spiritual revival eventually led her to build cross-denominational relationships. Consequentially, some of the criticisms she faced were based on her support of events and institutions outside Southern Baptist circles. Throughout Brazilian Baptist history, Baptists were critical of all forms of ecumenism and cross-denominational cooperation except when such cooperation represented a coalition against the bigger enemy: Roman Catholicism. In the late 1940s, tensions between Appleby and other Southern Baptist missionaries grew, and she was criticized for supporting events and institutions outside SBC circles.

---

[27] From Everett Gil, Jr. to Rolasee Appleby, September 16, 1943.

Everett Gill Jr. made the tensions with Appleby clear when he wrote her about complaints by other missionaries regarding some of her associations. In 1946, after visiting Belo Horizonte—the city in which Appleby worked—Gill wrote that "since returning to Rio, (my wife) Rachel and I have continued to talk about the glories of Belo Horizonte and Minas."[28] Similarly, one year later, he wrote Appleby affirming the FMB's joy for "the growing interest in a great spiritual awakening so needed in Brazil and all the world."[29] In 1948, however, Gill's tune changed. After chastising Appleby for her work involvement with a woman Presbyterian minister, Gill wrote:

> But beyond this, I fear that there are other factors which enter into the picture. For some years there has been a feeling on the part of members of the South Brazil Mission that you were possibly not in complete harmony with the way in which we were conducting our work. One illustration is the support which you have given to the Independent Seminary in Rio rather than our own institution which certainly needs all the help we can give it.[30]

The emphasis on the need for revival was not initially resisted, but Appleby's associations and alleged distance from fellow missionaries got FMB officials increasingly aware of the potential differences in particular understandings of what "revival" meant. "All of us are interested in a real revival in Brazil," Gill wrote, "and I believe that our missionaries as a whole are working toward that end. Of course, individual Christians may disagree on what exactly constitutes a revival."[31] The need for revival was never denied by FMB officials, but the particular ways in which the revival led by Appleby and her mentees developed eventually became an obstacle for the majority of Brazilian Baptists.

Gill's mention of Appleby's alleged involvement with a "Presbyterian lady preacher"[32] brings attention to the very contentious issue of woman leadership in Southern Baptist circles, because the SBC not only still does not ordain women today but also because Appleby was already operating

---

[28] From Everett Gill Jr. to Rosalee Appleby, November 22, 1946.
[29] From Everett Gill Jr. to Rosalee Appleby, October 2, 1947.
[30] From Everett Gill Jr. to Rosalee Appleby, June 15, 1948.
[31] From Everett Gill Jr. to Rosalee Appleby, June 15, 1948.
[32] From Everett Gill Jr. to Rosalee Appleby, June 15, 1948.

as an unmarried woman missionary since the death of her husband David in the 1920s. The literature documenting the resistance to women preachers in Southern Baptist circles suggests that, despite the space for women preachers provided by the more loosely gendered arrangements in the mission field, Appleby faced challenges in regard to her leadership role and leadership practices.[33] In terms of explicit resistance to Appleby in regard to her leadership practices *per se*, however, one struggles to find instances in which she was criticized by either male missionaries or locals. As a matter of fact, Appleby was taken to be a towering figure by both Brazilians who resisted the Spiritual Renewal movement and those who supported it.[34]

Although the non-SBC associations of Appleby were a matter of concern, the doctrinal issues surrounding her particular understanding of "spiritual renewal," were the main issue for some fellow missionaries and Foreign Mission Board (FMB) personnel. Some of Appleby's missionary colleagues even considered her to be mentally unstable.[35] Whereas FMB

---

[33] For treatments of women preachers in Southern Baptist circles see Elizabeth Hill Flowers, *Into the Pulpit: Southern Baptist Women & Power since World War II* (Chapel Hill: University of North Carolina Press, 2012); David Stricklin, *A Genealogy of Dissent: Southern Baptist Protest in the Twentieth Century* (Lexington: University Press of Kentucky, 1999), 114–42; Nancy Tatom Ammerman, *Baptist Battles: Social Change and Religious Conflict in the Southern Baptist Convention* (New Brunswick: Rutgers University Press, 1990), 72–99; Eileen Campbell-Reed, *Anatomy of a Schism: How Clergywomen's Narratives Reinterpret the Fracturing of the Southern Baptist Convention* (Knoxville: University of Tennessee Press, 2016).

[34] See Pereira, *História Dos Batistas*, 194; Ader Alvez de Assis, *Pioneirismo e Neopioneirismo: Cem Anos de Ação Missionária Batista Em Minas* (Belo Horizonte: Convenção Batista de Minas, 1989), 84; Tognini, *História Dos Batistas Nacionais*, 15–38.

[35] Another important note about gender dynamics is appropriate here. Although Appleby, as an independent woman operating in a thoroughly sexist, Southern Baptist environment, was uniquely vulnerable to charges of hysteria, mental weakness, and irrationality, similar charges were very often made of male charismatics. As a matter of fact, Appleby was shielded from public criticism probably because of her White American privilege (perhaps more clearly manifested in her strong support for Lost Cause mythology), which male locals—who were often attacked publicly—did not share. For examples, see "Seminário Teológico B. Do S. Do Brasil: Declaração," *Jornal Batista* 58, no. 48 (1958): 7; Junta Administrativa do Seminario Teologico Batista do Sul do Brasil, "Declaração," *Jornal Batista* 59, no. 1 (1959): 2; Ricardo Pitrowsky, "O Que Há Com o Movimento de Renovação Espiritual? Uma Séria Advertência," *Jornal Batista* 62, no. 1 (1962): 4; Editorial, "Uma Séria Advertência," *Jornal Batista* 62, no.

official Everett Gill Jr. never made her aware of the more damaging aspects of his conversations with leaders of the South Brazil Mission, he urged her to meet him when she returned to the United States in 1948. Appleby left Brazil to the United States allegedly in order to take care of her physical medical needs, and Gill told her that he was "naturally distressed"[36] about the conflicts that her movement of spiritual renewal generated in Belo Horizonte, but he concealed the claims of her alleged psychological weakness made by fellow Southern Baptist missionaries. The same day Gill wrote her about his desire to see her in the United States, he sent missionary M.T. Rankin a wire saying

> Mrs. Appleby is coming home definitely, leaving Brazil July 25, Cowsert and others feel that she is urgently in need of medical and psychiatric treatment. I am writing to her urging that she come to Richmond for a conference during this temporary furlough period. We are still fearful about the results of her so-called revival in Belo Horizonte, which may split our work.[37]

When Appleby was in the United States, Gill was blunter regarding how he felt about her continuous calls for a spiritual renewal movement in Brazil. He wrote to her saying that the FMB "does not believe that we need to organize an additional movement for that [spiritual renewal] purpose. Our whole denomination believes that we can best serve the kingdom of God by working through the channels of our local churches and denominational institutions and agencies."[38] Gill qualified his convictions by saying that Baptists never denied the need for power from the Holy Spirit, but they rejected an understanding that taught that such power had to be received in a specific way, as in expressions of Pentecostal doctrine. He also made clear to Appleby that he was disturbed by "the disruption of the work and division in our Brazilian churches"[39] that missionaries in Brazil associated with Appleby's initiatives.

Gill, like most Baptists in the second half of the twentieth century, rejected notions of baptism with the Holy Spirit as a post-conversion, *sui*

---

1 (1962): 2; Zacarias Campêlo, "Auto-Hipnose Por Pentecoste," *Jornal Batista* 62, no. 5 (1962): 5.

[36] From Everett Gill Jr. to Rosalee Appleby, July 20, 1948.

[37] From Everett Gill, Jr. to M. T. Rankin, July 20, 1948.

[38] From Everett Gill, Jr. to Rosalee Appleby, September 17, 1948.

[39] From Everett Gill, Jr. to Rosalee Appleby, September 17, 1948.

generis experience as well as what he perceived as the high emotionalism associated with Pentecostal worship styles. Showing his concern for what Appleby's calls for revival could mean for denominational life, Gill wrote that "if this movement in South Brazil results in another anti-missionary drive such as we experienced in North Brazil causing two conventions, I cannot see that this would be anything of which to be very proud, or an indication of the leadership of God's Spirit."[40] Appleby's stay in the United States did not serve to distance herself from her commitment to help bring a revival. On the contrary, during her time at First Baptist Church in Dallas in 1949, she experienced what she described as a one of the greatest revivals Dallas ever saw. The revival in Dallas, under the preaching of W.A. Criswell, gave her the conviction that she would be betraying God if she stopped working for a revival. Criswell's views on the role of the Holy Spirit in the lives of believers shifted over the course of his career, but during the time when Appleby was in Dallas, Criswell believed that Christians needed to seek and ask for "subsequent fillings of the Spirit to have the 'fullness of the Spirit,' or the enduement of 'Pentecostal power' to witness."[41] From Dallas, Appleby wrote Gill that, in regard to her work in Brazil, although "more care can be exercised and methods adapted,"[42] a revival was most certainly necessary—and to prove that she was not the only Baptist who believed that "the enduement of Spirit is necessary to power in Christian service,"[43] she sent him a folder with examples of other Baptists who espoused her position. In his response, Gill assured Appleby that he wasn't against proper revival, but that what was developing in Belo Horizonte under Appleby's watch was not producing true revival; rather it was "producing antagonisms, bitterness of spirit, and division."[44]

After talking personally with Appleby, Gill intentionally kept her in the United States until 1950, and contemplated sending her back not to Belo Horizonte, but to another city because of the issues surrounding her project for spiritual renewal.[45] After the FMB decided to send her back to Belo Horizonte, however, Gill wanted Appleby to commit to limit herself to working within the Southern Baptist fold. In March of 1950, Gill made

---

[40] From Everett Gill, Jr. to Rosalee Appleby, April 19, 1948.
[41] Weaver, *Baptists and the Holy Spirit*, 237.
[42] From Rosalee Appleby to Everett Gill Jr., April 14, 1949.
[43] From Rosalee Appleby to Everett Gill Jr., April 14, 1949.
[44] From Everett Gill Jr. to Rosalee Appleby, April 19, 1949.
[45] From Everett Gill Jr. to Rosalee Appleby, May 12, 1949.

it clear that the missionaries of the South Brazil Mission wanted her back to Belo Horizonte "but with the understanding that (she) would devote (herself) wholeheartedly to the promotion of the Baptist program."[46] The letter remained unanswered, and in a letter that continued his push for limiting Appleby's ecumenicity, Gill condemned Appleby's previous "meeting led by the Presbyterian lady [preacher], which was held with your full approval, your interest in the interdenominational Bethel Seminary in Rio, the times spent in promoting the interdenominational worldwide revival, etc." and ended with a strong argument in the name of the FMB:

> I am discussing the whole question, simply to emphasize the fact that when you return to Brazil the Foreign Mission Board will take for granted that you will devote yourself wholeheartedly to the extension of the denominational program fostered and supported by Brazilian Baptists, the members of the South Brazil Mission, and the Foreign Mission Board. Sincerely hoping and praying that you may be led to return on this basis, and confident that you will thereby render a lasting service to the Kingdom of God.[47]

Appleby, however, was not willing to agree to the FMB's expectations without testing her limits.

In Appleby's response to the FMB's clear expectations of sending her back to Belo Horizonte and limiting her commitments exclusively to Southern Baptist work, Appleby revealed that she was not convinced that her commitment to the SBC, as articulated by denominational workers, was God's own will. She emphasized that she couldn't go against God's lead and asked: "Would it be all right to go and decide after I get there, or go with the understanding that a change may be made at the close of the year?"[48] She thought that her work for revival was "the most valuable of the 25 (years I worked in Brazil) inspite of not being understood."[49] Gill told Appleby that he would "hold up any plans for travel preparation"[50] for her because she was unclear regarding her commitment to work exclusively within Baptist circles. Appleby's reply shows how astute and diplomatic she could be. She told Gill that she planned on giving her "wholehearted

---

[46] From Everett Gill Jr. to Rosalee Appleby, March 29, 1950.
[47] From Everett Gill to Rosalee Appleby, April 5, 1950.
[48] From Rosalee Appleby to Everett Gill Jr., April 15, 1950.
[49] From Rosalee Appleby to Everett Gill Jr., April 15, 1950.
[50] From Everett Gill Jr. to Rosalee Appleby, April 20, 1950.

cooperation and promote every interest of Christ and Baptists in Brazil," but she didn't want to lose or betray the vision that God "put on my heart nearly ten years ago for a Spiritual Awakening."[51] She committed to stay away from any "official relationship with any organization outside the denomination"[52] but she was clear that she thought that hostility to other denominations and institutions was not Christian. "Every time we gain the respect and confidence of other people—even other denominations," she wrote, "we have lifted higher and honored our own denomination."[53] Appleby clearly felt pressure to choose between denominational loyalty and loyalty to her sense of divine calling—and from her perspective those two were not always clearly the same.

Clarifying Appleby's doctrinal stances and resolving her disposition towards other denominations, however, was not everything. Gill had another concern with which to deal before Appleby left from the United States back to Brazil: her relationship with local leaders. Missionary unity was very important for Southern Baptist missionaries, and whenever a missionary was perceived as taking the side of Brazilians over the Mission, they were treated with suspicion by missionary personnel. Appleby's continuous correspondence with Brazilian Baptist leaders during her prolonged furlough in the United States brought that concern to light, as she may have suggested to Brazilian friends that she was returning to Belo Horizonte even before that was officially decided. Gill wanted to call this issue to attention as well:

> From the last report, both the Executive Committee and the Belo Horizonte missionaries feel that you should return to Minas. In fact, one of them writes that you have already agreed to rent a house in Belo Horizonte from some Brazilian. He may have been misinformed, but if this is true it is another illustration of the type of thing which worried our missionaries. One of them writes: "We missionaries have no such information, so it creates, or rather continues to place Mrs. Appleby as being friendly or confidential with Brazilians but alienated from the missionaries. Unless Mrs. Appleby is one with our mission, she will cause a separation between

---

[51] From Rosalee Appleby to Everett Gill Jr., April 24, 1950.
[52] From Rosalee Appleby to Everett Gill Jr., April 24, 1950.
[53] From Rosalee Appleby to Everett Gill Jr., April 24, 1950.

us and the Brazilians, or at least some of them."[54]

Appleby denied that she made living arrangements without the knowledge of FMB officials or field missionaries, but she was not apologetic about friendship with locals. Appleby was strongly opposed to missionary language of "us" against "them" and stated that "love and loyalty to Brazilians make no conflict as far as I can see in our loyalty and love to missionaries."[55] She agreed to go back to Belo Horizonte but made it clear that she would not stop working for spiritual renewal and that if she began to be accused of "imaginary things" she would "ask the Mission for removal."[56] Gill thanked her for agreeing to return with a renewed commitment to the denomination and he promised her the backing of the FMB to her missionary work.[57]

Appleby was back in Belo Horizonte, the capital of the state of Minas Gerais, by August of 1950 with the clear expectation that she was to work solely within Southern Baptist circles. During her prolonged furlough in the United States, however, Appleby became increasingly familiar with works of Baptists who agreed with her about the necessity of a special power from the Holy Spirit for service in the kingdom of God, which encouraged her further in her convictions that there was no necessary theological conflict between her Baptist identity and Spirit-filled language.[58] Appleby was, in other words, articulating a narrative that opened room for the possibility of being both Baptist and Spirit-filled—a narrative that her local mentees would appropriate and use. From then on, she would focus her defense for the Spiritual Renewal movement in Brazil as one deeply engrained in Baptist heritage.

From her return until the late 1950s, Appleby was affirmed and encouraged in her missionary work in Brazil by both Gill and his successor as FMB's Secretary for Latin America, Frank Means. She continued giving revival messages and explicitly waiting for the spiritual awakening she had been praying and working for since the 1940s. In her Annual Mission Report to the FMB ending in June of 1954, Appleby wrote that she maintained "the unchanging conviction of more than thirteen years that our

---

[54] From Everett Gill Jr. to Rosalee Appleby, May 8, 1950.
[55] From Rosalee Appleby to Everett Gill. Jr., May 13, 1950.
[56] From Rosalee Appleby to Everett Gill. Jr., May 13, 1950.
[57] From Everett Gill Jr. to Rosalee Appleby, May 26, 1950.
[58]From Rosalee Appleby to Everett Gill, Jr., April 19, 1949.

supreme need is a Spiritual Awakening and the assurance that it is near."[59] In her following report, one year later, Appleby continued to voice her strong commitment to "make some contribution toward the coming Spiritual Awakening."[60] In 1956, writing to the South Brazil Mission, she said that for "fifteen years of this time, a heavy burden has rested upon me to see a Spiritual Awakening in this country and there has been an inner certainty that it will come."[61] Soon before the event involving Appleby's mentee's that generated the beginning of the public controversy in the Brazilian Baptist Convention, however, signs of tension regarding Appleby's ministry started appearing again.

In 1957, one year before the controversy involving one of her mentees, José Rego do Nascimento, Appleby wrote Frank Means to ask permission to join revival meetings and "consecration weeks in preparation for revival meetings."[62] In her correspondence with Means, it became clear that a rift between her and her fellow Southern Baptist missionaries, who claimed she was supporting groups that opposed the Southern Baptist way of doing missionary work, had surfaced again. She told Means that she was being careful, but she could not stop the misrepresentations and rumors started by her fellow SBC missionaries. It also became clear that she was increasingly certain that the time for the Brazilian spiritual revival was near, and that if Southern Baptist missionaries did not cooperate for a church-centered revival, God would bring revival outside of the churches, "as in the time of Wesley."[63] Appleby did not want to miss God's timing for revival, which she had prayed for so much.

Appleby, Her Mentees, and Public Doctrinal Conflict

If the tensions regarding Appleby's ministry as it pertained to her emphasis on spiritual awakening were mostly managed in intra-missionary exchanges, the same could not be said for what happened when her two most

---

[59] Rosalee Mills Appleby, Annual Mission Report —July 1953 to end of June 1954, Archives of the International Mission Board in Richmond, Virginia.

[60] Rosalee Mills Appleby, Annual Mission Report—July 1954 to end of July 1955, Archives of the International Mission Board in Richmond, Virginia.

[61] Rosalee Mills Appleby, Report to South Brazil Mission From July 1955 to July 56, Archives of the International Mission Board in Richmond, Virginia.

[62] From Rosalee Appleby to Frank Means, June 8, 1957.

[63] From Rosalee Appleby to Frank Means, June 8, 1957.

THE GLOBAL MISSION OF THE JIM CROW SOUTH

prominent mentees became publicly engaged in continuing the quest for spiritual renewal she started. In the 1950s, two Brazilian Baptists who would continue Appleby's project for spiritual renewal, José Rego do Nascimento and Enéas Tognini, experienced what they called "baptism in the Holy Spirit."[64] In 1958, after Nascimento led a charismatic event in the South Brazil Baptist Seminary, the issue of baptism in the Holy Spirit—especially its correlated practices of speaking in tongues and divine healing—became a public point of contention in Brazilian Baptist life, eventually leading to a schism within the denomination in 1965. The contention regarding issues of spiritual renewal and baptism in the Holy Spirit, however, was framed by both sides as an issue about not only the proper understanding of Scripture but also about the proper stance on Baptist history and identity. Within this framework, both charismatics and traditionalists provided theological and historical arguments to either include or exclude those whose beliefs and experiences had been informed by the growing Pentecostal movement. The primary means of these disputes was the *Jornal Batista*.[65]

The charismatic event in 1958 led by Rosalee Appleby's mentee, José Rego do Nascimento, brought the issue of Baptist pentecostalization to the forefront of Baptist life in Brazil. Nascimento was a graduate of the South Brazil Baptist Theological Seminary (SBBTS), the most important Baptist theological seminary in the country, and in 1955 he had what he described as a "baptism with the Holy Spirit." As his prestige as a preacher and speaker grew, more Brazilian Baptists identified with a charismatic understanding of Christianity, which included the issues of speaking in tongues, healing, and prophesying. In 1958, following an invitation by students of the SBBTS, Nascimento led an on-campus meeting that resembled a Pentecostal service. Fearing a backlash from churches and pastors across the south of Brazil, the SBBTS printed a formal declaration in the *Jornal Batista* denouncing the "extreme emotionalism and disturbing excesses" that occurred during Nascimento's visit. The report ended with an unequivocal statement against charismatic practices:

---

[64] Enéas Tognini, *História Dos Batistas Nacionais: Documentário* (Brasília: Convanção Batista Nacional, 1993), 18.

[65] Israel Belo de Azevedo, "A Palavra Marcada: Teologia Política Dos Batistas Segundo *Jornal Batista*" (master's thesis, Seminário Teológico Batista do Norte do Brasil, 1983); J. Reis Pereira, *História Dos Batistas No Brasil (1882–1982)* (Rio de Janeiro: JUERP, 1982); Chaves, "Disrespecting Borders."

Also considering that this seminary has been mentioned in meetings where similar occurrences have been reproduced, the administration and the faculty wants to make public that they disapprove of the practices mentioned above (emotionalism and excesses) and they emphasize the need to distinguish between true spirituality and the excesses of emotionalism, which are dangerous distortions against which we must protect ourselves.[66]

In a letter that Nascimento sent to Enéas Tognini celebrating the event in the seminary as the beginning of Brazil's revival, he described that participants had visions, cried, made unusual noises, threw themselves onto the altar, and more.[67] On January 1, 1959, the Administrative Board of SBBTS published another note in the *Jornal Batista* reaffirming the previous declaration and making "an urgent appeal to the Brazilian Baptist churches" to avoid charismatic excesses and chiding Nascimento for conducting a charismatic meeting without previous approval from the seminary's director.[68]

Nascimento found a strong ally for "spiritual renewal" in the person of Enéas Tognini, who was director of the Baptist School of São Paulo and had served on the administrative board of the SBBTS. Tognini was also a charismatic Baptist who had been introduced to Spirit-filled experiences through Rosalee Appleby in 1958.[69] In a private letter to Tognini, Nascimento recounted the experience in the SBBTS library as the coming of Pentecost. Visions, speaking in tongues, and highly emotional expressions of worship took place that night. Nascimento also went preaching in local churches the next day and, in his own words, they also "received Pentecost." The letter makes it clear that Nascimento took these experiences as a divine sign that a revival was coming to Brazil. He was not naïve, however, regarding the denominational response that such practices would receive. By the time Nascimento wrote Tognini, he said that "a seminary

---

[66] Seminário Teológico B. do S. do Brasil, "Declarção," *Jornal Batista* 58, no. 48 (1958): 7.

[67] Correspondence from J. Rego do Nascimento to Enéas Tognini, October 22, 1958. A copy of this letter can be found in Enéas Tognini, *História dos Batistas Nacionais*, 19-21.

[68] Junta Administrativa do Seminario Teologico Batista do Sul do Brasil, "Declaração," *Jornal Batista* 59, no. 1 (1959): 2.

[69] Tognini, *História Dos Batistas Nacionais: Documentário*, 12.

professor already blamed the director for opening the seminary doors to a 'heretic.'"[70] But the director, Ben Oliver, was no friend of Pentecostal-like expressions of worship and he made his opinion on the matter known to the denomination in his article published in the *Jornal Batista* condemning charismatic practices.[71]

After this event, the mostly private discomforts that the Spiritual Renewal movement caused between Appleby and her fellow missionaries became a full-fledged dispute about what it meant to be Baptist and who could define Baptist identity. Although charges of emotionalism and excesses in practices that were described in ways that resembled moments in United States history in which Baptists were involved—such as the Second Great Awakening—were often voiced, Baptist criticism against charismatic-informed commitments had a doctrinal element.[72] Charismatic practices and commitments carried particular articulations of the doctrine of the Holy Spirit, which Baptists in general resisted. The administrative board affirmed the faculty open letter and warned Brazilian Baptist churches to "be careful and stay alert against any distortion to the glorious doctrine of the Holy Spirit" and the confusion that "can even cause schism in our beloved denomination."[73] The concerns against schism had two main sources: the Radical Movement of the 1920s–1930s[74] and, more importantly in this case, the alleged attempt to take over the Belém Baptist Church by Baptist pastors Gunnar Vingren and Daniel Berg in 1911— who went on to form two Pentecostal denominations in Brazil.[75]

---

[70] From José do Nascimento to Enéas Tognini, October 28, 1958.

[71] Ben Oliver, "Pentecoste E Pentecostismo," *Jornal Batista* 58, no. 50 (1958).

[72] As Weaver pointed out, Baptists sometimes criticized emotionalism in the Second Great Awakening as well (see Weaver, *Baptists and the Holy Spirit*, 122). For examples of the presence of emotionalism in the Great Awakening, see Paul S. Boyer et al., *The Enduring Vision: A History of the American People, Volume 1: To 1877, Concise* (Boston: Cengage Learning, 2009), 226; Dorothy A. Mays, *Women in Early America: Struggle, Survival, and Freedom in a New World* (Santa Barbara: ABC-CLIO, 2004), 167; and Sydney E. Ahlstrom, *Religious History of the American People* (New Haven: Yale University Press, 1972), 415–55.

[73] Junta Administrativa do Seminario Teologico Batista do Sul do Brasil, "Declaração," *Jornal Batista* 59, no. 1 (1959): 2.

[74] João Chaves and C. Douglas Weaver, "Baptists and Their Polarizing Ways: Transnational Polarization between Southern Baptist Missionaries and Brazilian Baptists," *Review & Expositor* 116 no. 2 (2019): 160–74.

[75] Premack, "'The Holy Rollers Are Invading Our Territory,'" 3–4.

Despite the criticisms directed at Nascimento after the event at SBBTS, Appleby defended him strongly to the FMB's Secretary for Latin America, Frank Means. Missionaries wanted Appleby to distance herself from Nascimento, but she refused. In a letter to Means, after praising the Shantung Revival and mentioning the twenty-four missionaries and native Chinese who were baptized in the Holy Spirit, Appleby said

> As to the request in reference to Pastor Nascimento, I felt it absurd and unchristian. He is a Baptist pastor in our city and highly esteemed, the judge of the supreme court of Brazil is a member there and a congressman [Dr. Vilas Boas and Elmir Maia]. It does not seem fair to me to be forced to renounce the friendship of his family and not hear his powerful messages that inspire. His wife, born near the date of David's birth, has been a daughter to me. Their children call me "grandmother." To be tied up by a promise or demand of non-cooperation may deprive opportunities that the Spirit leads to do. Such a promise I could not make of any of our workers.[76]

Appleby went on to say that in the fifty-three years she had been a Christian, she met but a few people "with the Spiritual power of this Brazilian pastor."[77] Appleby's correspondence with FMB officials suggests that, with the exception of Appleby, missionaries were united against Nascimento. She was criticized by missionaries for supporting Nascimento and missionaries thought that Appleby was, through her support of Nascimento, encouraging young people to be in favor of him.

In her letters to Frank Means, however, Appleby defended Nascimento as being not only a young pastor of great potential but also as being well within Baptist teaching and tradition.[78] Defending herself and Nascimento regarding the charges of heresy in their teaching, Appleby reminded Means that what she was teaching regarding the role of the Holy Spirit in Christian life had a long history within Baptist circles. She wrote:

> The so-called heresy was the teaching of the necessity of a Spirit-filled life, or enduement of power for living and serving. In face of a similar accusation in 1948, I studied in the seminary library and

---

[76] From Rosalee Appleby to Frank Means, March 1959.

[77] From Rosalee Appleby to Frank Means, March 1959.

[78] From Rosalee M. Appleby to Frank Means, April, 28, 1959; and From Rosalee M. Appleby to Frank Means, May 14, 1959.

discovered that a host of our finest Baptists in past had the same belief as to the Holy Spirit. Dr. Carrol in "Rivers of Life"; Dr. Scarborough, "With Christ After the Lost"; Dr. Dana in "The Holy Spirit in Acts"; A.J. Gordon in "The Ministry of the Spirit"; C.B. Jackson in a new book from the Dept. of Evangelism in Texas; Rice, Appleman, Earle; J.B. Lawrence in "The Holy Spirit and World Evangelization." The most powerful Christians of the past believed and appropriated the resources so abundantly provided. My belief is not because of them but through years of struggle and prayer before God's Word, trying to understand why such a small percentage of the world is converted (two percent evangelical Christian according to Stewart) when the divine provision is so abundant.[79]

In the second letter, Appleby added to the cacophony of Baptist voices, and she mentioned Christmas Evans' "Deeper Experience of Famous Christians," John Rice's "The Power of Pentecost," the Shantung Revival, and the revival in the Belgian Congo.[80] Appleby thought of herself as following within this strand of Baptist tradition, and implicitly trying to graft Nascimento within the same narrative. She never admitted that Nascimento was influenced by a Pentecostal understanding of the person and work of the Holy Spirit, and time would prove otherwise, but she also used language regarding the work of the Spirit that could clearly be interpreted as "Pentecostal friendly" language.[81]

The tension between Appleby and her fellow missionaries became too strong as the controversy developed, and Appleby was encouraged to retire in February of 1960, when she turned sixty-five, and to return to the United States soon afterwards. Frank Means made the tense context of Appleby's retirement clear in a letter he sent to Ione Gray in the month of Appleby's retirement. He told Gray that Appleby's retirement in 1960 was "an arrangement worked between her and her fellow missionaries as a result of these problems"[82]—by which he meant her involvement in controversies related to her work for spiritual renewal. Even after securing Appleby's retirement, however, there was a clear concern for how Appleby would work during the last months of her tenure as a missionary. After the

---

[79] From Rosalee M. Appleby to Frank Means, April 28, 1959.
[80] From Rosalee M. Appleby to Frank Means, May 14, 1959.
[81] From Rosalee M. Appleby to Frank Means, May 14, 1959.
[82] From Frank Means to Ione Gray, February 5, 1960.

decision for the retirement was made, Means wrote her:

> It is our hope that nothing will occur between now and that time
> [of your retirement] to mar the overall effect of your contribution
> to Brazilian Baptist life and the spiritual awakening for which you
> have prayed and worked these many years. It is our hope that your
> remaining days in Brazil will be days in which the consciousness of
> God's blessing upon you personally will be very real and that you
> will find it possible to work along with your fellow missionaries in
> such a way as to prevent any difficulties of a divisive nature.[83]

Means seemed to be less lenient with Appleby than his predecessor
as Secretary for Latin America, Everett Gill, Jr.. Gill had gone to seminary
with Appleby's late husband, David, and he and his wife Rachel were
clearly personal friends of Appleby. Appleby recognized this, and one
month before the official day of her retirement, Appleby asked Means to
reach out to her if he heard any negative gossip about her. She was simultaneously excited about the direction of spiritual awakening in Brazil and
careful about negotiating the repercussions of the controversy on her retirement and missionary legacy.[84] Appleby wanted to stay in Brazil until
the meeting of the Baptist World Alliance, but Means wanted her back in
the United States as soon as she retired, and encouraged her strongly in
that direction—she was back in the United States on April of 1960, before
the meeting of the Baptist World Alliance in Rio de Janeiro.

Baker J. Cauthen, who was an executive of the FMB from 1954 until
1979, told Appleby on February 11, 1960, that the FMB voted to make
her an emeritus missionary as of February 29, 1960.[85] Cauthen, however,
was also suspicious of Appleby. As a response to a letter he received from
Frank Means, who was in Brazil in March of 1960, Cauthen stopped press
releases related to Appleby. Cauthen wrote Ione Gray, who worked in the
FMB's Department of Press Relations, and shared a paragraph of the letter Means sent him from Brazil. For Means, Appleby had been engaged
in "associations she has formed with persons of peripheral ideas and prac-

---

[83] From Frank Means to Rosalee Appleby, May 13, 1959.
[84] From Rosalee Appleby to Frank Means, January 2, 1960.
[85] From Baker J. Cauthen to Rosalee Appleby, February 12, 1960.

tices" that had created divisions in Belo Horizonte, and Means was concerned about any good publicity given to Appleby by the FMB.[86] The article prepared by Ione Gray, entitled "Foster Mother to Young Churches: Rosalee Mills Appleby," highlighted Appleby's thirty-six years of work in churches in Brazil, her prolific literary output, and the good relationship with Brazilian Baptists. Gray's article illustrated the fact that Appleby was one of the greatest SBC missionaries in the history of Brazil and concluded: "She considers 'a life in the power under the direction of the Holy Spirit' the most essential characteristic of a Christian missionary."[87] The article was originally intended to be released with the news of Appleby's retirement in February of 1960, but Means was adamantly against its release. Means distributed a copy of the draft written by Gray to a number of South Brazil missionaries, and they were not happy with what they read. Means sent a letter to Gray two months after Appleby's retirement saying that "judging from the intensity of the feeling which is involved, as well as the fact that these missionaries do not feel the article is representative of Mrs. Appleby's work, my strong recommendation would be that nothing should be published either now or in the foreseeable future on Mrs. Appleby and her work."[88] Gray laid bare the depth of the anger other missionaries felt towards Appleby and, pointing out the inconsistencies of missionary criticism of her article, suggested that missionaries were allowing the controversy to "wipe out memory of the good of a person's earlier years."[89]

Appleby's personal papers show that she was clearly sad about her retirement. If it wasn't for the controversy regarding the trajectory of her spiritual awakening initiatives in Brazil, she would probably work as a missionary in the country for longer. Even when Appleby was back in the United States, however, she continued to work for a spiritual awakening, and the language of revival and power in the Holy Spirit continued to characterize her communication with FMB officials and local pastors. Soon after Appleby arrived in the US, she sent a copy of the book "Shantung Revival" to Frank Means as an attempt to show him how streams of

---

[86] From Baker J. Cauthen to Ione Gray, March 29, 1960.

[87] Ione Gray, "Foster Mother to Young Churches: Rosalee Mills Appleby," February 24, 1960 (unpublished manuscript).

[88] From Frank Means to Ione Gray, April 22, 1960.

[89] From Ione Gray to Frank Means, May 2, 1960.

spiritual revival movements were well within Baptist history and heritage. She told Means that revivals are often misunderstood, and, in the case of the Shantung Revival, missionaries were also against the manifestations of the Spirit. Appleby wanted Means to investigate the controversy in Brazil and asked him to be open to "the ones who have experienced His manifestations, especially the Brazilians, and have definite convictions on the subject."[90] Endorsing her mentees, Appleby wrote:

> Consult especially Sr. Eneas Tognini with an unprejudiced interpreter. He was against revival and had a visitation from above that changed him completely. The Lagoinha Church has had marvelous manifestations, if some of these who experienced a transformation could testify you might have an entirely different idea of things. Pastor Nascimento is a key person too. (I never found him anything but trustworthy).[91]

Appleby seemed open to the charismatic manifestations of her mentees, and the Lagoinha Church she mentioned, which was pastored by Nascimento, went on to be arguably the most famous charismatic church in the history of Brazil. Until her health deteriorated in the early 1980s, Appleby continued to write FMB officials, telling them of the importance of revival, spiritual awakening, and the powerful presence of the Holy Spirit. At times, she conceded that revivals sometimes came with mistakes—implying that this could have been the case with Brazil. Most times, however, she deemphasized a concern for doctrinal articulations and focused on the importance of experiencing the power of the Holy Spirit.

The intra-missionary tensions so apparent in the exchanges between Appleby, fellow missionaries, and FMB officials, however, didn't affect Appleby's public persona in Brazil. Appleby was never attacked in the *Jornal Batista*—especially given the fact that she was encouraged to retire only two years after the controversy on Pentecostal-informed doctrine became national. Lourival Terra praised Appleby as a true revivalist in the mode of the faithful Southern Baptist missionaries, as opposed to the revivalism of her mentees Tognini and Nascimento.[92] Ebenézer Cavalcanti, a harsh critic of Tognini, Nascimento, and their coreligionists, believed, somewhat

---

[90] From Rosalee Appleby to Frank Means, July 1, 1960.
[91] From Rosalee Appleby to Frank Means, July 1, 1960.
[92] Lourival Terra, "Renovação," *Jornal Batista* 62, no. 2 (1962): 5.

against Southern Baptist missionaries and FMB officials, that "that prim-
itive campaign for spiritual revival, to which Rosalee Appleby contributed
so much, and to which pastors and brothers of good faith had adhered, did
not have the goals of dividing or introducing strange doctrines."[93]
Throughout the years, Appleby's name was printed several times in the
Jornal Batista in ways intended to make a sharp distinction between her
work and that of her mentees.[94] Despite the fact that Appleby did not receive resistance from the Brazilian Baptist leaders who were against the
Spiritual Renewal Movement, her mentees and successors as leaders of the
growing charismatic tendencies in Brazilian Baptist life—Nascimento and
Tognini—were constantly under public attack.

In 1961, Tognini, who had not been so outspoken on the issue as
Nascimento and had a stronger record of denominational leadership in the
BBC, was elected to the Executive Board of the convention, and this gave
the movement for spiritual renewal a voice at the top of the denominational chain.[95] In the same year in the state of Minas Gerais, where Nascimento was a pastor, thirty churches left the state convention and formed
an alternative convention at the state level because of the issue of charismatic practices.[96] After this division, the *Jornal Batista* was flooded with
polemical treatises from the perspective of the non-charismatic group.[97]

---

[93]Ebenezer Gomes Cavalcanti, "Frutos Da Pentecostalização Dos Batistas," *Jornal Batista* 63, no. 51 (1963): 7.

[94]See, for example, Alzira Armindo, "Divergência Batista," *Jornal Batista* 64, no.
3 (1964): 5; 10; Samuel Figueira, "Centelhas de Avivemento Em Florianópolis," *Jornal
Batista* 72, no. 32 (1972): 4.

[95] "Junta Executiva Da Convenção Batista Brasileira," *Jornal Batista*, 61, no. 27
(1961).

[96] Pereira, *História Dos Batistas No Brasil (1882-1982)*, 197.

[97] For example, see Ernani Freitas, "Obra Normal Do Espirito," *Jornal Batista*
62, no. 1 (1962); Ernâni Freitas, "Não Entristeçais O Espírito Santo," *Jornal Batista*
62, no. 2 (1962); Gerson Rocha, "O Dom Você Já Tem," *Jornal Batista* 62, no. 1;
Editorial, "Uma Séria Advertência," *Jornal Batista* 62; Ricardo Pitrowsky, "O Que Há
Com O Movimento De Renovação Espiritual? Uma Séria Advertência," *Jornal Batista*
62; Lourival Terra, "Renovação," *Jornal Batista* 62, no. 2; Lourival G. Terra, "Espírito
Santo E Avivamento," *Jornal Batista* 62, no. 5; Francisco Mancebo Reis, "O Batismo
Do Espírito Santo," *Jornal Batista* 62, no. 2; "O Ministério Do Espírito Santo Em
Nossas Vidas I E Ii," *Jornal Batista* 62, no. 4; Delcyr de Souza Lima, "Calvário E
Pentecoste," *Jornal Batista* 62, no. 5; Zacarias Campêlo, "Auto-Hipnose Por
Pentecoste," *Jornal Batista* 62; and L.E. Maxwell, "Fé Ou Sinais," *Jornal Batista* 62.

Also in 1961, Nascimento's book on the doctrine of the Holy Spirit, entitled "*Calvário e Pentecoste*" (Calvary and Pentecost), began to be the focus of criticism. Pastor Delcyr de Souza Lima, for example, wrote a series of scathing reviews that were published in the *Jornal Batista*. After claiming that a former Baptist pastor became Pentecostal after listening to the radio show of the Spiritual Renewal Movement (once led by Appleby), Lima mentioned that spiritual renewal is not a negative goal if attained within the parameters of order and self-control, and he condemned heavily what he saw as Nascimento's defense of the doctrine of baptism in the Holy Spirit as a post-conversion experience.[98] In response to repeated attacks against the Spiritual Renewal Movement as well as their doctrinal stance on the Holy Spirit in the *Jornal Batista*, Tognini wrote a series of clarifications in 1961 regarding their position on the doctrine. These articles were among the very few articles from the perspective of the sympathizers of the Spiritual Renewal Movement printed by the most important denominational periodical.

In the articles, Tognini showed that he learned well from his mentor, Rosalee M. Appleby, as he also rooted their charismatic tendencies well within Baptist history and theology. He began his tour de force by raising the fact that Baptists did not have clarity regarding their stance on the doctrine of the Holy Spirit, and he quoted Baptist Augustus Strong on the matter. Tognini wrote:

> Have we Baptists a creed in relation to the doctrine of the Holy Spirit? Some clearly marked limit that the believer cannot cross? Is there, in our denomination, articles of faith, stereotyped and untouchable, voted by an infallible council and imposed on the believers' conscience? Or, to the contrary, we still have to agree with Augustus Strong, fifty years after, that "the doctrine of the Holy Spirit has never yet been unfolded," and that we are awaiting for a complete discussion on the topic, for which we are urged to recognize

---

[98]Delcyr de Souza Lima, "Calvário e Pentecoste I," *Jornal Batista* 61, no. 32 (1961): 4; Delcyr de Souza Lima, "Calvário e Pentecoste II," *Jornal Batista* 61, no. 40 (1961): 4; Delcyr de Souza Lima, "Calvário e Pentecoste III," *Jornal Batista* 61, no. 52 (1961): 4; Delcyr de Souza Lima, "Calvário e Pentecoste IV," *Jornal Batista* 62, no. 5 (1962): 4.

the work of the omnipotent agent in the historical revivals?[99]

Tognini then cited R.A. Torrey and Baptist H.E. Dana—whose book "The Holy Spirit in Acts" had been translated to Portuguese by the denominational label—as men whose doctrinal stance went against the normally-cessationist disposition of his Baptist rivals.[100] He then mentioned J.B. Lawrence—whose book on the Holy Spirit and missions was also translated into Portuguese—C.E. Matthews, W.A. Criswell, Billy Graham, B.H. Carroll, C.H. Spurgeon, F.B. Meyer, and Lee Scarborough as allies in his non-cessationist understanding of the gifts of the Spirit.[101]

Reflecting on the roots of his charismatic beliefs over three decades after the controversy began, Tognini listed names and events as remote and immediate causes for the movement. As remote causes, he listed the Spirit-filled hymns by Solomon Ginsburg; the miraculous healing of long-time editor of the *Jornal Batista*, W. E. Entzminger—who, according to him, was baptized in the Holy Spirit but did not have the theological language to name his experience as such; and Southern Baptist missionary O. P. Maddox, whose preaching and leadership influenced Rosalee Appleby herself to turn to Spirit-filled language and practice.[102] As immediate causes, he named Rosalee Appleby first; then, Tognini mentioned North American Methodist pastor George W. Ridout, who went to Brazil in 1930 and whose book *The Power of the Holy Spirit* was translated into Portuguese; J. Ewin Orr, a British Baptist revivalist whose book *Full Surrender* was also translated to Portuguese, was next in Tognini's list, followed by the ministry of Pentecostal pastor Raymond Boatright, whose ministry gave rise to a number of Pentecostal churches in Brazil. Finally, Tognini listed the ministry of British evangelist Roy Hession and two of his books that were translated into Portuguese: *My Calvary Road* and *We Would See*

---

[99]Enéas Tognini, "Posição Batista Em Face Da Doutrina Do Batismo No Espírito Santo I," *Jornal Batista* 61, no. 41 (1961): 4.

[100]Tognini, 4.

[101]Enéas Tognini, "Posição Batista Em Face Da Doutrina Do Batismo No Espírito Santo II," *Jornal Batista* 61, no. 42 (1961): 4; Enéas Tognini, "Posição Batista Em Face Da Doutrina Do Batismo No Espírito Santo III," *Jornal Batista* 61, no. 43 (1961): 4; Enéas Tognini, "Posição Batista Em Face Da Doutrina Do Batismo No Espírito Santo IV," *Jornal Batista* 61, no. 44 (1961): 4; Enéas Tognini, "Posição Batista Em Face Da Doutrina Do Batismo No Espírito Santo V," *Jornal Batista* 61, no. 45 (1961): 4.

[102]Tognini, *História Dos Batistas*, 14–16.

Jesus.[103] All of these individuals and events were, according to Tognini, answers to Rosalee Appleby's prayers, and she was the one who took upon herself to bear the responsibility of bringing revival to Baptist circles in Brazil.[104] Revival came to Baptists in Brazil through translated English, and in the Baptist fold, naming English-speaking roots was a means toward greater credibility for the Spirit-filled camp.

Resistance to the Charismatic Camp

Recruiting respected foreigners to a specific camp, however, was not a weapon exclusively used by defenders of the Spiritual Renewal Movement. Brazilian Baptist cessationists also used their English-speaking heroes to grant credence to their narrative. Gerson Rocha, for example, argued that D. L. Moody, Charles Finney, and Helena Edwig did not wait for the gifts of the Spirit, unlike the Baptists involved in the Spiritual Renewal Movement. According to Rocha, "there are already many in our denomination that are waiting their turn to speak in tongues, and others who are waiting on many other things. I know that one thing will happen: they will be hallucinated in their search for the gifts of the Spirit and will be empty of the Spirit of the gifts."[105] Lourival Terra also praised faithful foreigners. After making a clear distinction between Appleby and her mentees in the Spiritual Renewal Movement—a distinction she would likely not allow—Terra made an argument for what he called "true renewal" and said that not only Appleby but also other Southern Baptist missionaries wanted the power of the Spirit but not the pentecostalizing forces that were entering Brazilian Baptist life. He mentioned Z. C. Taylor, W. Entzminger, Solomon Ginsburg, and William Buck Bagby—some of whom were claimed to the charismatic side by Tognini—as advocates of true revival.[106] Z.C. Taylor, who together with William Buck Bagby began the sustainable part of the Southern Baptist mission in Brazil, was often cited by those who tried to resist the advances of the Spiritual Renewal Movement. In an editorial published in 1962, senior editor J. Reis Pereira mentioned Taylor as an authoritative figure whose opinion about the Holy Spirit went

---

[103]Tognini, 16–17.
[104]Tognini, 17.
[105]Gerson Rocha, "O Dom Você Já Tem," *Jornal Batista* 62, no. 1 (1962): 4.
[106] Terra, "Renovação."

against the direction of the Spiritual Renewal Movement.[107] In his many articles, Ebenezer Cavalcanti, one of the most vociferous critics of charismatic tendencies among Brazilian Baptists, used W. C. Taylor, E. C. Bouth, McConkey, A. B. Langston, Cyril Maskrey, and J. Oswald Sanders, among others in his attempt to build his argument against what he saw as doctrinal distortion.[108]

In Brazil, the proper Baptist stance on the doctrine of the Holy Spirit and the power of the denomination to exclude churches based on disagreements about the doctrine mirrored arguments and tensions in the English-speaking world to a great extent. Theologies nurtured in the English-speaking world in general, and among US Baptists in particular, carried unprecedented weight in the discussions of the denominational future in Brazil. The charismatic front was, many times, ahead of the curve in claiming themselves to be proper interpreters of the Baptist heritage. For example, in 1964, the editor of the *Jornal Batista* was surprised by an article printed in the *Minas Batista*—a regional Baptist periodical with charismatic tendencies—that translated the SBC's Baptist Faith and Message of 1963 (BFM 1963) and read it as allowing for charismatic beliefs and practices within the Baptist fold. The charismatic interpreters read the part of the section on the Holy Spirit in the BFM 1963, namely "He [the Holy Spirit] cultivates Christian character, comforts believers, and bestows the spiritual gifts by which we serve God through His church,"[109] as an indication that they could be charismatic and Baptist without any conflict.[110] The editor then commented that there is nothing wrong with the BFM 1963 article. In his attempt to identity the SBC as an ally of the anti-

---

[107] "O Ministério Do Espírito Santo Em Nossas Vidas," *Jornal Batista* 62, no. 4 (1962): 5.

[108] Ebenezer Gomes Cavalcanti, "Doutrina Do Espirito Santo No Pacto Das Igrejas Batistas Do Brasil," *Jornal Batista* 63, no. 19 (1963): 8–9; Ebenezer Gomes Cavalcanti, "Doutrina Definida," *Jornal Batista* 63, no. 27 (1963): 5; Ebenezer Gomes Cavalcanti, "O Sinal Das Línguas," *Jornal Batista* 63, no. 31 (1963): 7–8; Cavalcanti, "Frutos Da Pentecostalização Dos Batistas." McConkey's first name is unclear from the sources, but Cavalcanti relied on a treatise entitled "The Triple Secret of the Holy Spirit," authored by McConkey.

[109] Baptist Faith and Message 1963.

[110] "A Doutrina Do Espirito Santo Num Credo Batista," *Jornal Batista* 64, no. 7 (1964): 2.

charismatic wing of Brazilian Baptist life, he argued for a cessationist position writing that the issue is not whether the Holy Spirit bestows gifts or not, but rather the interpretation regarding their permanence and nature—which charismatics overstated.[111] The Brazilian Baptist Convention added the article on the Holy Spirit to their declaration of faith, copying the move made by the SBC. Almir Gonçalves let the Brazilian Baptist audience know of this development in an article published by the *Jornal Batista*. He wrote:

> In our edition of February 15, we addressed, in one of our editorials, the fact that an article of faith was added to our well-known Declaration [of Faith]. This article and others were added on the occasion of the [new articles introduced by the] Southern Baptist Convention, which met in Kansas, Missouri, in 7–10 of May.[112]

Appreciation for the United States in general and the SBC in particular was not uncommon in the Brazilian Baptist Convention, and the anti-American sentiments that characterized sections of Brazilian culture in 1960s Brazil were taken by many Baptists as proof of communist initiatives. What Alzira Armindo wrote to the *Jornal Batista* was representative of the Brazilian Baptist disposition: "My brothers, let us not escape the undeniable reality, which has roots in biblical prophecy: the American people represent today God's own Israel."[113] It would be expected, therefore, that both cessationists and charismatics wanted to claim their SBC heritage, the new Israel, to their side.

The Decision for Schism and its Ideological Consequences

When the 1962 national convention had its annual meeting, in which thirteen men were chosen to investigate the charismatic issue, the *Jornal Batista* stopped the anti-Pentecostal propaganda, and the editor offered a qualified apology for the journal's publishing practices.[114] The committee

---

[111] "A Doutrina Do Espirito Santo Num Credo Batista."

[112] Almir Gonçalves, "Declaração de Fé Batista," *Jornal Batista* 64, no. 11 (1964): 4.

[113] Alzira Armindo, "Religião Importada," *Jornal Batista* 65, no. 40 (1965): 3.

[114] Almir Gonçalves, "Convenção Batista Brasileira," *Jornal Batista* 65, no. 7; and "A Comissão Dos Treze," *Jornal Batista* 65, no. 8.

formed by the thirteen men presented their report at the 1963 national convention, but it did not resolve the controversial issue of spiritual renewal. The 1963 Annals of the BBC recorded the clash of opinions among pro- and anti-Pentecostal members of the committee formed in order to investigate the issue. Enéas Tognini and José Rego do Nascimento affirmed the doctrine of the baptism with the Holy Spirit. They had appropriated the doctrine of the "second blessing" with the possible, but not necessary, evidence of speaking in tongues, and the cessationist tendencies of other members of the committee fiercely resisted their position.[115] The committee recommended that the debate on the doctrine of the Holy Spirit end without any changes in the Brazilian Baptist "traditional theological stance on this matter."[116] The tone of the report is conciliatory, but it emphasized an anti-Pentecostal disposition. The NBBTS also weighed in on the matter, making public its commitment to the traditional Baptist stance. One of the recommendations of the committee was to include a clearer article on the doctrine of the Holy Spirit in the BBC's confession of faith, thus making official the denomination's resistance to the growing pentecostalizing forces within Brazilian Baptists.[117]

The division in Baptist ranks escalated during the following years, and in 1965 the churches that defended charismatic practices in their services were excluded from the BBC.[118] Under the leadership of Enéas Tognini and José Rego do Nascimento, another national body, the National Baptist Convention (henceforth NBC) could be seen as an alternative charismatic convention among Brazilian Baptists.[119] The pain of the 1965 schism could still be felt in Torgnini's rendition of the event. Writing in

---

[115] Anais da Convenção Batista Brasileira, 1963. A few years after the 1965 schism, Nascimento clarified the position of the Brazilian National Convention on the issue of evidence of tongues. He wrote that "speaking in tongues is evidence of Baptism with the Holy Spirit, but it is not an exclusive or obligatory sign. But once this sign is given, it is definite." José Rego do Nascimento, "O Dom de Línguas," *O Batista Nacional* 5, no. 7 (June 1971): 6.

[116] Nascimento, 6.

[117] Nascimento, 6.

[118] Southern Baptist missionary Lester Bell wrote about the influence of Pentecostalism in the BBC in 1965: "Brazilian Baptists have a doctrinal problem. Pentecostalism is flourishing in most countries in South America, and especially in Chile and Brazil." See Lester C. Bell, *Which Way in Brazil?*, Foreign Mission Graded Series, Adult 1965 (Nashville: Convention Press, 1965), 112.

[119] Pereira, *História Dos Batistas No Brasil (1882-1982)*, 200-1.

1993, he recalled:

> The Brazilian Baptist Convention, in January of 1965, in the city of Niterói, in the state of Rio de Janeiro, cast out around thirty-two churches from its ranks. By the end of 1965, the number reached 52 churches.... What was the reason for the division? A minor theological point—Baptism with the Holy Spirit as a distinct blessing of the new birth—a point on which there is no homogeneity among Baptists. And for that we were cast out as heretics, inconvenients, and dangerous.[120]

The National Baptist Convention came to stay, as the 1991 acceptance of the convention into the ranks of the Baptist World Alliance signaled. Though the animosity of the 1960s abated, the differences between the BBC and the NBC were by no means behind them.

As time went on, the identity of the NBC, in the mind of some prominent leaders, developed in opposition to the BCC. When the NBC first started in 1967, it also developed a major denominational journal—*Batista Nacional*—and a seminary called Brazil Evangelical Theological Seminary (BETS). José Rego do Nascimento made it clear that the BETS was not a Baptist seminary, although it was under the NBC's authority. He emphasized the fact that the seminary was not only interdenominational, but was the first in the country to emphasize spiritual renewal in its curriculum.[121] Despite the fact that the NBC developed its own publishing and educational institutions, its first leaders claimed that they were not forming a different denomination, and that they were proud to be as Baptist as members of the BBC.[122] As time went by, however, new leaders began to claim openly that the NBC was so different from the BBC that they should be considered a new denomination. In 1978, Rosivaldo de Araújo, then Secretary General of the NBC, affirmed that the NBC was a different denomination and that the only reason why it had taken so long

---

[120] Enéas Tognini, *História Dos Batistas Nacionais: Documentário* (Brasília: Convanção Batista Nacional, 1993), 11-12.

[121] José Rego do Nascimento, "Seminário Teológico Evangelico Do Brasil," *O Batista Nacional* 4, no. 6 (July 1970): 4.

[122] Enéas Tognini, "Enéas Tognini Conceitua Renovação Espiritual," *O Batista Nacional* 1, no. 1 (November 1967): 1; Wilmar Souza de Jesus, "Ainda Somos Batistas," *O Batista Nacional* 9, no. 22 (July 1975): 6.

to admit this fact was the conciliatory spirit of former NBC leaders.[123] By the early 1980s, the NBC began to focus on foreign missions and the convention sent its first foreign missionary to Italy in 1982, a fact that signaled a growing self-understanding that stood in opposition to the BBC, which by the 1980s had a successful program of foreign missions already in place.[124]

In the year of the NBC's official formation, the *Jornal Batista* began publishing anti-charismatic and polemic articles in a systematic and continuous manner. From 1967 until well into the 1980s, the major publication of the denomination aimed its voice toward the refutation of central Pentecostal doctrines such as divine healing, baptism with the Holy Spirit, and speaking in tongues as well as toward clarifying its position regarding such beliefs.[125] The publication never explicitly acknowledged the for-

---

[123] Rosivaldo de Araújo, "Batistas Nacionais," *O Batista Nacional* 12, no. 27 (August 1978): 3–4.

[124] "Pr. Antonio Acácio Na Itália," *O Batista Nacional* 16 (October 1982): 5.

[125] Jonathan Strassburg, "Falsificações Do Batismo No Espírito Santo," *Jornal Batista* 67, no. 4 (1967): 10; Philogomiro Lannes, "Sermão Do Espírito," *Jornal Batista* 68, no. 8 (1968): 1–2; Reynaldo Prestes Nogueira, "Renovação Espiritual," *Jornal Batista* 68, no. 7 (1968): 6–7; J. Reis Pereira, "Confusão Que Provoca Escândalo," *Jornal Batista* 68, no. 42 (1968): 3; Timofei Diacov, "O Batismo Do Espirito Santo," *Jornal Batista* 69, no. 1 (1969): 13; Philogomiro Lannes, "Atar e Desatar," *Jornal Batista* 69, no. 16 (1969): 5; J. Reis Pereira, "Sobre Curas," *Jornal Batista* 69, no. 4 (1969): 3; Antônio Lopes, "Igrejas Reavivadas," *Jornal Batista* 70, no. 23 (1970): 3; Reynaldo Prestes Nogueira, "Plenitude Do Espirito Santo," *Jornal Batista* 70, no. 6 (1970): 5; Pedro Bruno da Silva, "Milagres e Curas Nem Sempre São de Procedencia Divina," *Jornal Batista* 71, no. 28 (1971): 7; José Ednaldo Cavalcanti, "As Três Bençãos de Pentecostes," *Jornal Batista* 72, no. 28 (1972): 2; J. Reis Pereira, "Ação Do Espírito Santo," *Jornal Batista* 72, no. 49 (1972): 3; Antônio Maurício, "A Entreda Do Pentecostismo Em Portugal. Por Que Não Fui, Nem Sou, Nem Penso Ser Pentecostal," *Jornal Batista* 73, no. 16 (1973): 8; J. Reis Pereira, "Pentecostismo e Ecumenismo," *Jornal Batista* 73, no. 8 (1973): 3; David Gomes, "A Doutrina Da Cura Divina Biblicamente Apreciada," *Jornal Batista* 75, no. 27 (1975): 1;5; J. Reis Pereira, "Um Apelo de Criswell," *Jornal Batista* 75, no. 38 (1975): 3; J. Reis Pereira, "Ainda Os Curandeiros," *Jornal Batista* 76, no. 19 (1976): 3; J. Reis Pereira, "Males Do Curandeirismo Evangélico," *Jornal Batista* 76, no. 17 (1976): 3; Francisco Mancebo Reis, "Sobre O Dom De Cura," *Jornal Batista* 76, no. 27 (1976): 5; Gedeon Duarte, "Curas Em Que Não Creio," *Jornal Batista* 77, no. 46 (1978): 2; J. Reis Pereira, "Influências Carismáticas I," *Jornal Batista* 79, no. 26 (1979): 3; J. Reis Pereira, "Não Se Pode Mais Falar

mation of the NBC, nor did it pay much attention to the institutional development of the alternative Baptist body in Brazil, but it did sharpen its stance on charismatic and Pentecostal[126] practices.

To be sure, the BBC retained a qualified use of revivalistic terms, although calls for revivals in the *Jornal Batista* were statistically insignificant compared to condemnations of Pentecostal doctrine and practice.[127] Already in 1968, Reynaldo Nogueira argued that Enéas Tognini's claims that there was no emphasis on holiness in BBC circles was justified, and, not unlike.Rosalee Appleby, he criticized the growing formalism within the denomination.[128] Other similar observations were published in the *Jornal Batista* throughout the years,[129] but the qualification that such revival

---

No Espírito Santo?," *Jornal Batista* 79, no. 14 (1979): 3; Isaltino Gomes Coelho Filho, "Glossolalia—I," *Jornal Batista* 80, no. 19 (1980): 7; Isaltino Gomes Coelho Filho, "Glossolalia—II," *Jornal Batista* 80, no. 20 (1980): 4; Isaltino Gomes Coelho Filho, "Glossolalia—III," *Jornal Batista* 80, no. 21 (1980): 4; Isaltino Gomes Coelho Filho, "Glossolalia—4," *Jornal Batista* 80, no. 22 (1980): 4; Isaltino Gomes Coelho Filho, "Glossolalia—5," *Jornal Batista* 80, no. 23 (1980): 4; Isaltino Gomes Coelho Filho, "Glossolalia—6," *Jornal Batista* 80, no. 24 (1980): 4; Isaltino Gomes Coelho Filho, "Glossolalia—7," *Jornal Batista* 80, no. 25 (1980): 4; Isaltino Gomes Coelho Filho, "Glossolalia—8," *Jornal Batista* 80, no. 26 (1980): 4; Isaltino Gomes Coelho Filho, "Glossolalia—9," *Jornal Batista* 80, no. 27 (1980): 4; Isaltino Gomes Coelho Filho, "Glossolalia—10," *Jornal Batista* 80, no. 28 (1980): 4; José Alves da Silva Bitencourt, "A Doutrina Do Espirito Santo," *Jornal Batista* 82, no. 8 (1982): 4; José Alves da Silva Bitencourt, "A Doutrina Do Espirito Santo II," *Jornal Batista* 82, no. 9 (1982): 4.

[126] I use the term "Pentecostal" and "pentecostalized" for the purposes of this project in order to reflect the preference for the term by historical sources. The distinction between charismatic and Pentecostal practices, although helpful, is not common in the sources.

[127] Samuel Figueira, "Urgência de Um Avivamento," *Jornal Batista* 70, no. 51 (1970): 6; Stelleo Severino Da Silva, "Por Que e Como Um Reavivamento?," *Jornal Batista* 71, no. 39 (1971): 8; Severino Bello da Silva, "Lutamos Pelo Avivamento," *Jornal Batista* 72, no. 37 (1972): 2.

[128] Reynaldo Prestes Nogueira, "Queremos Avivamento?," *Jornal Batista* 68, no. 49 (1968): 1–2.

[129] Antônio Lopes, "Igrejas Frias," *Jornal Batista* 71 (1971); Samuel Figueira, "Centelhas de Avivemento Em Florianópolis," *Jornal Batista* 72, no. 32 (1972): 4; and Assis Cabral, "Obstáculos a Um Avivamento Espiritual," *Jornal Batista* 81, no. 15 (1981): 8.

should not look like the Pentecostal expressions of worship that were taking over the country from then on was mentioned more explicitly.[130]

The understanding of both the place of Pentecostalism within Baptist circles and the value of Pentecostal doctrine and practice was sharpened progressively in the denomination, and the *Jornal Batista* was the denominational tool that implemented the project of delegitimizing Pentecostalizing tendencies. In 1967, Ebenezer Ferreira lamented not that the convention was unable to find a peaceful way forward with the charismatic churches that were excluded from the convention, but that the issue of spiritual renewal had not been crushed sooner.[131] Ferreira feared that the charismatic issue would be a longstanding issue for the BBC, and he was correct. Over the coming years, non-Pentecostal Protestants in Brazil would increasingly challenge the aggressive growth of Pentecostalism in the nation. But rather than compromising, the BBC's first reaction was to resist vociferously anything that would make them look like Pentecostals. In other words, the rise of Pentecostalism was a significant part in the creation of a distinct Baptist denominational self-understanding that was articulated as being essentially anti-Pentecostal.

The resistance to Pentecostal doctrine and experience came from different angles. When it came to the practice of speaking in tongues, Sóstenes Barros, for instance, wrote in 1969 that the tongues that were spoken in Pentecostal services were psychologically induced.[132] Assis Cabral stated that the Pentecostal practice of speaking in tongues was not applicable to contemporary times,[133] and denominational leader Isaltino Gomes Filho published a ten-article series on the practice of glossolalia that argued against the practice in contemporary churches.[134] The *Journal Batista* also

---

[130] J. Reis Pereira, "Dá-Nos Um Avivamento," *Jornal Batista* 68, no. 47 (1968): 3; Pereira, "Males Do Curandeirismo Evangélico," 3; Pereira, "Influências Carismáticas I," 3; and Pereira, "Não Se Pode Mais Falar No Espírito Santo?," 3. As editor of the *Jornal Batista*, J. Reis Pereira constantly qualified any statement in the journal that could be interpreted as an endorsement of charismatic practices.

[131] Ebenezer Soares Ferreira, "Os Perigos Atuais Que Ameaçam a Obra Batista No Brasil," *Jornal Batista* 67, no. 16 (1967): 1.

[132] Sóstenes Pereira de Barros, "As Línguas, Idiomas Dos Anjos? Do Espírito Humano? (Conclusão)," *Jornal Batista* 69, no. 17 (1969): 8.

[133] Assis Cabral, "Línguas Estranhas," *Jornal Batista* 74, no. 6 (1974): 4.

[134] Filho, "Glossolalia—1," 7; Filho, "Glossolalia—2," 4; Filho, "Glossolalia - 3," 4; Filho, "Glossolalia—4," 4; Filho, "Glossolalia—5," 4; Filho, "Glossolalia—6," 4;

heavily criticized the Pentecostal practice of divine healing, as it was known in denominational parlance, the practice generally being considered either misguided or fraudulent.[135] The NBC and the NBC's adoption of the practices of healing and speaking in tongues, in itself a symptom of the growing influence of Pentecostalism in the country, energized the development of an anti-Pentecostal stance in BBC leadership circles. In the second half of the twentieth century, cooperating with the Brazilian Baptist Convention generally came to mean being necessarily non-Pentecostal and many times outspokenly so.

Conclusion

The history of global evangelicalism is often characterized by the overbearing shadow of the English-speaking world. In the case of Brazilian Baptists, the Southern Baptist Convention was the sun around which their world orbited. It is not surprising, therefore, that the influence of both charismatic and anti-charismatic forces within Baptist circles in Brazil came from United States Baptist circles. Although Appleby and her mentees—Tognini and Nascimento—also allowed non-Baptist literature produced in the US and Great Britain to inform their defense of their view of the doctrine of the Holy Spirit, they insisted throughout their ministries that they were thoroughly Baptist. When Tognini wrote the history of the charismatic National Baptist Convention, he still felt the need to affirm his Baptist self-identification. In the preface, Tognini wrote:

> God knows what we are and what we have always been. I was born in a Baptist church, I studied in a Baptist seminary, and I always worked among Baptists. I am still Baptist and will never stop being a Baptist, except in heaven, where there will not be Baptists or any other group whatsoever. I didn't abandon even one comma of the Baptist position. I added two realities, and if they are Baptist, I do

---

Filho, "Glossolalia - 7," 4; Filho, "Glossolalia - 8," 4; Filho, "Glossolalia - 9," 4; Filho, "Glossolalia - 10," 4.

[135] Gomes, "A Doutrina Da Cura Divina Biblicamente Apreciada," 1; David Gomes, "A Doutrina Da Cura Divina Biblicamente Apreciada: Comclusão," *Jornal Batista* 75, no. 28 (1975): 1–2; Antônio Maurício, "Memírias de Um Missionário: Curas Emocionais--Curas Fraudulentas--Curas Divinas," *Jornal Batista* 76, no. 29 (1976): 8; Pereira, "Males Do Curandeirismo Evangélico," 3; Pereira, "Ainda Os Curandeiros," 3; Duarte, "Curas Em Que Não Creio," 2.

not know, but I know they are biblical: Baptism in the Holy Spirit, distinct blessing of the new birth. This reality I experienced in 1958 and cannot deny it. And the second reality is that of the gifts of the Spirit described by Paul in I Corinthians 12 and 14 as blessings for today.[136]

As Appleby had done in her time, Tognini read himself as being deeply within Baptist history and heritage.

Brazilian Baptists who opposed charismatic forces, however, tended to question the Baptist identity of their Spirit-filled counterparts. Cavalcanti encapsulated well the disposition of the majority of the Brazilian Baptist Convention that eventually excluded those who wanted to remain Baptist and to experience simultaneously the gifts of the Spirit:

> Our Declaration [of Faith] characterizes Baptists also in regard to the doctrine of the Holy Spirit. It endured and overcame the tremendous Pentecostal impact of 1911, in Belém do Pará, which also began from the inside out, as it is now becoming clear in the inappropriately-named Spiritual Renewal Movement. They pretended to diminish their activities so that they could better establish themselves in the Baptist fold and in it be nourished. Diplomacy sometimes can avoid impact. We adopted the policy of peaceful coexistence. Soon we will pay the price with interest in terms of a bigger exodus, when the innovator group considers itself numerically strong enough to impose conditions and profit freely from the spiritual and institutional patrimony of the octogenarian Baptist Denomination in Brazil.[137]

In Brazil, the Spirit was imported through English-speaking means and resisted by similar mechanisms. Throughout the history of Baptists in Brazil, bearing the Baptist name meant, to a great extent, being able to read one's history as being in line with the identity narrative of the Southern Baptist Convention. Traditionalist cessationists and charismatic innovators, no matter where they stood, were more often than not conditioned to connect the legitimacy of their positions to the approval of different sets of imported plausibility structes.

---

[136]Tognini, *História Dos Batistas*, 12.

[137]Ebenezer Gomes Cavalcanti, "Doutrina Do Espírito Santo Na Declaração de Fé Das Igrejas Batostas Do Brasil," *Jornal Batista* 63, no. 20 (1963): 7.

CONCLUSION

The first one hundred years of Baptist life in Brazil and, partially through Brazilian influence, in Latin America, was characterized by Southern Baptist influence through missionary presence. Missionaries arrived in Brazil in the last decades of the nineteenth century and brought with them a number of cultural dispositions from the Southern United States, where the majority of FMB missionaries were born and raised. They established institutions that had in their organizational culture the soul of the South, with their disposition toward Southern superiority, conservative social imagination, racially informed biases, male dominated leadership, and theologically fundamentalist leanings. To expect a different approach from Southern Baptist missionaries in their foreign mission endeavors in the nineteenth and most of the twentieth century would be to expect missionaries to transcend their context in ways that most of them could not. Furthermore, in Brazil they found a context that mostly encouraged, rather than challenged, the racial biases that undergirded a number of additional aspects of Southern Baptist theopolitical imagination.

For the first several decades of Brazilian Baptist history, Southern Baptist missionaries did not face widespread, organized local resistance against the White supremacist leanings that permeated their initiatives and institutions. In the early 1920s, however, a number of locals and one "rogue" Southern missionary, D.L. Hamilton, organized against the imbalance in denominational power. From the perspective of Hamilton and the Brazilians who organized in what came to be known as the Radical Movement, Southern Baptist missionaries intentionally and aggressively kept Brazilian Baptists away from a number of leadership positions, and Brazilians wanted more denominational power and autonomy. Eventually, given the pressure that the Radical Movement imposed on missionaries and FMB officials, as well as the limitations created by the financial strain of the Great Depression, locals got some of the qualified autonomy they wanted. Missionaries, however, were mostly resentful of the success attained by the Radical Movement and the denominational arrangements that followed.

After Brazilians took leadership of major denominational committees and the most important institutions of cultural output (seminaries and publications), missionaries began to work toward a resurgence. In just a few years after locals became leaders of major denominational initiatives and institutions, missionaries were again holding undisputed denominational power and guiding the shaping of the Brazilian Baptist Convention. When missionaries were back leading the denomination, however, they had an advantage in the fact that unlike the Brazilians of the Radical Movement, they didn't need to organize a public movement of resistance to get back the power they had lost. Missionaries regained the denominational power they had lost in the 1930s through backstage maneuvers that included financial support of missionary-friendly initiatives and the quiet exclusion of locals that were perceived as threats to missionary power from positions of leadership in the denomination and its institutions. In 1982, when the Brazilian Baptist Convention celebrated its one hundred years of history, missionaries stood as unqualified heroes of the denomination, and the more questionable aspects of their work in the country were—and remain—unknown by the vast majority of Brazilian Baptists.

Despite the general doctrinal unity that characterized the first one hundred years of the Brazilian Baptist Convention, one issue generated a definite spit in the denomination: the doctrine of the Holy Spirit. In the 1950s and 1960s the Brazilian Baptist Convention would enter in the public controversy that resulted in the creation of the charismatic National Baptist Convention. Following the legacy and direct influence of Southern Baptist missionary Rosalee Mills Appleby, Brazilians Enéas Tognini and José Rego do Nascimento would spearhead a struggle for the inclusion of the gifts of the Holy Spirit—particularly speaking in tongues—in the self-understanding of Brazilian Baptist doctrine and practice. The majority of Brazilian Baptists, together with an overwhelming number of Southern Baptist missionaries, resisted the charismatic notions that Tognini, Nascimento, and a few other Baptist ministers wanted to incorporate into the Brazilian Baptist Convention. In 1965, a number of churches would be excluded from the BBC and later these churches created an alternative denomination that supported its own publication, seminary, and foreign mission initiative. The role played by Rosalee Mills Appleby and other English-speaking theologians and ministers illustrates the extent of the importance of Southern Baptist figures in Brazilian Baptist thinking. Both the agreements and disagreements within the Brazilian Baptist Convention were informed and guided by sensibilities born within and legitimized by Southern Baptist circles.

The Southern Baptist shaping of Brazilian Baptist identity was deep-seated and manifested itself strongly in the first century of Brazilian Baptist history. Since 1982, both the Southern Baptist Convention and the Brazilian Baptist Convention have developed their own institutional identities but remained strongly connected. These connections deserve a separate study, but it is appropriate to notice that the grip of Southern Baptist imagination that shaped Brazilian Baptist thought still permeates the Brazilian Baptist Convention in its theological articulations, social dispositions, and institutional commitments. As the history of both of these deeply connected denominations progressed, the Southern Baptist Convention remained the father to which Brazilian Baptists looked up for the legitimation of its own self-perception.

The mostly unqualified praise for missionaries continued in the pages of the *Jornal Batista* throughout the years. The support for the "conservative resurgence" that divided the Southern Baptist Convention as well as for the conservative theological stances that Southern Baptists, despite the diversity within their ranks, continued to espouse even after the sharper edges of the controversy waned, are also characteristic of Brazilian Baptist denominational leaders. The literature produced by the publication house of Brazilian Baptists is characterized by an overwhelming presence of translated works that originated within the American evangelical camp. The struggle against an imagined form of modernist threat was part and parcel of the continuing shape of both the Southern Baptist Convention and of Brazilian Baptist identity. The imposition of religiously legitimized heteronormativity is blatantly evident in both conventions until today. The resistance against full equality for women, despite differences in emphasis and strength, characterizes both the SBC and the BBC. General commitment to conservative politics and politicians, with the strong SBC support of Donald Trump and the support given by most Brazilian evangelicals to Jair Bolsonaro, are indicators of a common history and identity. In addition, independent and denominationally sponsored cooperation between Southern Baptists and Brazilian Baptists in the areas of missions and theological education continue to take place.

As technology made access to transnational religious goods easier, the connection between the SBC and the Brazilian Baptist Convention continues to develop. For Baptists in general, the commonality between Southern and Brazilian Baptists seems to be the fruits of a natural connection created around common understandings of the Gospel of Christ and its cultural and social ramifications. Careful historical analysis, however, reveals that much of these common dispositions were constructed and maintained by Southern Baptist missionaries who went to Brazil and operated in an environment that did not challenge foundational aspects of Southern culture in general and the form of White supremacy so common among nineteenth and twentieth century Southern Whites in particular.

Baptists in Brazil, however, were not just recipients of Southern Baptist orthodoxy. Brazilian Baptists returned the favor of their Southern Baptist fathers and mothers and also took the Southern gospel abroad. The World Mission Board of the Brazilian Baptist Convention had, by the time Baptists in Brazil celebrated one hundred years of history, missionaries in Chile, Portugal, Paraguay, Bolivia, Mozambique, Angola, Azores, Uruguay, Argentina, Rhodesia, Venezuela, France, Spain, Canada, South Africa, the United States, Peru, and Ecuador. Brazilian Baptists are mission-minded people, another legacy of the Southern Baptists who helped shape their identity and theology. Baptists in Brazil also helped form people, such as C.D. Daniel and J.F. Plainfield, who became denominational workers of great influence in the United States. As such, the Brazilian Baptist place in the dissemination of Southern Baptist orthodoxy became multidirectional in a short period of time, as Baptists with connection to Brazil moved simultaneously from and to a wide range of places. Eventually, Southern Baptist faith moved simultaneously from the United States to Brazil, from Brazil to the United States, from Brazil to Portugal, from Brazil to several Latin American countries, from other Latin American countries to the United States, from Brazil to Africa, from the United States to other Latin American countries, and etc. The transnational, multidirectional nature of Southern Baptist orthodoxy is hard to trace exhaustively due to its many connections, but the central place of Brazil in the global transmission of Southern Baptist influence is undeniable.

The role of the missionary in the dynamic of Southern Baptist influence abroad is often understated or uncritically celebrated. The global ambassadors of Southern faith were the marketers and institutionalizers of Southern Baptist presence abroad. They were extremely effective in the way in which they conceptualized and maintained the Southern ethos in other countries and in how they convinced converts foreign to their way of life that their culturally-embedded message was the direct word of the Christian God. Southern and Latin American Baptist believers are often fascinated and mystified by the towering, heroic figure of the missionary.

These men and women were indeed courageous, intelligent, committed, and struggled with the existential challenges familiar only to those who have lived in countries that are not their own. They were also limited by an imagination that was shaped by the Southern culture that formed them.

True, authentic appreciation for these men and women is not appropriately conveyed in the mostly uncritical works produced by denominationally affiliated scholars. The hagiographic portrayals of missionaries so common among Baptist circles have functioned as a tool that keeps locals from developing an appropriate self-perception. Rather, it is better to acknowledge the contextual inadequacies of those who built the roads of Baptist faith abroad. The roads of Southern Baptist faith in the mission field were built with the mixed and sometimes contradictory bricks of racial violence, true love for Christ, White supremacy, commitment to the foreign convert, exclusionary theologies, tears shed in foreign lands, institutional domination, courage to face the challenges of missionary living, misogyny, willingness to face religious persecution, disdain for other religious bodies, initiatives of poverty alleviation, homophobia, the building of orphanages and hospitals, American nationalism, and educational initiatives. Mixed legacies need mixed stories. The souls of Southern Baptist missionaries were sold out to Christ and the South. Separating God from nation, however, was not a quality that missionaries often shared. For them, God spoke English, and English with a Southern drawl. Only a recognition of the ramifications of this realization will free those who were conditioned to worship the Christian God of the South to look to their own contexts honestly as sources for theologies that can respond to the material challenges ahead of them. As Global South evangelicalism grows rapidly, with it grows the shadow of sensibilities spread globally by Southern Baptists and their foreign converts.

BIBLIOGRAPHY

Archives
International Mission Board, Richmond, VA
James P. Boyce Centennial Library at Southern Baptist Theological Seminary,
    Louisville, KY
Marconi Monteiro's Private Collection, San Antonio, TX
North Brazil Baptist Theological Seminary Archives, Recife, PE, Brazil
Southern Baptist Historical Library and Archives, Nashville, TN
Wright Library at Princeton Theological Seminary, Princteon, NJ
The Texas Collection and University Archives at Baylor University, Waco, TX

Primary Sources in Portuguese: Newspapers, Periodicals, and Reports
A Nova Vida
Anais da Convenção Batista Brasileira
As Boas Novas
Boletim do Seminário Teológico Batista do Norte do Brasil
Correio Nacional
O Batista Nacional
O Jornal Batista
Revista Teológica
Visão Missionária

Primary Sources in Portuguese: Manuscripts
Appleby, Rosalee Mills. *Filhas do rei,*. Rio de Janeiro: Casa Publicadora Batista,
    1946.
———. *Florilégio cristão: compilação*. Rio de Janeiro: Casa Publicadora Batista,
    1970.
———. *Labaredas de fogo*. São Paulo, Brazil: Renovação Espiritual, 1963.
———. *Meditacoes do crepusculo*. Rio de Janeiro: Edicao da Escola Bíblica do ar,
    1970.
———. *Melodias no alvorada*. Rio de Janeiro: Casa Publicadora Batista, 1954.
———. *O ensino da palavra*. *"Lampada para os meus pes a tua palavra e luz para o
    meu caminho" (Sal. 119: 105)*. Rio de Janeiro: Casa publicadora Batista,
    1967.
———. *Sarça ardente*. São Paulo, Brazil: Edições Enéas Tognini, 1966.
Appleby, Rosalee Mills and Stella Camara Du Bois. *A vida vitoriosa,*. Rio de
    Janeiro: Casa Publicadora Batista, 1954.
Appleby, Rosalee Mills and Stela Câmara Dubois. *Asas resplandecentes*. São

Paulo: Renovação Espiritual, 1962.

Crabtree, A.R. *História Dos Baptistas Do Brasil*. Vol. 1. Rio de Janeiro: Casa Publicadora Baptista, 1937.

Mesquita, Anônio Neves de. *História Dos Baptistas Do Brasil*. Vol. 2. Rio de Janeiro: Casa Publicadora Baptista, 1940.

Mesquita, Anônio Neves de. *Historia Dos Baptistas Em Pernambuco*. Recife: Typographia do C.A.B., 1930.

Tognini, Enéas. *História Dos Batistas Nacionais: Documentário*. Brasília: Convanção Batista Nacional, 1993.

Primary Sources in English: Newspapers, Periodicals, and Reports
Annals of the Southern Baptist Convention
Annual Report of the Foreign Mission Board
Christian Index
Foreign Mission Journal
Home and Foreign Fields
The Commission
Toronto Star

Primary Sources in English: Manuscripts

Appleby, Rosalee Mills. *Flaming Fagots*. Nashville: Broadman Press, 1943.

————. *Orchids and Edelweiss*. Nashville: Broadman Press, 1941.

————. *Rainbow Gleams*. Nashville: Sunday School Board, 1929.

————. *Sarça ardente*. São Paulo, Brazil: Edições Enéas Tognini, 1966.

————. *The Life Beautiful*. Nashville: Broadman, 1936.

————. *The Queenly Quest*. Philadelphia: Judson, 1933.

————. *White Wings of Splendor*. Nashville: Broadman Press, 1962.

————. *Wings against the Blue*. Nashville: Broadman Press, 1942.

Bell, Lester C. *Which Way in Brazil?* Foreign Mission Graded Series. Adult 1965. Nashville: Convention Press, 1965.

Bratcher, L. M. *Francisco Fulgencio Soren: Christ's Interpreter to Many Lands*. Nashville: Broadman Press, 1938.

Carver, William O. *Syllabus of Lectures on Missions*. Louisville: Southern Baptist Theological Seminary, 1905.

Cox, Ethlene Boone, and Rosalee Mills Appleby. *Star Trails to Life Beautiful,*. Nashville: Broadman Press, 1936.

Gill, Everett. *Europe and the Gospel*. Richmond: Foreign Mission Board, 1931.

————. *Pilgrimage to Brazil*. Nashville: Broadman Press, 1954.

Ginsburg, Solomon L. *A Wandering Jew in Brazil: An Autobiography of Solomon L. Ginsburg*. Nashville: Sunday School Board of the SBC, 1922.

Harrison, Helen Bagby. *The Bagbys of Brazil*. Nashville: Broadman Press, 1954.

Mein, David. *O Que Deus Tem Feito*. Rio de Janeiro: JUERP, 1982.

Oliver, A. Ben. *Baptists Building in Brazil*. Nashville: Broadman Press, 1942.

Plainfield, J.F. *The Stranger Within Our Gates*. Atlanta: Home Mission Board of the Southern Baptist Convention, 1938.

Sampey, John R. *Southern Baptist Theological Seminary*. Baltimore: Wharton, Barron & Company, 1890.

Taylor, Zachary Clay. *The Rise and Progress of Baptist Missions in Brazil, an Autobiography*. Unpublished manuscript.

Tupper, H. Allen. *Armenia: Its Present Crisis and Past History*. New York: John Murphy & Company, 1896.

Theses and Dissertations

Azevedo, Israel Belo de. "A Palavra Marcada: Teologia Política Dos Batistas Segundo O Jornal Batista." Master's thesis, Seminário Teológico Batista do Norte do Brasil, 1983.

Beck, Rosalie. "The Whitsitt Contorversy: A Denomination in Crisis." PhD diss., Baylor University, 1984.

Cameron, David J. "Race and Religion in the Bayou City: Latino/a, African-American, and Anglo Baptists in Houston's Long Civil Rights Movement." PhD diss., Texas A&M University, 2017.

Chaves, Joao B. "Disrespecting Borders for Jesus, Power, and Cash: Southern Baptist Missions, The New Immigration, and the Churches of the Brazilian Diaspora." PhD diss., Baylor University, 2017.

Lamkin Jr., Adrian. "The Gospel Mission Movement Within the Southern Baptist Convention." PhD diss., Southern Baptist Theological Seminary, 1979.

Landers, John M. "Eric Alfred Nelson, the First Baptist Missionary on the Amazon, 1891-1939." PhD diss., Texas Christian University, 1982.

Martins, Mário Ribeiro. "O Radicalismo Batista Brasileiro." Master's thesis, Seminário Teológico Batista do Norte do Brasil, 1972.

Monteiro, Fávio Marconi Lemos. "Radicalism in Pernambuco: A Study of the Relationship Between Nationals and Southern Baptist Missionaries in the Brazilian Baptist Struggle for Autonomy." Master's thesis, Baylor University, 1991.

Moore, Christopher C. "Apostle of the Confederacy: J. William Jones and the Question of Ecumenism and Denominational Identity in the Development of Lost Cause Mythology." PhD diss., Baylor University, 2016.

Nash Jr., Robert Norman. "The Influence of American Myth on Southern Baptist Foreign Missions, 1845-1945." PhD diss., Southern Baptist Theological Seminary, 1989.

Oliveira, Zaqueu. "The Persecution of Brazilian Baptists and Its Influence on

Their Development." PhD diss., Southwestern Baptist Theological Seminary, 1971.

Premack, Laura. "'The Holy Rollers Are Invading Our Territory': Southern Baptist Missionaries and the Early Years of Pentecostalism in Brazil, 1910-1935." Master's thesis, University of North Carolina at Chapel Hill, 2007.

Pruitt, Nicholas T. "Open Hearts, Closed Doors: Native Protestants, Pluralism, and the 'Foreigner' in America, 1924-1965." PhD diss., Baylor University, 2017.

Silva, Célio Antonio Alcantara. "Capitalismo e Escravidão: A Imigração Confederada Para o Brasil." PhD diss., Universidade Estadual de Campinas, 2011.

Wedeman, Walter. "A History of Protestant Missions to Brazil, 1850-1914." PhD diss., Southern Baptist Theological Seminary, 1977.

Secondary Sources

Adeney, Miriam. *Kingdom without Borders: The Untold Story of Global Christianity*. Downers Grove: IVP Books, 2009.

Adogame, Afeosemime U., and Shobana Shankar, eds. *Religion on the Move! New Dynamics of Religious Expansion in a Globalizing World*. International Studies in Religion and Society, v. 15. Leiden: Brill, 2013.

Ahlstrom, Sydney E. *Religious History of the American People*. New Haven: Yale University Press, 1972.

Alencar, Gedeon. *Matriz Pentecostal Brasileira: Assembleias de Deus, 1911-2011*. Rio de Janeiro: Novos Dialogos, 2013.

———. *Protestantismo Tupiniquim*. São Paulo: Aret Editorial, 2007.

Alexandre, Ricardo. *E a verdade os libertará: Reflexões sobre riligião, política e bolsonarism*. São Paulo: Mundo Cristão, 2020.

Ammerman, Nancy Tatom. *Baptist Battles: Social Change and Religious Conflict in the Southern Baptist Convention*. Rutgers University Press, 1990.

Anjos, Maria de Lourdes, and Carlos Henrique Carvalho. "Ações Educacionais Dos Missionários Batistas Norte-Americanos No Início Do Século XX No Brasil." In *Contribuições Do Protestantismo Para a História Da Educação No Brasil e Em Portugal*, edited by Cesar Romero Amaral Vieira and Ester Fraga Vilas-Bôas Carvalho do Nascimento, 207–32. Piracicaba: UNIMEP, 2017.

Araújo, João Pedro Gonçalves. *Batistas: Dominação e Dependencia*. São Paulo: Fonte Editorial, 2015.

———. *Historias, Tradições e Pensamentos Batistas*. São Paulo: Fonte Editorial, 2015.

Assis, Ader Alvez de. *Pioneirismo e Neopioneirismo: Cem Anos de Ação Missionária*

Batista Em Minas. Belo Horizonte: Convenção Batista de Minas, 1989.

Azevedo, Israel Belo de. *A Celebração Do Indivíduo: A Formação Do Pensamento Batista Brasileiro*. Piracicaba: Editora Unimpep, 1996.

Baker, Robert A. *The Southern Baptist Convention and Its People, 1607-1972*. Nashville: Broadman Press, 1974.

Bakker, Janel Kragt. *Sister Churches: American Congregations and Their Partners Abroad*. Oxford: Oxford University Press, 2014.

Bandeira, Moniz. *A Presença Dos Estados Unidos No Brasil (Dois Séculos de Hisória)*. Rio de Janeiro: Civilização Brasileira, 1973.

Barbosa, José Carlos. *Slavery and Protestant Missions in Imperial Brazil: "The Black Does Not Enter the Church, He Peeks in From Outside."* Translated by Fraser G. MacHaffie and Richard K. Danford. Lanham: University Press of America, 2008.

Barger, Lilian Calles. *The World Come of Age: An Intellectual History of Liberation Theology*. Oxford University Press, 2018.

Barreto Jr., Raimundo. "A Ética Social e Sua Relevância Para a Igreja Hoje." *Episteme* 3, no. 2 (2001): 65–80.

Bebbington, David W. *Evangelicalism in Modern Britain: A History from the 1730s to the 1980s*. London: Routledge, 1989.

Blight, David W. *Race and Reunion: The Civil War in American Memory*. Cambridge: Belknap Press, 2002.

Bosch, David Jacobus. *Transforming Mission: Paradigm Shifts in Theology of Mission*. Maryknoll: Orbis Books, 1991.

Bowen, Kurt. *Evangelism and Apostasy: The Evolution and Impact of Evangelicals in Modern Mexico*. Montreal: McGill-Queen's University Press, 1996.

Boyer, Paul S., Clifford E. Clark, Sandra Hawley, Joseph F. Kett, and Andrew Rieser. *The Enduring Vision: A History of the American People, Volume 1: To 1877, Concise*. Boston: Cengage Learning, 2009.

Brinsfield Jr., John Wesley. *The Spirit Divided: Memoirs of Civil War Chaplains*. Macon: Mercer University Press, 2006.

Butler, Anthea. *White Evangelical Racism: The Politics of Morality in America*. Chapel Hill: University of North Carolina Press, 2021.

Campbell-Reed, Eileen. *Anatomy of a Schism: How Clergywomen's Narratives Reinterpret the Fracturing of the Southern Baptist Convention*. Knoxville: Univ Tennessee Press, 2016.

Carter, Greg. *The United States of the United Races: A Utopian History of Racial Mixing*. New York: NYU Press, 2013.

Cathcart, William. *The Baptist Encyclopedia*. Paris: The Baptist Standard Bearer, 1881.

Chaves, João B. *Evangelicals and Liberation Revisited: An Inquiry into the Possibility of an Evangelical-Liberationist Theology*. Eugene: Wipf & Stock Pub, 2013.

————. *Migrational Religion: Context and Creativity in the Latinx Diaspora.* Waco: Baylor University Press, 2021.

————. "Where Should We Go Next?: A Call for the Critical Investigation of Possible Racial Encounters Between Anglo-American and Mexican American Baptists in Texas During the Pioneer Period." *Baptist History and Heritage* 49, no. 3 (Fall 2004): 23–38.

Chaves, João, and C. Douglas Weaver. "Baptists and Their Polarizing Ways: Transnational Polarization between Southern Baptist Missionaries and Brazilian Baptists." *Review & Expositor* 116, no. 2 (May 1, 2019): 160–74.

Collins, Travis. *The Baptist Mission of Nigeria.* Ibadan: Associated Book-Makers Nigeria, 1993.

Corten, André. *Le pentecôtisme au Brésil.* Paris: Karthala, 1995.

————. *Pentecostalism in Brazil: Emotion of the Poor and Theological Romanticism.* New York: St. Martin's Press, 1999.

Corten, André, and Ruth R. Marshall-Fratani. "Introduction." In *Between Babel and Pentecost: Transnational Pentecostalism in Africa and Latin America*, edited by Andre Corten and Ruth R. Marshall-Fratani, 1–21. Bloomington: Indiana University Press, 2001.

Cowan, Benjamin A. *Moral Majorities Across the Americas: Brazil, the United States, and the Creation of the Religious Right.* Chapel Hill: University of North Carolina Press, 2021.

Dawsey, Cyrus, and James M. Dawsey. *The Confederados: Old South Immigrants in Brazil.* Tuscaloosa: University of Alabama Press, 1998.

Dias, Zwinglio Mota, and Rodrigo Portella. "Apresentação." In *Protestantes, Evangélicos e (Neo) Pentecostais: História, Teologias, Igrejas e Perspectivas*, edited by Zwinglio Mota Dias, Rodrigo Portella, and Elisa Rodrigues, 19–26. São Paulo: Fonte Editorial, 2014.

Dias, Zwinglio Mota, Rodrigo Portella, and Elisa Rodrigues, eds. *Protestantes, Evangélicos e (Neo) Pentecostais: História, Teologias, Igrejas e Perspectivas.* São Paulo: Fonte Editorial, 2014.

Dip, Andrea. *Em nome de quem?: A bancada evangélica e seu projeto de poder.* Rio de Janerio: Civilização Brasileira, 2018.

Dubois, Stela Câmara. *Rosalee Mills Appleby.* Lapa, São Paulo, SP: Edições Enéas Tognini, 1991.

Du Mez, Kristin Kobes. *Jesus and John Wayne: How White Evangelicals Corrupted a Faith and Fractured a Nation.* New York: Liveright Publishing, 2020.

DuRocher, Kristina. *Raising Racists: The Socialization of White Children in the Jim Crow South.* Lexington: University Press of Kentucky, 2011.

Durso, Pamela R, and Keith Durso. *The Story of Baptists in the United States.* Brentwood: Baptist History and Heritage Society, 2006.

Eighmy, John Lee, and Samuel S Hill. *Churches in Cultural Captivity: A History of the Social Attitudes of Southern Baptists.* Knoxville: University of Tennessee Press, 1987.

Enns, James C. *Saving Germany: North American Protestants and Christian Mission to West Germany, 1945-1974.* Montreal: McGill-Queen's University Press, 2017.

Esposito, Karina. "Confederate Immigration to Brazil: A Cross-Cultural Approach to Reconstruction and Public History." *Public History Review* 22 (2015): 23–37.

Fath, Sébastien. "The Impact of Charismatic Christianity on Traditional French Baptist Identity." In *Baptist Identities: International Studies from the Seventeenth to the Twentieth Centuries,* edited by Ian M. Randall, Toivo Pilli, and Anthony Cross, 77–91. Milton Keynes: Paternoster, 2006.

Flowers, Elizabeth Hill. *Into the Pulpit: Southern Baptist Women & Power since World War II.* Chapel Hill: University of North Carolina Press, 2012.

Fuller, A. James. *Chaplain to the Confederacy: Basil Manly and Baptist Life in the Old South.* Baton Rouge: LSU Press, 2000.

Gallimore, A.R. "The Hakkas, the Anglo-Saxons of China." *Home and Foreign Fields* 11, no. 4 (1927): 5–7.

Goldman, Frank. *Os Pioneiros Americanos No Brasil: Educadores, Sacerdotes, Covos e Reis.* São Paulo: Pioneira, 1972.

Griggs, William Clark. *The Elusive Eden: Frank McMullan's Confederate Colony in Brazil.* Austin: University of Texas Press, 1987.

Hallock, Edgar Francis, and Ebenezer Soares Ferreira. *Historia Do Seminario Teologico Batista Do Sul Do Brasil: 1908 a 1998.* Rio de Janeiro: JUERP, 1998.

Harter, Eugene. *The Lost Colony of the Confederacy.* College Station: Texas A&M University Press, 2006.

Harvey, Paul. *Redeeming the South: Religious Cultures and Racial Identities in the South, 1865-1925.* Chapel Hill: University of North Carolina Press, 1997.

Hefner, Robert. "Introduction: The Unexpected Modern—Gender, Piety, and Politics in the Global Pentecostal Surge." In *Global Pentecostalism in the 21st Century,* edited by Robert Hefner, 1-36. Bloomington: Indiana University Press, 2013.

Helgen, Erika. *Religious Conflict in Brazil: Protestants, Catholics, and the Rise of Religious Pluralism in the Early Twentieth Century.* New Have: Yale University Press, 2020.

Hill, Lawrence F. "Confederate Exiles to Brazil." *The Hispanic American Historical Review* 7, no. 2 (1927): 192–210.

Hollinger, David A. *Protestants Abroad: How Missionaries Tried to Change the World but Changed America.* Illustrated edition. Princeton: Princeton University Press, 2017.

Horne, Gerald. *The Deepest South: The United States, Brazil, and the African Slave*

Trade. New York: NYU Press, 2007.

Jardilino, José Rubens Lima, and Leandro de Proença Lopes. "Protestantismo e Educação, Construção de Um Campo de Pesquisa: Algumas Observações e Teses Inclusas." In *Contribuições Do Protestantismo Para a História Da Educação No Brasil e Em Portugal*, edited by Cesar Romero Amaral Vieira and Ester Fraga Vilas-Bôas Carvalho do Nascimento, 291–322. Piracicaba: UNIMEP, 2017.

Jarnagin, Laura. *A Confluence of Transatlantic Networks: Elites, Capitalism and Confederate Immigration to Brazil*. Tuscaloosa: University of Alabama Press, 2008.

Jenkins, Philip. *God's Continent: Christianity, Islam, and Europe's Religious Crisis*. Oxford: Oxford University Press, 2010.

———. *The Next Christendom: The Coming of Global Christianity*. Oxford: Oxford University Press, 2007.

Jones, Judith Mac. *Soldado Descansa! Uma Epopéia Norte-Americana Sob Os Céus Do Brasil*. São Paulo: Fraternidade Descendência Americana, 1998.

Jones, Robert P. *White Too Long: The Legacy of White Supremacy in American Christianity*. New York: Simon & Schuster, 2020.

Kirkpatrick, David C. *A Gospel for the Poor: Global Social Christiantity and the Latin American Evangelical Left*. Philadephia: University of Pennsylvania Press, 2019.

Lacerda, Marina Basso. *O novo conservadorismo brasileiro: de Reagan a Bolsonaro*. Porto Alegre: Zouk, 2019.

Lancaster, Daniel. *The Bagbys of Brazil: The Life and Work of William Buck and Anne Luther Bagby*. Austin: Eakin Press, 1999.

Lee, Erica. *America For Americans: A History of Xenophobia in the United States*. New York: Basic Books, 2019.

Leonard, Bill. *Baptists in America*. New York: Columbia University Press, 2005.

———. *God's Last and Only Hope: The Fragmentation of the Southern Baptist Convention*. Grand Rapids: W.B. Eerdmans, 1990.

Leonard, Emile G. *O Protestantismo Brasileiro: Estudos de Eclesiologia e Historia Social*. São Paulo: ASTE, 1963.

Li, Li. "From Southern Baptist Indentity to Chinese Baptist Identity, 1850-1950." In *Baptist Identities: International Studies from the Seventeenth to the Twentieth Centuries*, edited by Ian M. Randall, Toivo Pilli, and Anthony Cross, 241–56. Milton Keynes: Paternoster, 2006.

Lima, Paulo-Tarso Flecha de. "Liberalism versus Nationalism: The Prodevelopment Ideology in Recent Brazilian Political History (1930-1997)." *Presidential Studies Quarterly* 29, no. 2 (1999): 370–88.

Lowe, John. "Reconstruction Revisited: Plantation School Writers, Postcolonial Theory, and Confederates in Brazil." *The Mississippi Quarterly*, Winter 2003, 5–25.

Lukes, Steven. *Power: A Radical View*. New York: Palgrave Macmillan, 2005.

Lynch, John. *New Worlds: A Religious History of Latin America*. New Haven: Yale University Press, 2012.

Machado, José Nemésio. *Educação Batista No Brasil: Uma Análise Complexa*. São Paulo: Colégio Batista Brasileiro, 1999.

Martins, Mário R. *História Das Idéias Radicais No Brasil*. Recife: Acácia Publicações, 1974.

———. *Missionários Americanos e Algumas Figuras Do Brasil Evangélico*. Goiânia: Kelps, 2007.

Marx, Anthony W. *Making Race and Nation: A Comparison of South Africa, the United States, and Brazil*. Cambridge: Cambridge University Press, 1998.

Mays, Dorothy A. *Women in Early America: Struggle, Survival, and Freedom in a New World*. ABC-CLIO, 2004.

McAlister, Melani. *The Kingdom of God Has No Borders: A Global History of American Evangelicals*. Oxford: Oxford University Press, 2018.

McCann, Frank D. *The Brazilian-American Alliance, 1937-1945*. Princeton: Princeton University Press, 1973.

Mello, José Antonio Gonsalves de. *Tempo Dos Flamengos*. Recife: Governo do Estado de Pernambuco, 1978.

Melo, Mário. *A Guerra Dos Mascates Como Afrimação Nacionalista*. Recife: Governo do Estado de Pernambuco, 1984.

Mendonça, Antônio G. "Evolução Histórica e Configuração Atual Do Protestantismo Brasileiro." In *Introdução Ao Protestantismo No Brasil*, edited by Antônio G. Mendonça and Prócoro Velasques Filho, 11–60. São Paulo: Edições Loyola, 1990.

Mendonça, Antônio Gouvêa, and Prócoro Velasques Filho. *Introdução Ao Protestantismo Brasileiro*. São Paulo: Loyola, 1990.

Mesquida, Peri. *Hegemonia norte-americana e educação Protestante no Brasil: um estudo de caso*. Juiz de Fora: Editora da Facultade de Teologia da Igreja Metodista, 1994.

Miller, Donald E., Kimon H. Sargeant, and Richard Flory, eds. *Spirit and Power: The Growth and Global Impact of Pentecostalism*. New York: Oxford University Press, 2013.

Moore, Christopher C. *Apostle of the Lost Cause: J. William Jones, Baptists, and the Development of Confederate Memory*. Knoxville: University of Tennessee Press, 2019.

Motta, Roberto. "Social Scientists and Disenchanters: Some Basic Themes of Brazilian Sociology of Religion." In *Sociologies of Religion: National Traditions*, edited by Giuseppe Giordan and Anthony J. Blasi, 76–106. Leiden: Brill, 2015.

Muller, William A. *A History of Southern Baptist Theological Seminary*. Nashville: Broadman Press, 1959.

Nagai, Tyrone. "Multiracial Americans Throughout the History of the US." In *Race Policy and Multiracial Americans*, edited by Kathleen Odell Korgen, 13–28. Bristol: Policy Press, 2016.

Nielssen, Hilde, Inger Marie Okkenhaug, and Karina Hestad Skeie, eds. *Protestant Missions and Local Encounters in the Nineteenth and Twentieth Centuries: Unto the Ends of the World*. Leiden: Brill, 2011.

Noll, Mark A. *God and Race in American Politics: A Short History*. Princeton University Press, 2010.

———. *The New Shape of World Christianity: How American Experience Reflects Global Faith*. Downers Grove: IVP Academic, 2009.

Norris, Kristopher. *Witnessing Whiteness: Confronting White Supremacy in the American Church*. Oxford: Oxford University Press, 2020.

Oliveira, Ana Maria Costa de. *O Destino (Não) Manifesto: Os Imigrantes Norte-Americanos No Brasil*. São Paulo: União Cultural Brasil-Estados Unidos, 1995.

Oliveira, Betty Antunes de. *Antonio Teixeira de Albuquerque: O Primeiro Pastor Batista Brasileiro*. Rio de Janeiro: Edição de Autora, 1982.

———. *Centelha Em Restolho Seco*. São Paulo: Vida Nova, 2005.

Oliveira, Zaqueu Moreira de. *Desafios e Conquistas Missionárias: 100 Anos Da Junta de Missões Nacionais Da CBB*. Rio de Janeiro: Convicção, 2007.

———. "Os Batistas: A Versão Histórica de Sua Origem." *Refexão e Fé* IV, no. 4 (Dezembro 2002): 9–20.

———. *Ousadia e Desafios Da Educação Teológica: 100 Anos Do STBN*. Recife: STBN Edições, 2002.

———. *Perfil Histórico Da Educação Teológica Batista No Brasil*. Fortaleza: ABIBET, 2000.

———. *Perseguidos, Mas Não Desamparados: 90 Anos de Perseguição Religiosa Contra Os Batistas Brasileiros (1880-1970)*. Rio de Janeiro: JUERP, 1999.

Oliveira, Zaqueu Moreira de, André Ramos, and João Virgílio. *Panorama Batista Em Pernambuco*. Recife: Departamento de Educação Religiosa de Junta Evangelizadora de Pernambuco, 1964.

Padilla, Elaine, and Peter C. Phan, eds. *Christianities in Migration: The Global Perspective*. Christianities of the World. New York: Palgrave Macmillan, 2016.

Parker, Calvin F. *The Southern Baptist Mission in Japan, 1889-1989*. Lanham: University Press Of America, 1990.

Parsons, Mikeal C. *Crawford Howell Toy: The Man, the Scholar, the Teacher*. Macon: Mercer University Press, 2019.

Pinheiro, Jorge, and Marcelo Santos, eds. *Os Batistas: Controvérsias e Vocação Para a Intolerância*. São Paulo: Fonte Editorial, 2012.

Porto, José da Costa. *Os Tempos Da Praieira*. Recife: Secretaria do Estado de Pernambuco, 1981.

Premack, Laura. "'The Holy Rollers Are Invading Our Territory': Southern Baptist Missionaries and the Early Years of Pentecostalism in Brazil." *Journal of Religious History* 35, no. 1 (March 2011): 1–23.

Robert, Dana L. *Christian Mission: How Christianity Became a World Religion*. Chichester: Wiley-Blackwell, 2009.

Sanneh, Lamin O. *Disciples of All Nations: Pillars of World Christianity*. Oxford: Oxford University Press, 2007.

Santos, João Ferreira. "A Teologia Protestante No Brasil Nesse Ultimos Trinta Anos." *Episteme* 3, no. 1 (2001): 29–40.

Santos, Marcelo. *O Marco Inicial Batista*. Coleção Sem Fronteiras. São Paulo: Convicção, 2003.

Seigel, Micol. *Uneven Encounters: Making Race and Nation in Brazil and the United States*. Durham: Duke University Press Books, 2009.

Siepierski, Paulo D. "Localização Histórica Do Racismo No Protestantismo Brasileiro." *Episteme* 2, no. 1 (2000): 61–72.

Silva, Célio Antonio Alcantara. "Confederate and Yankees under the Southern Cross." *Bulletin of Latin American Research* 34, no. 3 (2015): 270–304.

Silva, Elizete da. *William Buck Bagby: Um Pioneiro Batista Nas Terras Do Cruzeiro Do Sul*. Editora Novos Diálogos, 2011.

Silva, Graziella Moraes, and Marcelo Paixão. "Mixed and Unequal: New Perspectives on Brazilian Ethnoracial Relations." In *Pigmentocracies: Ethnicity, Race, and Color in Latin America*, edited by Edward Telles. Chapel Hill: The University of North Carolina Press, 2014.

Simmons, Charles Willis. "Racist Americans in a Multi-Racial Society: Confederate Exiles in Brazil." *The Journal of Negro History* 67, no. 1 (1982): 34–39.

Simmons Jr., Donald C. "Confederate Exiles in Latin America." In *Encyclopedia of U.S. - Latin American Relations*, 1:914–15. Thousand Oaks: Sage Publications, 2012.

———. *Confederate Settlements in British Honduras*. Jefferson: McFarland & Company, 2001.

Skidmore, Thomas E. *Black into White: Race and Nationality in Brazilian Thought*. Durham: Duke University Press, 1993.

Smith, Andrew Christopher. *Fundamentalism, Fundraising, and the Transformation of the Southern Baptist Convention, 1919-1925*. Knoxville: The University of Tennessee Press, 2016.

Smither, Edward L. *Brazilian Evangelical Missions in the Arab World: History, Culture, Practice, and Theology*. Eugene: Wipf & Stock Pub, 2012.

Souza, Alverson de. *Thomas Bowen: O Primeiro Missionário Batista No Brasil*. Rio de Janeiro: Novos Dialogos, 2012.

Spencer, Jon M. *The New Colored People: The Mixed-Race Movement in America*. New York: NYU Press, 2000.

Spyer, Juliano. *Povo de Deus: Quem são os evangélicos e por que eles importam*. Rio de Janeiro: Geraçao Editorial, 2020.

Stone, Bryan. *Evangelism after Pluralism: The Ethics of Christian Witness.* Baker Academic, 2018.

Stricklin, David. *A Genealogy of Dissent: Southern Baptist Protest in the Twentieth Century.* University Press of Kentucky, 2015.

Stroope, Michael W. *Transcending Mission: The Eclipse of a Modern Tradition.* Downers Grove: IVP Academic, 2017.

Sunquist, Scott W., and Mark A. Noll. *The Unexpected Christian Century: The Reversal and Transformation of Global Christianity, 1900-2000.* Grand Rapids: Baker Academic, 2015.

Sutton, Matthew Avery. *American Apocalypse: A History of Modern Evangelicalism.* Cambridge: Belknap Press, 2014.

Telles, Edward E. *Race in Another America: The Significance of Skin Color in Brazil.* Princeton: Princeton University Press, 2014.

Topik, Steven. "Middle-Class Brazilian Nationalism, 1889-1930: From Radicalism to Reaction." *Social Science Quarterly* 59, no. 1 (1978): 93–104.

Tota, Antonio Pedro. *The Seduction of Brazil: The Americanization of Brazil During World War II.* Austin: University of Texas Press, 2009.

Trexler, Melanie E. *Evangelizing Lebanon: Baptists, Missions, and the Question of Cultures.* Waco: Baylor University Press, 2016.

Tull, James E. *High-Church Baptists in the South: The Origin, Nature, and Influence of Landmarkism.* Macon: Mercer University Press, 2000.

Vieira, Cesar Romero Amaral, and Ester Fraga Vilas-Bôas Carvalho do Nascimento. "Apresentação." In *Contribuições do Protestantismo para a História da Educação no Brasil e em Portugal,* edited by Cesar Romero Amaral Vieira and Ester Fraga Vilas-Bôas Carvalho do Nascimento, 15–21. Piracicaba: UNIMEP, 2017.

———, eds. *Contribuições do Protestantismo para a História da Educação no Brasil e em Portugal.* Piracicaba: UNIMEP, 2017.

Weaver, Blanche Henry Clark. "Confederate Emigration to Brazil." *The Journal of Southern History* 27, no. 1 (February 1961): 33–53.

Weaver, C. Douglas. *Baptists and the Holy Spirit: The Contested History with Holiness-Pentecostal-Charismatic Movements.* Waco: Baylor University Press, 2019.

———. *In Search of the New Testament Church: The Baptist Story.* Macon: Mercer University Press, 2008.

Willis, Alan Scot. *All According to God's Plan: Southern Baptist Missions and Race, 1945-1970.* Lexington: University Press of Kentucky, 2005.

Willis, Gregory A. *Southern Baptist Theological Seminary, 1859-2009.* Oxford: Oxford University Press, 2009.

Wilson, Charles. *Baptized in Blood: The Religion of the Lost Cause, 1865-1920.* Athens: University of Georgia Press, 2009.

Xavier, João Leão dos Santos. *Colunas da renovacao: Rosalee Appleby, José Rego do Nascimento, Enéas Tognini, Achilles Barbosa, Rosivaldo de Araújo, Ilton Quadros, Renê P. Feitosa, Achilles B. Júnior.* Belo Horizonte, MG: LER-BAN, 1997.

Yamabuchi, Alberto Kenji. *O Debate Sobre a História Das Origens Do Trabalho Batista No Brasil: Uma Análise Das Relações e Dos Conflitos de Gênero e Poder Na Convenção Batista Brasileira Nos Anos 1960-1980.* São Paulo: Novas Edições Acadêmicas, 2015.

INDEX